GW00597176

THE FAITH

by the same authors

The Unwanted
In the Night Season

THE FAITH

Christiaan Barnard
and Siegfried Stander

HUTCHINSON
London Melbourne Sydney Auckland Johannesburg

Hutchinson & Co. (Publishers) Ltd

An imprint of the Hutchinson Publishing Group

17–21 Conway Street, London W1P 6JD

Hutchinson Group (Australia) Pty Ltd
30–32 Cremorne Street, Richmond South, Victoria 3121
PO Box 151, Broadway, New South Wales 2007

Hutchinson Group (NZ) Ltd
32–34 View Road, PO Box 40-086, Glenfield, Auckland 10

Hutchinson Group (SA) Pty Ltd
PO Box 337, Bergvlei 2012, South Africa

First published 1984
© Christiaan Barnard and Siegfried Stander

Set in Linotron Ehrhardt by Wyvern Typesetting Ltd, Bristol

Printed and bound in Great Britain by Anchor Brendon Ltd, Tiptree, Essex

British Library Cataloguing in Publication Data
Barnard, Christiaan
The faith
I. Title   II. Stander, Siegfried
823'.914[F]   PR6052.A/

ISBN 0 09 155630 9

Authors' Note

The enigma and the conflict which form the basis of this book are very real. Some of the events depicted have happened or are happening today. The state Bapangani, its geography and its people are, however, imaginary.

PART ONE

Prelude to a journey of exploration

1

The air conditioning had broken down again. He lay awake and tense in the midnight heat, knowing that sleep was far away. He thought crossly about tomorrow. It was important that he should be rested and clear-headed, for the day would be long and exhausting, with the ministerial conference at the head of its agenda of irritations. But he could not sleep in this heat.

He toyed with the idea of taking a Valium. It was a temptation to which he had succumbed too often recently, and he was worried about his increasing dependence on pills to sleep and tablets to wake and capsules to prevent worry. Later, he decided. If it really gets bad I'll take something.

His briefcase stood open on the bedside table. On top of the pile of papers was a financial report due to be discussed at tomorrow's meeting. So far he had given it no more than a cursory examination. He turned the pages wryly. The long list of figures and balances would probably be as effective a soporific as the drug he had resisted. But trying to make sense of it would call for all his concentration. He put the report aside and instead picked up a medical journal which had arrived in this morning's mail. An article on the problems of hospital administration in rural America briefly held his attention. There were parallels with his own situation. He wondered, a little cynically, how that other administrator would cope with the extra complications of political unrest and civil strife. Had rioters ever stoned his ambulances and tried to burn down his hospital?

He read another article, on the diagnosis of pituitary micro-adenoma, with waning interest.

On the ceiling directly over the bed was a streaky, rust-brown stain. It had been there when he first occupied this room, and he still wondered about its cause. Was it a fault in the plumbing system, or had a guest on the floor above had an accident with his bathwater? At first he had amused himself, during bouts of sleeplessness like the present, by trying to find shape, a face or an animal, a coat of arms, a human body, in its amorphous outline. In time he had ceased to be aware of it, had come to accept it as he accepted other symptoms of rawness and newness about the hotel and the country: the uncertain elevator service, the dining-room windows which were still unglazed, the scaffolding and piled half-bricks which made the main entrance to the lobby a perilous trap.

Now he studied the stain again and realized what he had missed all along. It was a mirror image of the map of Africa, with the bulge to the east, the horn to the west. By squinting a little it was possible to imagine the curl of the Cape of Good Hope transported to the right-hand side. A further stretch of the imagination converted the whole thing into the semblance of an old-fashioned duelling pistol. Was it coincidence that the pistol was cocked and that its barrel pointed south?

That kind of grim oddity had caused political cartoonists morbid fun after this country had come into being. The scythelike shape, curving along the frontier of its white-ruled neighbours, was an obvious symbol, and Bapangani had at once been nicknamed Pangaland, a reference to the bush-cutting panga which had been the secret dread of white men during the Mau Mau terror in Kenya.

For Bapangani was a black homeland, one of the string of ministates created by South Africa in fulfilment of the desperate dream of apartheid. Here, so the theory ran, on land which had long tribal associations, the Bapa'hanga people (the erosion of history had abbreviated the national name to Bapanga, derogatively shortened to Panga) would eventually gain their independence and the political rights and privileges from which they were disbarred within white South Africa. Here, perhaps, the blade would be blunted, would never be used to slash at white skins.

Could one find significance in the curious colour of that stain on the ceiling? An Africa with the colour of congealed blood?

He had to get to sleep. He sat up and rapidly fanned the top sheet, hoping to get at least an illusion of coolness and airiness. Then he rolled over again with determination and reached for the switch.

10

The telephone rang.

He said: 'Oh, hell!' and pushed the sheet away. The woven reed mat was rough under his bare feet. He walked naked to the telephone in the narrow hallway.

He said: 'Yes?'

A woman's voice asked hesitantly: 'Dr Brand?'

'Speaking.'

'This is Dr Karim.'

'Who? Oh. Yes.'

'I'm sorry to trouble you at this time of night, doctor.'

'That's OK. What's the problem?'

The bathroom door stood open and he could see his reflection in the mirror over the washbasin. He sucked in his belly a little.

The woman said: 'I have a patient here I'm very worried about.'

He tried to keep irritation out of his voice. 'Isn't there a consultant on duty?'

'I discussed the case with Dr Hauge earlier this evening. But he's not available now.'

'Who is on second call?'

There was a momentary hesitation. Then she said, her voice emotionless: 'Dr Hamilton.'

Russell Hamilton was the chief surgeon. He was an American, a man with a self-confident and caustic manner. He was not liked, especially among the junior doctors.

'Have you spoken to him?'

'He's seen the patient. But I don't agree with his diagnosis. I would like your permission to change his orders.'

'Oh.' He grimaced at the man in the mirror. Well, the girl was frank enough. What else would she like? Maybe her air ticket back to where she had come from?

'What's wrong with your patient?'

'I'm not sure. But Dr Hamilton suggests it's typhoid. I . . . I can't agree with him. The onset has been far too acute.'

'You're being rather awkward.' A senior man's decision could not be so casually overridden.

'I know,' she said, and disarmed him. 'That's why I feel we should have another opinion. Could you come out to see the patient?'

He sighed. 'Let me speak to Dr Hamilton.'

11

'He said that if I disobeyed his orders he was washing his hands of the case. The orders were to transfer the patient to the ID hospital in town. I simply can't do that.'

Brand understood, only too well, the reasons for her misgivings; 'hospital' was a misnomer for the Infectious Diseases establishment, a ramshackle collection of huts and military prefabs, inadequately staffed and poorly equipped.

Nevertheless, open defiance could not be allowed to pass.

'What do you *think* is wrong with the patient?' That sounded too placatory, so he added, with ironic emphasis, 'Doctor.'

'I suspect it to be some kind of contagious disease.'

'Then what's the argument about?' He was relieved. 'Even if it's not typhoid, if it's infectious then the ID hospital is clearly the right place for it.' He tried a jocular tone of voice. 'We don't want to risk having to go into quarantine, do we?' Be a good girl now, do as I tell you and all will be forgiven.

'The patient is desperately ill. And besides, she's one of our nurses. One of the local black nurses.'

'How does that change the situation, doctor?'

'There's more to it,' she persisted. 'This nurse looked after a patient here a week ago and the patient died only hours after admission.'

Brand was puzzled. 'So?'

'I believe there's a connection. The symptoms are practically identical. It was an African child, a young boy. The history was one of sudden malaise and muscular pains. He developed a high fever, conjunctivitis and a generalized rash – '

Testily he interrupted the over-clinical presentation. 'Yes, yes. But what was the diagnosis?'

'Measles.'

He laughed disbelievingly. 'And I suppose you disagreed with that too?'

She said, without hesitation: 'It was my own diagnosis. Originally.' She played her trump card. 'But I was wrong. The autopsy finding contradicted me. It wasn't measles. But it definitely wasn't typhoid either.'

There was silence except for the sighing of the telephone wires between them.

'Then what was it?' he asked finally.

12

'The histology isn't through yet. But Dr Hauge . . .' She paused fractionally and said in an offhand way: 'He did the postmortem, by the way . . . Dr Hauge found widespread involvement of most of the organs. He was especially puzzled about signs of necrosis in the liver and spleen. And also about evidence of a haemorrhagic tendency.'

The forthright admission that she had made a mistake, which implied, did it not, that Hamilton too was capable of error; the slightly calculated way in which she held back the information about the autopsy until last – he was not sure that he cared much for Dr Karim.

He thought about her. A Malayan woman, small and slim. She had come here from a London hospital. Was there a Malay community in England? She was very attractive in a taut, rather daunting way. She kept herself aloof and he knew that some of the staff, particularly the nurses, thought her to be arrogant. What else did he know about her? She spoke with a British accent. The British had ruled Malaya once, of course. One tended to forget. She was young, but she seemed to be capable at her job. That was really all he knew about Dr Karim. Was it enough?

'You mentioned having spoken to Dr Hauge. What does he think?'

'That was much earlier.'

Had there been an unexpected note of reticence? He decided to press her a little.

'Did he think it was typhoid?'

'He didn't give an opinion.'

'Did Dr Hauge see the patient, doctor?'

She defended, vainly, the crumbling walls of discretion. 'She was not in a critical condition at that stage. He thought we should admit her for observation.'

He began to understand what had happened. Dr Hauge had little time for the routine of day-to-day clinical medicine. The old man's interests were his pathology department and his laboratory work. He would have been content to leave the problem in Dr Karim's hands and go away thinking about something else.

The patient had become worse and she had consulted Hamilton. There was a long-standing feud between the surgeon and Hauge. Perhaps he had seen an opportunity of showing up his enemy in a

13

bad light. Perhaps he had been genuinely anxious to avoid a typhoid outbreak. He had ordered the patient to be sent away.

Dr Karim had been caught between loyalty to one superior and defiance towards another.

Brand looked at his watch. Half-past eleven.

'All right. Perhaps I'd better come and sort this out. Where have you got the patient?'

'In the Emergency Unit.'

'Keep her there. But take infectious precautions.'

'I'd like to move her. She needs a special.'

He thought, with exasperated amusement: this girl doesn't let up. Make one concession and she's got the next demand all polished and ready.

'Listen,' he said sharply. 'Don't do a damn thing until I get there. I'm leaving right away.'

'What about the curfew?'

He sighed wearily. He had forgotten the emergency regulations, enforced during the riots and now seemingly perpetuated, which made it forbidden to be on the streets after ten at night. Some of the patrols were black and there were stories of whites who went out in defiance of the curfew, on the haughty assumption that it did not apply to them, and had been handled less than gently.

He looked at his watch again.

'I'll arrange something. It might take a while, but I'll be out there as soon as I can.'

She said, 'Thank you, doctor,' with such evident relief that he became sceptical once more. Inexperienced doctors were notorious for contriving obscure diseases from commonplace symptoms.

He stood for a moment, frowning and holding the receiver against his cheek. Then he shrugged, and dialled the switchboard.

The man on the hotel exchange, preparing to go off duty at midnight, was sulkily reluctant to start the complicated procedure of getting him connected to a number that did not appear in the directory. Only Brand's vow of securing his instant dismissal, a threat both of them knew to be hollow, finally moved him to action.

The buzzing ring seemed to go on interminably. The exchange broke in to say in tones of gloomy satisfaction: 'No reply.'

14

'Ring it again,' Brand told him implacably.

He listened to the ringing. At last there was a click and a sleepy voice.

'Hullo?'

'Is that Mr Makaza?'

'Who is that?'

'This is Dr Brand from the AID unit. I need your help, Mr Makaza.'

'*Monsieur le Directeur*,' the other man said, his voice now wide awake. A moment of speculative silence. 'You need my help?'

'A . . .' Brand paused deliberately. 'A problem has arisen at the hospital and I need to go out there urgently. But as you know it is well after curfew time.'

'It is very late,' Makaza said, but whether in agreement or reprimand it was hard to tell.

'I shall need an escort or at least a pass or something to get me through the patrols. Can you arrange that for me?'

Again the silence. Finally Makaza said: 'It will not be easy. At this time of night.'

'Mr Makaza, I am sure that a word from you to the police by telephone would be more than sufficient.'

'You flatter me, doctor. The Police Commissioner is a very important officer.' This time the silence was very deliberate. Then: 'He is also a white man.'

They were both aware that Makaza had no need to go to the Chief of Police and that, even if he did, that officer would not ignore a direct request from a member of the cabinet, irrespective of skin colour. It was a game you had to play, although its purpose was undefined.

'I realize that, Mr Makaza. Nevertheless – '

'It is very late. And on a Sunday night too.'

'Unfortunately disease is not a clock-watcher.'

'Naturally you as a doctor and myself with my interest in matters of health would understand. But the Commandant might not.'

Makaza was enjoying the situation. Suddenly Brand became weary of fencing. He said sharply: 'Mr Makaza, I'm making a very modest request. If you can't help me, you force me to wonder why we are in your country in the first place.'

If he had expected the African to display anger or even

15

discomfiture he was disappointed. There was only surprise and a trace of curiosity in Michael Makaza's voice.

'Naturally we don't want that. Have you perhaps spoken to Dr Van Jaarsveld at the Bureau of Health?'

'This matter has only just come up. And besides, Mr Makaza, I believe in going to the top.'

Makaza laughed, flattered. His subordinate, the Director of the Health Bureau, was, like the Police Commissioner, a white man.

'Very well. I'll see that someone is sent to fetch you. You are staying at the hotel?'

'Yes. Thank you.'

'My pleasure, *Monsieur le Directeur*. Good night.'

The man's use of the fanciful title irritated Brand, as it had done before. It was based on a pretended misunderstanding on Makaza's part of Brand's precise role within the Paris-based Agence pour l'Alléviation de Détresse Internationale, which employed him. He suspected that the African used the French as a private joke.

'Good night, Mr Minister,' he said.

He replaced the receiver in vexation, knowing that Makaza would relish having got under his skin.

Shahida Karim had used the telephone in the Emergency Unit duty room. The room had served an unknown purpose, either ecclesiastic or educational, in the days when these buildings had housed a mission school. Its fittings had been replaced by the clinical clutter of hospital needs, and three of the walls had been painted a flat white, to improve the poor lighting or simply in the belief that a hospital should have a sterile look. The fourth wall, however, still bore a reminder of the past, in the shape of a mural depicting Christ as a shepherd with a flock of lambs.

There were times when Shahida wished that whoever had wielded the white brush could have overcome his scruples about obliterating the pious work of his predecessor. The mural was badly drawn and its symbolism so heavy (the lambs had all been black originally; age and the damp which seeped up the stone walls had turned them a uniform grey and given the ethereally white Christ a sickly pallor) that it both amused and annoyed her.

She did not leave the room immediately after ending the

16

conversation with the director, but instead sat at the night supervisor's desk a moment longer, contemplating the painting.

What had Dr Brand thought, she wondered. I hope I didn't sound too emotional. Does he think I'm only a hysterical young woman making impossible demands about nothing?

Perhaps she should ignore instructions and give the orders to have the patient transferred to the intensive care ward. But what if she was wrong?

She could not bear to be still. What might have happened to the patient in the meantime?

The woman was still in the Emergency Room, lying on a trolley with its sides down. Shahida was annoyed to find that there was no nurse in attendance. The patient was delirious at times and needed a restraining hand. She picked up the temperature chart. The fever had increased to more than 40°C. The absence of a corresponding rise in the pulse rate puzzled her. It was still slow: 65 to 70 beats a minute.

Again she looked at her notes, taken hurriedly earlier when the woman had still been lucid enough to give a history. Nurse Jakavula had been off duty for the weekend, at the end of a spell of work on the night shift. She had gone home to her village in spite of being troubled by a headache and a nagging pain in the back. By last night she had felt decidedly unwell, but she had been reluctant to end her holiday prematurely. Today she had felt very hot and had developed diarrhoea with blood in the stools. Relatives had brought her back to the hospital. She was very sick.

Shahida put down the notes.

The history was similar to that of typhoid fever. The only symptom which did not match was the startlingly rapid deterioration. She had never heard of a typhoid patient going downhill so fast. It had been exactly the same with the little black boy last week. All over in a matter of hours.

But what if the woman had been sick for much longer than she claimed? She hadn't wanted to miss her weekend off duty. These black people were accustomed to discomfort and suffering. Often they complained only when a disease was well established.

She turned at the sound of footsteps.

'Where have you been, nurse? You can't just leave the patient lying here.'

17

'I haven't got help. I went to test the urine.' The nurse held her face averted and her voice was sullen. Since the riots the black staff had regarded the whites with resentment. Shahida's own situation was particularly delicate. Did they classify her with the whites or the blacks?

She tried not to show that she had noticed. 'What is the urine result?'

'There's plus plus albumen and plus plus plus blood.'

'Any other lab tests back?'

'It's on the chart.'

Shahida had not noticed. She picked up the chart again and examined the column headed 'Special Investigations'. The haemoglobin was down. But what caused her to wince uneasily was the low white cell count. Another symptom of typhoid fever.

'Have you collected faeces for the lab?'

'Yes.' The nurse wrinkled her nose in distaste. 'She smells like a typhoid to me.'

The woman had probably overheard the argument with Dr Hamilton. She was trying to needle.

'Move her to the side room,' Shahida said coldly. 'Dr Brand is coming to see her. And, nurse. . . .'

The woman waited indifferently.

'Pull up the sides of that trolley,' Shahida said.

She went back to the duty room to wait. The eyes of the painted Christ were turned heavenwards. The artist, striving for an expression of exaltation, had instead achieved one of fastidious disdain, as if the Shepherd was repelled by the grey and no doubt smelly flock at his feet.

She thought again about the child. When had he been admitted? On Tuesday night. If Nurse Jakavula had been taken ill on Friday, as she claimed, the incubation period could be no longer than two or three days. She had read up the literature on typhoid incubation this evening. It was usually longer than a week, but with a large inoculum it could be much shorter.

But she was sure the woman had the same disease as the child. And he had not died of typhoid. If it had been typhoid there would have been lesions in the small bowel for the pathologist to identify. And if it wasn't typhoid, what was it?

2

The section of tarred road was a token, intended to impress tourists arriving by air. It started at the landing strip on the flats above the town, skirted the hillside where the hotels stood, then broadened into brief grandeur as a double carriageway named Government Avenue before petering out as a sandy track along the river's edge.

The police van had reached the end of the tar. Its brake lights came on three or four times in quick succession as it pulled over to the shoulder. The vehicle stopped, motor running and headlights still switched on. The light beam showed the empty track curving away into darkness.

Brand drew his car obediently alongside. He waited for a moment but the policemen remained in their vehicle. He got out. The driver put his head through the window.

'This OK, doc?' He was a sergeant, a white man, and he had a drawling Boland accent which overlaid a 'gh' sound over every other syllable.

Brand hesitated. He had hoped that the police escort would accompany him all the way out to the hospital. Danger did not end once one was out of reach of the curfew patrols. Only two days ago there had been reports of a series of apparently motiveless stone-throwing attacks on cars along the road south.

Yet he did not wish the young man to think him foolishly afraid. He struggled between pride and caution. He raised his head. 'Yes. OK.'

The policeman nodded. He was obviously impatient to be gone. 'Will you need an escort back?'

'I really can't tell. It depends on circumstances.'

A radio inside the van chattered briefly, but the driver ignored it. Beside him an African constable sat motionless.

'OK. You call the station when you're ready, hey? We'll come and fetch you.'

'I'll let you know.'

19

The policeman lifted his finger to his cap in a sketchy salute and pulled away too fast. Dust rose from the spinning rear wheels. The van made its turn. Its lights swept over Brand, where he stood beside his car, and then it went tearing past and left him to the darkness.

He climbed back into his car and started the motor, but did not immediately switch on the lights. Was this a trick of Makaza's? Had he deliberately given the police wrong instructions? More probably the sergeant was simply in a hurry to be rid of an unwanted responsibility. Or perhaps he had merely misunderstood.

There were lots of misunderstandings in this damn country.

He drove off, not happy about the prospect of the long and lonely circuitous journey ahead.

The hospital lay within sight of the town, across a bend in the river. From his hotel room he could see its lights, but he had to travel twenty miles on bad roads in order to reach it. Town and hospital were separated by a wilderness of marshland, trackless and impenetrable.

The physical separation was deliberate: the product of a mental attitude as tangled and obscure as the maze of swamps.

The AID medical unit's role in Bapangani was ambiguous. AID teams operated elsewhere in Africa but this was the first to venture into the politically sensitive climate of the white-dominated south. Bapangani had been provided with key health staff, ranging from administrators and nurses to experts on everything in the medical alphabet from abdominal surgery to zoonotic diseases. And their salaries were paid elsewhere.

However, although the Health Bureau of the Bapangani government was nominally under the control of a black minister, the real power was in the hands of its white director, a holdover from the previous South African administration. Dr Van Jaarsveld was a stiff and dour Afrikaner who behaved as if he regarded the situation as an attempt to embarrass him personally. If it was so essential that medical services should suddenly be imported, was this an implication that he had not been doing his job?

At times it seemed to Brand that there was a policy of deliberate neglect towards the AID unit. By coming to this country it had achieved South Africa's political purpose and after that it was only a nuisance factor. The original plan had been that the AID team would integrate into existing and projected local health services, but this had come to nothing.

A new modern hospital was being built with money from South Africa, but it was still far from completion. It was also, in Brand's opinion, too expensive; the cost of the elaborate, wood-panelled entrance hall alone would have paid for an entire outpatient clinic.

Dr Van Jaarsveld had blocked any suggestion that AID doctors should staff the new hospital. Instead he had offered only the use of the abandoned mission station upriver, beyond the marshes. Working there, within sight of the town but remote from it, was a constant frustration. Many of the specialists on the staff had given up and left.

It was very dark, with no moon and no lights except those of the car, searching the road ahead. He could not see beyond the edge of the road but he knew that the marshes were there, a presence rather than a mere geographical feature. He could almost feel them in the night. By day, oddly, the marsh was not remarkable. Indeed, it was possible to pass by without even knowing it was there, for you needed high ground to be able to trace the intricate course of the waterways.

They stretched far to the north, nearly 3000 square miles in extent. Once only hunters had come to them, seeking elephant and hippo and rare game such as *situtunga* and *lechwe* and Chobe bushbuck. Where the new town of Leruarua now stood there had been a guest house, safely on the hillside above the plaguing mosquitoes, which had served the hunting parties as jumping-off ground for the great northern swamps.

Leruarua meant, in the Sesangani language, 'Big Fish'. Most of the new town had risen round the folds of the low hills overlooking the great river which flowed out of the marshes, wide and powerful, before its waters joined the Chobe and then the Zambesi to plunge into the chasm of the Victoria Falls. In the old days, however, there had been only a string of villages, inhabited by a handful of fisherfolk. They could not use their primitive nets in the fast, deep water of the main channel, so their huts had been built at the edge of the swamps. Here, among the labyrinth of shallow channels which sliced the land into a thousand reed-plumed islands, they had made their catches when the river gods willed and for the rest of the time lived hungrily but passively on dried fish and fruit.

21

Other fishermen had come: missionaries who had built, with more devoutness than good sense, on a spur of headland close to the marsh-dwellers for whose souls they angled. It was on the site of the old mission that the AID unit was now housed. The designer of more than half a century before had been a monk who had carried a memory of central Europe in his mind. The mission buildings – chapel, priory, school, oratory – stood squatly and solidly on the alien soil. Yet there was an impermanence about them, as if they were part of a stage setting transported to a landscape of *makalani* palms and reeds and papyrus.

The land had rejected the transplantation. Malaria was endemic to the swamps. The black people died of it too, but they were many. The white fathers were few. They died, one by one. The fishermen returned to their nets and their old ways.

The next invaders had been fishers in different waters, the entrepreneurs and politicians who picked on Leruarua first as a tourist resort, later as the site of the future capital, once independence had been achieved. In this dry land the river was a miracle. It was also a place of quite spectacular beauty, its long banks fringed by tropical vegetation of the kind that decorated advertising photographs in travel magazines.

The Bapangani people were not, by custom, orientated towards the river. Even the swamp people, the fishermen of Leruarua, owned primitive dugout canoes. But with the coming of the town the river had become a road and the ferry owners its highwaymen, for they made their own rules and set their own prices. The ferrymen operated according to their own highly flexible time-tables, but that did not really matter in a land where time spent waiting was not counted as time wasted, provided there was companionship and laughter and perhaps food and drink to share. All day long there were throngs of waiting passengers and their baggage, or perhaps cargo, live chickens in a woven reed coop, fruit for the market, battered cardboard boxes or lumpy grain bags, on the river banks or on the few rickety jetties.

Then came the riots. The mobs had burned down schools and buildings in the town and finally a party of the more determined among them had found their way to the hospital too.

The police had kept them away from the main buildings and they had managed to set fire only to the old chapel, closer to the river.

But the consequence had been the installation of harsh searchlights and the razing of the garden, for fear its trees and shrubs should give cover to future marauders. It was a brutal fact of life in this country: beauty always had to make way for security.

First there had been the maddening frustration of attending to the riot casualties, of removing bullets and buckshot, amputating limbs and taking out bits of shattered bowel, while all around were people sick with dysentry, with malnutrition and its attendant diseases, people who were dying from a hundred other ills and with no one to care for them.

But that ended in time and the wounded had been sent home. There had been high hopes that, at last, the AID unit could tackle the task they had come to perform. Instead there had been a sudden and puzzling drop in the outpatient numbers.

Investigation brought to light the apparently mundane reason. Ferry fares had soared. A crossing which had cost a few bits of copper before the hospital had opened had gone up ten, twenty times in price. And, whether pushed by greed or fear, the boatmen had been persuaded to form a cartel and to maintain their prices.

Brand had darkly suspected Dr Van Jaarsveld's hand somewhere in the affair, but there was no proof. Official complaints had produced little more than official shrugs. Nothing could be done. The country was, unlike others not far away, not run by a socialist dictatorship. Amidst the pious double talk a message came across clearly: whoever had originated and profited from the ferry price rise was not one of those who had to pole a boat along the river for a living.

As for the road, the motor service had suddenly improved. New buses had made their appearance on the long road between the town and the old mission. There was talk that the road would be graded, perhaps even tarred. The transport company was given a state subsidy to buy new ambulances.

Brand found Dr Karim waiting for him at the main door. She was standing in the dimly lit porch between the old arched doorway and the modern glass swing doors which led to the lobby, as if this enclosed space was a trap which she knew he would have to enter.

A black hospital porter sat half asleep behind the reception

23

counter. He straightened up, blinking, when he saw Brand, and scratched for papers with which he could seem to be occupied. Brand nodded at the man, then turned back to Dr Karim.

Again he was reminded how small she was. Her body was shapeless under a hospital coat too large for her. Her olive skin was unlined, but there were rings of fatigue under her eyes. She carried a clipboard and a record file.

'How is the patient?' he asked.

'She's deteriorated a lot since I spoke to you. I kept her in the Emergency Unit, but I've moved her to one of the side rooms.'

'Has Dr Hamilton seen her again?'

'No.'

'I think he should know that I'm here.'

She nodded, tight-lipped. 'I'll see that he is informed.' She walked to the desk, where the porter was now busy with a box of file cards. She picked up the telephone.

When she rejoined him she said, in a voice without emphasis, 'Dr Hamilton will meet us in the Emergency Unit.'

They walked side by side down the echoing corridor.

'Tell me about the child,' Brand invited.

'He was a black child, about eleven, admitted in a terminal condition. The family's name was . . .' – she consulted the file cover–'Moremi. As I told you on the phone, I diagnosed measles, with bronchial complications.'

'Was there a history of contact with measles?'

She said defensively: 'We haven't got much of a history, I'm afraid. The people who brought him were not very . . . not very co-operative.'

"Oh. Who brought him here?'

'An old couple. An elderly man and a middle-aged woman. Not his parents. They claimed to be relatives, but they were very vague about how he became sick. Or even how long he'd been sick.'

The Emergency Unit was housed in a separate building, connected to the main block by a covered way. The walls were towering and virtually windowless. The operating block was here too. Surgeons, like emergency patients, did not need a view.

The building was chilly after the warm night air. As if by common consent neither made a move to go beyond the door. They

24

stood facing one another. Dr Karim clutched her clipboard and the file as if to shield herself.

'I should have pressed them harder.' She seemed compelled to shoulder blame. 'The history is unsatisfactory. I know that. But there were language problems . . . the nurse who interpreted for me couldn't seem to get them to understand what I wanted. And besides . . .' She hesitated for a moment. 'It was as if they didn't want me to understand. As if they were hiding something.'

'What do you mean?'

'I can't define it exactly. It's just that they were evasive. They seemed scared of something. I put it down to superstition.' She shrugged. 'I don't know.'

'The child was dying by then?'

'There was no time to take a proper history. I had to do what I could to save the patient.' She shrugged again, with an element of despair in the gesture. 'But it was too late. And afterwards, when I wanted to speak to them again, they had disappeared.'

'Disappeared?'

'They simply walked out and nobody thought to stop them.'

'Leave a dying child behind? That's most unusual.'

'Yes.' But her toneless voice made it clear that she had not really been surprised, that nothing that happened here could surprise her.

'Have they been traced, do you know? Or have the parents been found?'

'We have a name and address. But I don't know if it was followed up.'

It was unimportant and yet the fact that the child had been abandoned bothered him. 'Oh well,' he said. 'Let's get on with it. Was there anything unusual about the case?'

'Well, the rapid deterioration, for one.'

'But the history was unreliable, so the duration could have been far longer than you thought.'

'It's possible,' she said dubiously. After a moment she added: 'There was also a marked bleeding tendency. He had purpura, epistaxis, bleeding into the mouth and also into the bowel.'

'The platelet count?'

'It was low. And there was marked leukopenia too.'

'Consistent with measles. Or typhoid for that matter.'

25

'Yes. Except that it wasn't either.'

His eyebrows lifted slightly. No one could accuse Dr Karim of inconsistency.

'Anything else?'

'There was one other thing. A subcutaneous bruise at the side of the neck. I would say it was a bite of some kind. And there were incision wounds, partly healed, on both hands and on the fingers.'

He stared at her, puzzled. 'Bites?'

'Looked like bites to me. Sharp teeth, like those of a small animal. Dr Hauge noticed them as well, when he did the postmortem.'

'Did he attach any significance to them?'

She pulled up her shoulders. 'No.'

'And the people who were with the child? Did they say anything about it?'

'I tried to ask them. But they knew nothing. Or anyway they said they knew nothing.'

'Did they . . . ?' He hesitated. He did not really know what question he had intended asking. So, instead, he said: 'I assume the cause of death was bronchial?'

'We put it down to broncho-pneumonia, following complications of measles. But at the postmortem . . .' She quoted from the file. '"On surveying the macroscopical findings, the morphological diagnosis taken separately or in combination did not show a characteristic pattern which would allow classification into any group of diseases."'

Brand sighed inwardly. Trust old Hauge to be as long-winded as possible about saying: 'I don't know.' He said: 'I guess the histology will give us the answer.'

'I hope so.'

He nodded. 'Well, we'll see. OK, where's your patient?'

'This way.'

Painted arrows along the wall, colour-coded for the guidance of the illiterate, led to the Emergency Unit.

'When did the child come in?' he asked.

She was walking a little ahead of him, leading the way with swift strides.

'On Tuesday.'

'And when did this nurse become ill?'

26

'She had the weekend off. But she was already feeling unwell when she left here on Friday.'

He whistled. 'An incubation period of two or three days? That's very short.'

'I know.'

He glanced sideways at her. Her fine-drawn features, seen in profile, had a stubborn, unyielding look. She was undoubtedly a very pretty young woman, but how much medicine did she know?

The door from the operating block, controlled by a pneumatic device, had opened with a hiss and a thump, and Russell Hamilton came plunging towards them on tall, impatient legs. He was carelessly dressed, but whether this was because of the urgency of the summons or a deliberate demonstration of his anger at being disturbed, Brand could not tell. The surgeon did not bother with polite greetings.

'James, this whole performance is utterly unnecessary. I'm telling you, the woman's got typhoid. I've never seen a more typical, clear-cut case.' He glared at Dr Karim and asked, in his most abrasive tones: 'Are the lab tests back?'

She did not flinch and her voice was controlled. 'Only the blood count. The haemoglobin is low and so is the white cell count. It's 2500.'

Hamilton's mouth tightened in grim satisfaction. He turned back to Brand. 'What more do you want?'

Brand found himself at a loss. Hamilton read his silence as assent.

'I told Miss . . . Miss What's-her-name here hours ago to send the patient out. She belongs in the ID hospital, not here. Why were my instructions not carried out?'

Dr Karim's expression became even more remote. Brand felt his anger grow.

'Hold it a minute, Russ. Dr Karim suspects the woman has picked up something from a child she nursed last week. You know about this?'

'Of course I know about it. She came to me with the same story. But it's cockeyed. There's nothing to substantiate it. Except feminine intuition, I suppose.'

Dr Karim said, in the same dispassionate tones with which she

27

had reported the laboratory results: 'I saw the child. You didn't – and the child didn't die of typhoid.'

Hamilton asked her insultingly: 'Where did you work before you came here?'

'In London.'

'London, England? I suppose you saw a lot of typhoid in London, England?'

She flushed suddenly. 'I've worked elsewhere. In Malaya, for instance. I saw typhoid cases there.'

Brand interrupted. 'Now wait, wait, wait. I don't think the point is who has seen what disease and where. I think what – '

Hamilton's face had set. 'If you're going to accept the opinion of this inexperienced young woman before that of a senior member of your staff, then go ahead.'

'I think you should see the patient again and then you might revise your own opinion.' Dr Karim addressed them both. 'We're standing here wasting time. This woman is very sick.'

Brand looked at her and saw only concern. She was prepared to risk offending her seniors to secure her patient's welfare. Blame and responsibility could be allotted after the larger issue of life had been decided.

He made up his mind.

'Let's see the patient.'

A nurse sat on an anaesthetist's swivel chair probably filched from the surgical block. She swung it around as they came in, clearly making up her mind whether or not to rise. When she saw the two men she got slowly to her feet.

In silence broken only by the hissing of the steam autoclave, they donned the sterile gowns and disposable paper masks which she offered them.

The woman lay on her side on the high trolley, legs drawn up close to her chest, motionless. A chart with the vital life signs monitored every five minutes hung at the foot of the trolley, but there was no need to look to it for verification. She was close to death.

Hamilton ripped the chart free from its clipboard and stared as if he could not credit its ominous message of rapidly rising temperature and respiratory rate and slowing pulse.

'What the hell's going on here?' He stabbed an accusing finger at the spiky graph and glowered at Dr Karim. 'Why wasn't I told about this?'

'You said you didn't want to be disturbed again.'

'That's not true.' He turned to Brand and said angrily: 'I gave definite instructions that I should be called if there was any change. Obviously she's perforated an ulcer.' The black nurse stood behind them. Hamilton swung round to her. 'Sister, let the theatre know I have an emergency laparotomy and they are to get everything ready. Get hold of my registrar. I want him down here to pass a naso-gastric tube.' He eyed the bottle on the drip-stand suspiciously and, ignoring Dr Karim, asked the nurse: 'What have you got in there?'

Hamilton, in full and furious action, was behaving as if he were the only doctor in the room. Brand realized that the situation was slipping beyond his control. He saw Dr Karim watching him, concern in her eyes.

He moved towards the trolley. The sick woman stirred and he looked at her uncertainly, not knowing what to hunt for or whether, even if he found something, it would change what was happening.

'Hullo, sister.' His voice sounded falsely jovial. 'How do you feel?'

He heard Hamilton utter a disdainful grunt and tried to ignore it.

The woman struggled to turn on to her back. The Emergency Unit sister, unsure whose orders to obey, and hoping to ingratiate herself with someone, moved quickly to help. Sunken eyes opened and squinted at him.

There were crusts of blood on the lips. Brand picked up a limp arm and felt for the radial pulse. It was so weak as to be almost undetectable. Very slow and irregular.

He turned inquiringly towards the nurse. She pushed forward a stainless steel trolley with an array of instruments. He selected a spatula. 'Have you a torch?'

The patient had closed her eyes. She breathed in slow, deep gasps. A trickle of blood seeped from the corner of her mouth.

He depressed her lower jaw and tongue. The torch had a faulty switch and he had to work it several times to produce a light.

The mucous membrane of the mouth and pharynx were red and oedematous. There were crusts of dried blood on the soft and hard

29

palates and more blood oozed from her gums. He asked himself, puzzled: why so much blood?

'The trouble is in her belly,' Hamilton said loudly.

Brand pretended not to have heard. He pulled the covering sheet down off the limp body. There were sporadic petechiae all over the skin, developed in some places into large haematomas. The abdomen was distended, but when he palpated it he found no rigidity of the abdominal muscles.

He took up a stethoscope from the trolley, fumbling with it for a moment as if it were strange to him. Through it he could hear the rumble of active peristalsis.

'No signs of acute peritonitis,' he said.

Hamilton said impatiently: 'We've caught it early.'

'Then how do you explain her condition?' Dr Karim asked with apparent innocence.

Hamilton flushed. It was obviously a clinical discrepancy, but he offered no explanation.

Brand pulled down the stethoscope, leaving it hanging round his neck. He surveyed his patchy recollection of the signs and symptoms of typical typhoid fever. The so-called 'rose spots' were almost a hallmark of the disease. Leukopenia and anaemia were characteristic. So was relative bradycardia, and there was usually a weak, dicrotic pulse, giving the impression of a double beat.

All of them were present, like a row of figures on a ledger, adding up to an inevitable and ominous total.

'I'm afraid Dr Hamilton is right,' he said, half apologetically. 'This looks like typhoid to me.'

Hamilton said, with heavy sarcasm: 'I'm delighted by your faith in my diagnostic abilities, doctor. Meanwhile we'd better get moving with the operation.' He snapped his fingers at the nurse. 'My God, are you still here? Didn't I tell you to call my registrar?'

She scurried away, obviously relieved to be removed from the conflict.

Dr Karim said: 'No.'

The two men stared at her wordlessly. Hamilton gave an exasperated sigh and turned his eyes to the ceiling. Brand fidgeted uncertainly with the dangling stethoscope. He felt a curious mixture of weariness and boredom. He wished he was rid of the whole damn business. Dr Karim and her obsessions were more than anyone should have to bear.

She faced them with an appearance of complete calm.

'I'm sorry, but I'm convinced this is not a typhoid. In my opinion an operation would be a terrible risk.'

Hamilton, too, seemed resigned rather than angry. He ignored the woman and spoke to Brand, tersely, but with a touch of good humour, almost of commiseration.

'Look, James, I'm not prepared to stand here arguing all night. You'd better sort this out. The ball's in your court. If you want me to operate I'll be available. You know where to find me.'

The door banged behind him.

Brand turned irresolutely back to the woman on the trolley. He had to do something for her, but what?

His eyes met those of Dr Karim. She had arching eyebrows set in a permanent expression of ironic detachment. There was nothing obviously oriental about the features concealed by her mask, apart from the skin like dark honey, and yet he was aware of a subtle difference between them. Did it lie in their present conflict or in racial antipathy, in a feeling that they inhabited separate worlds? Or was it even more simple: that they were a man and a woman?

They worked together throughout the night, attempting every life-sustaining regimen they could devise. Early in the morning, when Brand had to leave for his meeting with the Minister of Health, their patient still had a precarious hold on life.

3

'It must surely be obvious', the Director of Health said sourly, 'that in emergencies we have to make use of all available medical services.' Dr Van Jaarsveld kept his head lowered as he spoke, occasionally shifting the papers on the table in front of him. 'I can't see why there should be objections.'

Brand sighed inwardly. All that remained to complete the

31

familiar cycle was for him to give the same old reply. His mind felt as gritty as his eyes from lack of sleep.

'I'm afraid the director has missed the point.' He addressed the minister, hoping to take the sting out of his words by strict adherence to parliamentary procedure. 'Naturally my staff do not object to treating any disease or any injury, irrespective of its cause. What they do object to is being politically involved with one side or the other. They don't want to appear to be tools of the apartheid system.'

Van Jaarsveld said: 'It's not a question of enforcing apartheid. It's a matter of maintaining law and order.'

Makaza said tartly: 'Surely that's a job for the police, not for hospitals?'

Brand interrupted. 'Minister, you have pointed a finger right at the basic problem.' No harm in flattering a potential ally. 'We're running a health service, not a law enforcement office.'

The meeting was being held in the Health Bureau offices, one of the row of identical, dormitory-like buildings which housed the administration of the new state. Like most buildings in the capital it was at a stage of frenzied half-completion. The town reminded Brand of the toy engineering construction sets of his youth, all girders and struts and stray bits and pieces. As he spoke, a jack hammer started deafeningly somewhere outside. Michael Makaza frowned and motioned to one of his aides. The young black man got up hastily to close the windows. The jack hammer clattered on, its noise hardly diminished.

Brand raised his voice for emphasis as much as in competition.

'I'm sure you are all aware that AID is sponsored by governments and churches and business undertakings, but it is apolitical, interdenominational and, as the name implies, international in its structure and also in its aim.'

He knew that his voice had taken on the sonorous tones of a lecturer reciting a familiar beginning-of-term speech to yet another new class. The director, after a brief, suspicious glance, was fiddling with his papers again. Makaza delicately hid a yawn behind his hand, perhaps as a pointed reminder that he had been woken in the middle of the night.

You had a lot more sleep last night than I did, Mr Minister, Brand thought. You can listen to me now, for a change.

Suddenly he was weary of the trite phrases, the endless repetition of noble but shallow concepts. They were fine and admirable, but they did not belong to the real world of suffering and subterfuge, the world with which he was forced to deal. He ended his speech abruptly, and was aware of the slightly puzzled pause which resulted.

Van Jaarsveld took up his former theme, unshaken and stubborn. His attitude was that of an official who had been given his orders and would carry them out, ignoring all opposition, whether he believed in them or not. 'Minister, it's all very well Dr Brand saying he doesn't want anything to do with politics. But you can't get away from it all that easily. The riots were instigated by communists. It's been proved. And if they're given half a chance they'll start more riots. And what will happen to his hospital then, if there isn't law and order?'

At what stage, Brand wondered, did a doctor become a bureaucrat? Was it when papers became more important than people? Was he guilty of the same offence?

Before the start of the meeting he had received the telephone call he had half expected, half dreaded. He had been in the committee room waiting, like the others, for the minister's arrival, when a clerk had come to call him out of the room.

Dr Karim had been on the line. She had not wasted time on preliminaries.

'Nurse Jakavula has just died.'

He had known, of course, of whom she was speaking, but he had been unable to stop himself asking: 'Who?' After a night spent fighting to save a woman's life he had not even known her name. Where to move her; how to isolate her; what to do with her: these had been the urgent questions. Quickly, quickly, there's a file out of place in the filing cabinet; put it back, straighten it out in line with all the other files.

But after all the file had been closed.

He had given curt orders for an immediate autopsy and gone, with sick reluctance, back to the committee room. It was difficult to concentrate, to simulate interest in Van Jaarsveld's obstinate argument or to search for the hidden motives, the clues to other, more complex manoeuvring.

Brand himself was an administrator, a committee man, and part of his mind could not be kept from following after Van Jaarsveld's spoor, sniffing at the tracks to distinguish the real scent from the false.

Makaza interrupted his director, asking searching questions. Why should the police need authority over doctors, even during a riot? Could the Health Bureau cope with AID's problems in addition to its own, especially during an emergency?

Van Jaarsveld began to flounder and to make protesting noises. Makaza's comments were sharp.

'It seems to me we're lucky to have these people in our country. It seems to me we shouldn't try to chase them away by demanding that they conform to foreign ideologies. Shouldn't we just be grateful for what they're doing for us?'

It was a bear-baiting performance. That sideswipe at 'foreign' ideology must have stung, Brand thought. And the gracious reference to AID's role in the country, he recognized, was Makaza's private signal to him, a reference to last night's telephone call. He had no illusions about the motives of his unexpected ally. The minister was scoring a political point. Rumour said that he had ambitions beyond his present position.

Van Jaarsveld grumpily proposed an adjournment of the discussion to allow him to prepare a report. Makaza gave his smiling, mock-approving consent. Then he steered the meeting on to other, less contentious matters. There was little further discussion and the meeting closed. Makaza withdrew, with his entourage and with Van Jaarsveld in tow. Brand could not be sure but he believed that he caught the shadow of a wink from the African as they made their farewells. Was Makaza trying to tell him that he understood it was all a game?

He had risen to shake hands with the minister. The man who had sat silently beside him throughout the meeting was still seated. He spoke now, for the first time.

'The minister and his director are not on good terms today,' Helmut Fissher observed mildly. But there was a flash of malice from the eyes obscured by the thick spectacles. 'I wonder why?'

Brand looked down at the seated man. Fissher was reaching for his cane.

'I don't know,' Brand said. 'I don't think Makaza gives a damn either way. He was just showing off.'

Fissher smiled thinly. He was looking across the room to the door where Van Jaarsveld was seeing the minister out.

'Nevertheless it would be interesting to discover the reason for their disagreement. Dr Van Jaarsveld is a very stubborn man.'

Van Jaarsveld turned back to them. Brand wondered uncomfortably whether the man realized he had been the subject of the conversation. He made a special effort to smile amicably.

Van Jaarsveld answered the smile with one of his own which was little more than a spasmodic tightening of the cheek muscles. He stood in silence, as if waiting for them to go away.

The hell with you, Brand thought. Why should I bother to be polite?

'I'm disappointed that the ferry question has been shelved again,' he said. 'Frankly, that was the only urgent and important item on the agenda. We can't continue putting it off.'

Brand's idea of providing a free ferry service for genuine hospital patients had produced real consternation when he had first suggested it as a solution to the transport problem. There had been pursed lips and ominous head-shaking around the committee table. A multitude of problems were foreseen. Where would a suitable vessel be found? Who would do the administrative work? The real reason, of course, was that the bus company's profits would suffer, but this was not mentioned. Dr Brand was thanked for his suggestion and it was deferred for later consideration, after investigation and a full report.

Van Jaarsveld spread his hands in a gesture of resignation. 'We'll see,' he said vaguely.

Brand stooped to draw out a chair for Fissher, who was leaning on his cane and struggling to rise.

Fissher nodded his thanks.

They went to the door, moving slowly to keep pace with Fissher's laboured progress. Brand saw a brief look of irritation on the older man's face.

'Go on, go on,' Fissher said testily. 'There is no need to wait for me.'

Brand and Van Jaarsveld were both awkwardly silent. As much to overcome the uneasy moment as for any other reason, Brand said: 'We had a bit of a crisis on our hands during the night.'

Van Jaarsveld gave him a blank, uninterested look.

35

'Really?'

'One of our nurses. One of the local women, in fact. I've just heard that the poor woman has died. We suspect typhoid.'

The other man's expression changed with dramatic suddenness. They had reached the head of a shallow flight of steps leading down to the main entrance. He stopped on the stairs, so abruptly that an African in a clerk's grey jacket, coming up from the door, had to dodge to avoid cannoning into him. The clerk went by with a reproachful glance.

'Typhoid! Why was my department not informed?' His voice had gone high with indignation.

'I'm informing you now, am I not?' Brand looked at Van Jaarsveld's angry face. It was typical of the man's civil service mentality that he should be more concerned about what he perceived as a clerical error than about the fate of a patient. There was no point in sarcasm. 'Anyway, it's only a query typhoid at this stage. It's not been confirmed.'

'You've missed the point,' Van Jaarsveld said haughtily, and Brand was intrigued to find his own words flung back at him. He had used the phrase towards Van Jaarsveld during the meeting. He had not realized how much it had rankled. 'The point is that infectious diseases are a state responsibility.'

Fissher had joined them at the steps and stood leaning on his cane, looking attentively from one to the other.

'Might I suggest a meeting on the matter as soon as possible?' he said diplomatically. 'I think what Dr Brand means is that from the point of view of efficiency it would be better if the Bureau should act in a consultative capacity.'

This solution, combining compromise with the promise of meetings and memoranda to come, seemed to satisfy Van Jaarsveld. He nodded his acceptance and took his leave with stiff courtesy.

Sunlight was hard and flat outside and the heat, after the artificial cool of the building, was almost tangible. They made their way to the car. There was no shade on the street. Young trees had been planted within protective boxes along the pavement, but they were seldom watered and had grown withered and stunted.

Getting into the car was like climbing into a furnace. Brand felt sweat beading on his forehead. Fissher sat down heavily in the passenger's seat.

He winced as he drew his legs in through the door, then slammed it. 'This tin object,' he muttered beneath his breath.

Brand, uncertain whether the reference was to the car door or to the metal prosthesis which served as Fissher's left leg, remained tactfully silent. He knew vaguely that the loss was due to a wartime injury, but had never learnt the details. Fissher managed well enough with the cane once he was on his feet, but he had difficulty in rising or sitting down and at times appeared to experience pain.

Helmut Fissher was in charge of administration for the AID unit and did most of Hauge's non-medical work, even assisting the old man in his laboratory. Fissher was reticent about his origins. His English was correct, if pedantic. Brand assumed he was German. He had a dry, somewhat secretive manner but, in spite of their age difference, he and Brand got on well together.

Both Fissher and Hauge had quarters at the hospital and seldom left its premises. They had come out to Africa together as an advance guard to prepare for the arrival of the AID unit, and Fissher was better informed about Bapangani social and political nuances than anyone else on the staff. Most of what he knew he kept to himself, but Brand had learned to value his executive officer's unobtrusive skill in negotiations with the country's officialdom.

He remembered that he had at first been dubious about both Fissher and Hauge. He had expressed his doubts to the man who had interviewed him on behalf of AID. It had been in Paris, in an opulent hotel suite overlooking the Tuileries. His prospective employers were paying all expenses, including the hotel and air ticket from Montreal, and he had been suitably impressed. The priest who was his host had turned from contemplation of the evening traffic on the Rue de Rivoli and asked: 'When will you be able to travel to South Africa, doctor? We would like you to go as soon as possible.'

Brand had composed his expression to show a suitable mixture of pleasure and confidence. He did not want to appear over-anxious.

'There are some minor matters to be cleared up at home,' he had said. 'But as you know I am already free from the university, so I should be able to leave pretty soon.'

37

'Good,' Monsignor Pauchet had said with an approving nod. 'We're anxious that you should relieve Dr Hauge as soon as possible.'

Brand had hesitated. 'About this Dr Hauge. Do I understand correctly that he is to remain as my deputy?'

'That is correct. And Mr Fissher is to serve as your administrative officer.'

'Will they not resent my appointment? They have worked together doing the spadework, so to speak.'

'That will not be a problem. Dr Hauge has chosen to remain, for various reasons, but he is an elderly man and he went out originally on the understanding that he would be replaced as soon as we had found a suitably qualified person.' Monsignor Pauchet had a round face with somewhat popping eyes of great intensity. He had fixed his gaze on Brand, contradicting the benign smile which accompanied the fulsome tones. 'We believe that you are that person.'

'You say "We". What does that mean?'

'Oh, myself and others, of course,' Pauchet said airily. He had continued his song of praise, dismissing the interruption. 'We particularly appreciate what you are sacrificing in order to come to us. We value the great work you have been doing at McGill, creating virtually a new field in organizing medical services for developing countries.'

Brand had noted the skill with which the man had dodged the risk of being forced into answering a question about his fellow directors on the board which ran AID. So far he had met none of them except Pauchet. He knew from the brochures he had studied who they were: one or two members of European royalty, a scattering of politicians, a few bankers, businessmen whose names were familiar from *Time*, some church and medical leaders. But Monsignor Pauchet seemed to be in sole charge. He had met Brand at Charles de Gaulle Airport, had brought him to this hotel, had interviewed him deftly, asking questions to elicit information he obviously already possessed, and finally made the oblique offer of the post of director of the AID unit in a riot-plagued homeland within the Republic of South Africa.

This fact alone made a valid reason for secrecy. Was this why there had been so much caution about his journey from Montreal

38

and the way of his reception in Paris? Or was the truth that AID was one of those right-leaning, crank organizations that believed in racial superiority even as they proclaimed humanitarian ideals?

He did not really believe this. It all seemed genuine enough – both the ideal and the reality. Money was genuinely donated (and the luxury of his present surroundings, while it pricked his conscience, indicated that there was enough of it) and genuinely spent among the sick and needy in Africa.

He was puzzled, too, by what seemed a hint from Pauchet that they shared this need for discretion.

'One other factor in your favour is, of course, that you are a free man,' the priest had said. 'You can move easily around the world, without the need to tell others where you are bound.'

At the time Brand had assumed that this was a delicate reminder that Pauchet knew about his recent divorce. I understand, the priest seemed to be saying, why a man like you should throw away his eminent position to run a mission hospital in the depths of Africa. You, too, are in search of Lambaréné. He had not cared to pursue the subject. Later he was to wonder whether this was what Pauchet had meant.

As Brand started the car Fissher said: 'The director appeared unduly alarmed. Why, when we must have had half a dozen typhoid cases in the last few months?'

'I wish we were sure this is typhoid.'

'There is a chance it is not?'

'A slight chance.'

'What does that mean?'

'If it isn't typhoid we don't know what it is except that it's contagious and damned virulent.'

Fissher looked at him without saying anything.

On the opposite side of Government Avenue, set within the beginnings of a landscaped garden, stood the parliamentary buildings, a gift from the South African government. It had been a prime target during the riots; the rioters had struck here with the advantage of surprise, for no one in authority, not even the white police, had really expected them to destroy something of their own.

But the modern glass-walled building (the glass was tinted against the sunlight and the result was similar to an airport control tower) was seen as a symbol of repression, and so the stones and petrol bombs had been ritually hurled. One wing, intended to house the directorate and the future parliamentary library, had been destroyed by fire. Scaffolding showed where it was being rebuilt. Discreet but sturdy wrought-iron screens had been incorporated into the new design in case of future violence. It was an African adjustment: the hope of good order hand in hand with preparation for disorder.

The line of traffic consisted mostly of pick-up trucks, with the occasional Land-Rover or jeep, a reminder that outside town lay rough and primitive country.

As he waited for a gap, Brand said: 'The riots must have cost a lot of money. Where is it coming from?'

'South Africa, I assume.'

'Generous of them.'

Fissher did not appear to sense the sarcasm. He said with a shrug: 'They have paid so much already.'

'So they have to protect their investment, eh? But is this country really viable?'

'The same could be asked about many other African states.'

Brand turned on to the track which led alongside the river. Both he and Fissher were momentarily silent in the unconscious tribute which men pay to the sight of a large expanse of water in a dry land. They watched the grey-green stream sliding past. The river was low, for the rains were late. Deep erosion ditches sliced the bare soil below the tree line and there were mud banks in the shallows. The opposite bank was hazy with smoke from bush fires deep inside the marshes.

Half a dozen jetties reached out towards the deep centre channel. Most of them were rudimentary: logs, poles and planks haphazardly wired and nailed together. But the last of the row was sturdier than its neighbours and moored alongside it, startlingly incongruous in this African setting, was a Mississippi paddle-wheel steamer. The vessel, slowly rotting away on a foreign river, was all that remained of an ingenious scheme devised by an American entrepreneur with a flair for showmanship.

Three Gay Ladies, she was called; a name apparently as mystifying as the plan behind her presence here. Ostensibly the shallow-draught vessel, built by a Cape Town shipwright and laboriously transported up-country by rail and road, was meant to serve as a floating hotel to carry tourists on game-watching cruises into the marshes. The reality had been much more shrewd, with a fair chance of success. The borders of five countries came to a near-common meeting point on the river. The then white-ruled states reached out across the continent as if to shake hands over a black sea. Gambling was officially frowned upon by the white nations, tolerated by their black neighbours. In the maze of waterways and islands, much of it disputed territory with ill-defined frontiers, who would keep watch on one vessel, even if it happened to be as unmistakable and eccentric as a paddle-wheel steamer turned casino?

The names of the frolicsome threesome became more evident. They were Clotho, Lachesis and Atropos, the fates whose busy hands determined, among other things, the fall of the cards and the spin of the roulette wheel.

By being too subtle the American had outwitted himself. The head of an international hotel chain had dispensed with subtlety. He had gone directly to the Chief Minister and sold him on the idea of tourists by the thousands and hundreds of thousands pouring money into Bapangani. There was only one small obstacle, he had pointed out. The laws against gambling.

The obstacle was removed.

The chain had bought out the existing hotels and provided money for the construction of a magnificent new building, designed with great architectural skill to give the impression of a walled village against the hill above the river, its colour that of the African earth, its shape the cones of African mud-huts. The hotel was still incomplete, as Brand knew to his cost, but its casino did a thriving business. Some people looked sourly at the new building and, remembering the lovely landscape it had replaced, called it a tragedy. Others thought it a joke. And yet others said the joke was on South Africa and that the real reason why the Chief Minister fell so easily for the hotel man's wiles was that the old man, resentful of the fragmented condition of his nation, had scored a point off South Africa for delaying the amalgamation of certain white-

41

owned farms on the western border. It was all part of the complicated game on which politicians place their bets. *Three Gay Ladies* had been the loser.

They drove past the angular, upright silhouette of the steamer, as dissonant here as a honky-tonk tune in the middle of a pastorale.

'What's going to happen to that thing?' Brand asked.

Fissher laughed. 'Who knows? Perhaps the hotel will buy her eventually, when the price is right.'

'It's a shame to see a boat go like that.' Brand said.

Fissher laughed again. 'There is a new joke about her. People have renamed her *Faith*. Three Sad Ladies. Faith, Hope and Charity. Which is what keeps her afloat.'

Brand said reflectively: 'You know, that was a topic we were supposed to discuss at the meeting this morning. The question of a free ferry service to the hospital. One of the objections they keep raising is that there's no suitable boat. But what's to stop us hiring this thing?'

Fissher twisted his lips dubiously. 'The boat is probably sinking as it lies here. Or the engines are rusted.'

Brand was not to be deflected from his sudden enthusiasm.

'At least we can make inquiries. There's a guy I've seen around the place who's supposed to be in charge of her. What's his name? He's a Spaniard, isn't he?'

'Portuguese. Da Costa. Captain Da Costa.'

'Do you know him?'

'I have met him.'

'I've seen him drinking at the hotel. I'm damned if I'm not going to speak to him about it next time he turns up.'

'I do not know whether you will have success. He is not a . . . communicative person.'

'What is his background?'

'I understand he was a game ranger in Portuguese territory.'

'Not a sailor?'

'It seems he was a seaman in his youth. Merchant navy, I assume.'

'So the title is honorary?'

Fissher laughed. 'Many people had strange titles when the Portuguese were here.'

42

'Well, I think I'll have a chat with *Capitane* Da Costa in any case.'

A message was waiting on Brand's desk. It was terse to the point of rudeness. Dr Hauge acknowledged the instructions regarding a postmortem on Nurse Jakavula. Interested parties were informed that he would be performing the autopsy at 12h00.

Brand suppressed his irritation at the arrogant tone. That was the man's habitual manner. Meeting Erik Hauge for the first time, he had imagined that the old man resented him as a stranger taking control of the AID unit. But he had come to realize that the quick temper and scathing contempt towards opposition were ingrained. Hauge had the look of an aging, rumpled bear, from the forests of his native Norway. The resemblance did not stop there. He was, Brand thought, a bear with a permanently sore head.

The mortuary was inconveniently isolated in an austere building at the far end of the old mission complex. Hauge was already at work over the opened cadaver when Brand silently joined the others in the autopsy room.

He saw Dr Karim's unhappy expression and tried to smile reassuringly, but managed no more than an ambiguous grimace under his mask. Dr Hamilton stood opposite the pathologist, grimly silent. He was there to prove that his diagnosis had been correct and that, in not allowing him to operate for a perforated ulcer, Brand was guilty.

Hauge straightened up and made a weary, flexing movement of his back.

'Nothing there,' he said flatly. And then, in dictating tones to the secretary standing behind him: 'Examination of the gastro-intestinal tract revealed no lesions typical of typhoid fever.'

In the frozen silence which followed, Brand felt only sick relief. He could not look at Hamilton's face, not even for the satisfaction of seeing an opponent discomfited.

Then Hamilton said in a strangled voice: 'I don't believe you.' Before anyone could move he snatched up a scalpel and started to rummage inside the corpse as if it were no more than a bundle of dirty washing.

The look of astonishment and outrage on Hauge's face would have been comic under any other circumstances. He flung out his

43

hands in an agonized attempt to intervene. Hamilton's scalpel slipped. He hissed with pain. Before all their eyes he withdrew his hands from the gaping abdominal cavity. A thin slit across the palm of his left-hand glove showed where he had cut himself. Hauge gave the surgeon a single disgusted glance. The autopsy room attendant handed Hamilton a fresh pair of gloves. No one said anything.

Hauge was still fuming as he and Brand walked away from the mortuary.

'The man is a fool. By what right does he question my judgement? He has not even sense to keep his hands out of the way.'

Remembering the macabre moment made Brand feel queerly ashamed, as if he had somehow shared in the surgeon's humiliation.

He asked: 'Can we definitely rule out typhoid?'

Hauge went abruptly from fury, or its simulation, to professional caution.

'Ah. Not so quick. The postmortem does not show this, but I wait for the lab results to be sure.'

'Naturally. But the chances are that it was something else. The question is: what?'

Hauge hunched his shoulders and spread his hands. He held the exaggeratedly baffled gesture for a moment. Then he said: 'As you say: what?'

'I think the main point is to establish whether it really is a contagious disease.'

'I have not said that,' the pathologist said quickly.

'Yes, but clinically it does seem . . . Dr Karim is very definite that the woman had the same symptoms as the dead child.'

'She is very young,' Hauge said disparagingly.

It was you, you self-centred old bastard, who wouldn't be bothered about that same young woman's fears last night, Brand thought. He did not care to remember that he had entertained doubts of his own.

Brand asked: 'Can we establish a link between the two deaths? Other than on clinical evidence?'

44

'If there is a link we will find it. Already we are working on this in the lab.'

'How? Of course with the woman there would be no problem, but in the case of the child. . . .'

'Some specimens were kept and frozen after the postmortem. Portions of the liver, the spleen and so forth. Always I do this, when the results are not conclusive.'

Brand was relieved and also impressed. Say what you would about the old man, he was a scientist.

He had contrived to make the meeting seem accidental, as if he were merely passing through the Emergency Unit on his way to more important business elsewhere. He found Dr Karim in the duty room, writing up records at a desk which stood beneath the ceiling-high religious mural. A desk light was switched on and it made a private place for her hands and bowed head with the glossy dark hair.

Like last night, she again had on an oversized white coat, and he noticed how vulnerable it made her look. He now knew differently, he thought wryly.

Her expression was coldly questioning.

Brand said: 'Hullo, Shahida.'

She looked surprised, and he smiled.

'I had to go through the records to discover your name. It's a very beautiful name.'

'It is not uncommon among Malay people.'

She was not making it easy for him. He said awkwardly: 'It seems we owe you an apology.'

Those arching eyebrows lifted fractionally. She did not speak.

Feeling a lumbering idiot, he stumbled on. 'About Nurse Jakavula, I mean.'

'What about her?'

'The fact that she didn't have typhoid.'

'Oh, that.' She seemed indifferent and he was faintly disappointed. He had expected some reaction.

'Dr Hauge tells me he has set up a study to establish if there's a link between the nurse and the child, as you suspected.'

'Why they died?'

45

'Yes.'

'I would like to know that, yes.' But still she had that air of apathy and it occurred to him that she was not really interested in technical explanations after the fact; what mattered was that she had lost a patient, not the reasons why.

'However, we have encountered a problem about the child,' he told her.

'What problem?'

'Someone from the Health Bureau has been to check but there's no trace of any Moremi family at the address you were given. So it's going to be a battle to find contacts, if we have to.'

She made a tired gesture. 'I wrote down what the old people told me. But, as I explained to you, I wasn't sure of their story.'

'Some of these people lie as a matter of course.'

'Perhaps they are afraid.'

'Why should they be?'

'There is much fear in this country. Of anything unusual, anyone who asks questions.'

He did not have a ready answer. He made preparations to leave. 'Well, I hope you have an easier night of it than last night. I could do with some sleep myself.'

'You must be exhausted,' she said sympathetically. 'All last night and all day long.'

Sympathy was not unwelcome, but he pretended he had not sought it. 'At least I don't have a whole night ahead of me as you do.'

She gave a twisted smile. 'A whole night of what?' She indicated the record sheets. 'Of filling in papers? I'll be done with these in half an hour and then I'll go to bed and the chances are I won't be called until morning.'

'You don't seem overjoyed at the prospect of a good night's sleep.'

'I didn't come to this country to sleep.'

'I don't suppose you did.' He paused uncertainly. 'Would you be interested to know that I have a scheme which might shake us all awake a little?'

The sudden brightening of her face gave the answer.

'Do you know that old paddle steamer downriver?' he asked. He told her about his idea, vague until now, to convert the riverboat

46

into a permanent ferry to serve the hospital. She listened closely, without interrupting.

'I think it's a marvellous idea,' she said at last.

He said on impulse: 'I was thinking of going to meet the captain and at the same time looking over his boat. Would you like to come with me?'

'Yes.'

'Tomorrow morning, perhaps, if you don't have too busy a night?'

'I'd like to do that very much.'

4

Before now he had only seen the ship from a distance and had not realized it was quite so tall. The hull itself stood not much higher than the jetty, but above it towered three decks of overhanging superstructure, like a Victorian hotel, with the bridge perched on top as if the architect had belatedly decided to add a glass conservatory on the roof of his teetering mansion.

They walked in silence to the end of the jetty, staring at the blunt bows and up at the elaborate trelliswork of the promenade deck.

'Weird-looking, isn't she?' Brand said.

Dr Karim was looking apprehensively at the huge scabs of old green paint peeling from the upper works.

'Will it sail?'

He grinned.

'Looks as if it might sail straight down to the bottom, doesn't it? Shall we see if there's anyone aboard?'

A length of unplaned timber hardly a foot across, held in place by two ends of greasy-looking rope, did service as a gangplank forward of the boxed-in portside paddle wheel. Brand eyed it dubiously, testing it with a foot and measuring the distance from jetty to deck. There was a light wind on the river this morning and small waves slapped against the jetty pilings. If Shahida had not been there he would have swallowed his pride and called until someone came.

'I'll have a look,' he said with assumed ease. 'You stay where you are.'

The plank was more secure than it seemed, but halfway across he made the mistake of looking down and for a moment ship and deck and gangplank seemed to be in lurching, independent motion. He launched himself across the grey water in a desperate leap, clutching for the tall pillars which supported the middle deck. He caught hold of some unidentified bit of woodwork and hung on, feet scrabbling for purchase.

A gruff voice said 'Hah!' and an arm reached out to haul him ignominiously on to the deck. He tripped over the coaming and, with his last dignity gone, landed sprawling against the rail. His rescuer had already turned away and, with outstretched hand, was helping Shahida across. To his chagrin Brand saw her negotiate the gap with light-footed ease.

Feeling foolish, he straightened up and made an effort to present a confident smile.

'Captain Da Costa?'

The man who faced him, unsmiling, with a look of deep suspicion on his dark face, was shorter than average but as broad as a barrel. He reminded Brand of an old, weathered wine cask, for there was a sour wine smell about the captain of the *Three Gay Ladies*, although it was not yet ten o'clock in the morning.

Da Costa did not reply or even nod acknowledgement, and Brand uneasily introduced himself and his companion. The hostile expression softened somewhat as the man examined Shahida, and Brand thought that his impulsive invitation to her might have been a wise move. Nevertheless he was surprised to find himself resentful of the look in Da Costa's eyes.

He explained the purpose of their visit. The other man heard him out in complete silence, standing with legs defiantly astride, occasionally glancing at the woman, or, as if to underline his disinterest, staring at the dark line of the bush across the river. He wore a pair of filthy denim jeans and a cotton singlet with 'Three Gay Ladies' stencilled in faded gothic type over the bulge of his considerable belly.

'Do you think it's a proposition?' Brand asked.

Da Costa scratched contemptuously at the grizzled chest hair which showed at the neck of his vest. He looked at Shahida again,

48

then past Brand at the great height – the full three decks of the vessel – of the paddle wheel. On its box the ship's name was painted in the same typeface as the lettering across his chest.

'Naturally we have to discuss a price before we can come to an agreement,' Brand said despairingly. The other showed no sign of having understood or even of having heard. I wonder if the stupid bastard can speak English, Brand thought.

'Well, what do you think?' he asked again. It was a mistake to have come. The master of the ship was as much a useless hulk as his vessel.

Da Costa stuck out his lips and made a sucking sound. Brand wondered whether this was some obscure Portuguese insult. But the skipper was only removing a shred of foreign matter from between his teeth. He completed the task with a fingernail, then jerked his head at them in peremptory command.

They followed, in silence, through an entryway and then down a panelled passage as far as another, much more imposing door of glass and carved wood. He pushed it open and directed them inside with another jerk of his hand.

The main saloon (and Brand guessed that it had been designed as the casino, had the ship ever been allowed to carry out her primary mission) stretched the full width of the vessel and reached up through two decks. It had been decorated in the style of the river-boat period, with heavy emphasis on brocade and tinselled mirror and carved pillars, although neglect showed these to be fake, for many of the moulded and glued trimmings had come adrift, revealing bare plywood beneath. In spite of the tatty appearance there was a rakish, devil-may-care air about the cavernous chamber.

Da Costa did not pause to give them time to admire the lost trappings of what might have been. Already he had crossed to the further end of the saloon, where a well-proportioned branching staircase led to the upper decks. He guided them not up, however, but down, descending a spiral stairway of rusty and unadorned steel. Their shoes clattered on the steel rungs, causing echoes within the empty spaces of the hull. Da Costa himself wore rope-soled shoes and moved without a sound. Brand became apprehensive. Where the hell was the fellow taking them?

They stopped at a hatch beyond which was another cavernlike

49

hold filled with large, antiquated-looking machinery. Their guide pointed, and Brand examined the confusion of beams and levers and jointed shafts uncomprehendingly.

'Engine,' Da Costa said, as if this explained everything.

Brand nodded and tried to look smart.

The captain saw that he had been misunderstood and muttered something under his breath, then tried again.

'Steam engine. Very old. Come from stateside, America. Very old.'

'Do you mean it might break down?'

Da Costa, making it clear that he was abandoning all hope of communicating with a fool, addressed himself to Shahida.

'Burn very much wood,' he told her. 'Old engine take very much wood.'

'I think perhaps it would be expensive to . . . what is the phrase? . . . get up steam,' Shahida told Brand. 'It's an old-fashioned engine and therefore wasteful. I think that's what he means.'

The Portuguese nodded admiringly at her.

'*Si, si.* Very much wood. Cost very much money.'

'How much wood?' Brand asked suspiciously.

Eyes narrowed, Da Costa examined him for a moment.

'One thousand kilos?' It was a question rather than a statement.

Brand turned impatiently to Shahida. 'This is obviously a con. How much does wood cost?'

'I have no idea.'

He told the other man firmly: 'I will discuss it with the government. They will know how much to pay.'

In turning, he had caught Da Costa looking at him reflectively. There was a flash of acute intelligence in the dark eyes, which was as quickly gone. The oafish expression returned.

Da Costa shrugged.

'You come.'

He led them back to the upper decks and from there, up a steeply angled ladder, to the bridge. Brand was a little surprised to see that it was fitted out in modern fashion, with a conventional ship's wheel, compass in a binnacle, a clutter of miscellaneous electronic gear, VHF radio and swivel-mounted spotlights on the wings. No *Robert E. Lee* nonsense up here. He wondered how well Captain Da Costa coped with all the gadgetry.

50

A bottle of red wine was produced from a cabinet which also held a pair of binoculars, and Da Costa, suddenly effusive, found two not very clean glasses and a plastic mug.

They drank the sour wine, looking down at the river flowing silently and secretly past the ship's bows. If you ignored the jetty and looked only at the moving water, Brand thought, you could almost imagine yourself at sea.

'How many cabin passengers does she carry?' On the way up to the bridge they had passed a row of cabins, each facing out to the deck, with windows instead of portholes.

Da Costa was not interested in past prospects. 'Thirty, forty. Who knows? But' – slyly – 'she take plenty deck passenger. Plenty.'

'We'll see about it,' Brand told him evasively. He was conscious that Shahida was as disappointed with his reply as Da Costa.

On the way back to hospital Brand told Shahida of the new joking name for the river boat: *Faith*, short for Faith, Hope and Charity. She did not seem to find it very amusing.

For a time they travelled in silence. Brand searched his mind for a safe topic of conversation.

'Did you live in Malaya for long?'

She turned with a startled look.

He said defensively: 'You mentioned the other night you'd worked there.'

'Yes, of course. But it's weird you should have asked just now. I was thinking about Malaya.'

He laughed. 'ESP.'

'Must have been.'

'What made you think about it.'

'Going aboard that wreck of a ship, I guess. It reminded me of a shipload of refugees that landed at the camp where I worked.'

'A refugee camp?'

'For the boat people from Vietnam. I was a medical officer there.'

He looked at her with new respect. At the same time he made a swift historical calculation. He would have to revise his estimate of her age. He had thought her to be in her mid-twenties. But if she had been involved with the Vietnam refugees she must be thirty at least.

'Tough job.'

'It was.'

She was silent again and after a while he prompted her.

'You mentioned a shipload of people.'

'Yes. They'd been boarded by pirates off the Thai coast. The women were raped and most of the men killed.'

Contemplating the horrors she must have witnessed, he in turn was silent. At last he said awkwardly: 'The things people do to one another.'

'Yes.'

'How did they get to be in Malaya? Isn't it quite a way from Thailand?'

'The Thais left them adrift in the Gulf with no one to work the ship and hardly any water. Even not counting those who were shot, there were nearly two hundred of them crowded on a ship not much bigger than Captain Da Costa's paddle steamer. They were at sea forty days.'

'Dear God. How were they rescued?'

'A Malayan gunboat spotted them. But they weren't allowed ashore at first. They spent another month anchored in quarantine off Redang Island. Then they came to the camp. Those who survived.'

'At least some of them were lucky.'

She laughed shortly. 'If you can call it lucky to be an inmate of a refugee camp.'

'Unpleasant thought.'

'Yes.' She looked fixedly through the windscreen and her hands were clenched tightly in her lap. 'You know, there were times, when I looked at those people, that I wished I could have had a ship of my own.'

'A ship?'

'One big enough to take all the sick and the hungry.'

'Tall order. It would have to be very big indeed.'

'Yes. The size of half the world.'

Brand left Shahida at the entrance to the nurses' home. It was deserted at this time of day and she made her way down echoing corridors to her room. He had seemed embarrassed when he took his leave and she wondered whether the reason was her bringing up the subject of the refugees in Malaya. Some people did not care to be reminded how terrible life could be for the poor and the homeless. There were times when even she tried her best to forget.

Another memory came to mind. It dated back to when she had been very small, probably not more than three or four years old. She'd had a small friend then, a year or two older. His name was Sharif and they played together every day. Her family and Sharif's family had been neighbours in the Malay Quarter in Cape Town.

She had not told anyone here that she had been born in South Africa. She did not think anyone knew. The AID administrators had been interested only in qualifications and experience, not in race or creed or origin. She had been a British national for a long time now, ever since her father had sold his business and left the land of apartheid.

It had been a winter's morning and it had rained, an icy grey Cape Town drizzle. They had been forced to play indoors, in Sharif's mother's house, and they were bored. Shortly before the noon gun the rain had stopped and there had even been patches of watery blue over the mountain. Sharif's mother had fitted them into their coats and, gratefully, sent them into the back yard. The coats were very special, bright red and brand new, with warm linings. Sharif had been given his coat first and then she had to have one too, identical. Once the wish had been granted she had not really cared much about the coat and she sensed that Sharif liked his more than she liked hers. It was different for him; his father was not rich and there were lots of older children in the family from whom he received hand-me-down clothing. The red coat was new and it was his own.

There had been puddles on the crack-starred concrete of the yard and they had amused themselves splashing in the water until Sharif's mother had come out and scolded them. A warm cooking smell followed her from the kitchen. She was famous in the neighbourhood for her cooking, particularly festival dishes, biriani and kabobs and *smoored snoek* and all the variety of sweet cakes and pastries which went with Malay great occasions. But that had been an ordinary working day, so the aroma Shahida believed she could still smell had probably been no more than a curry or a bobotie simmering on the immense black wood stove.

They had been quiet after the scolding, and quickly bored again. They were forbidden to go beyond the latched gate and out into the busy street, but there was a chicken run against the wall in a corner of the yard and from its roof they could see over the wall and watch people and traffic passing on the other side.

Sharif had helped her on to the rusty corrugated iron roof, impatient because she could not climb as well as he. They had crawled across to the parapet and peered over it, taking care not to be seen because sometimes bigger children spotted them and threw stones at them. The Quarter was a respectable neighbourhood, but there were gangs of young hooligans who sometimes made trouble.

Diagonally across the street was a vacant plot on which vendors set up their stalls in defiance of the licensing authorities and the police. Today, however, the rain had driven the illegal traders elsewhere and only a few roughly shaped skeleton stalls, hung with soaked canvas rags, marked their centre of commerce.

In the tall grass beyond the market place a vegetable dealer had discarded the contents of a bag of oranges too far gone to attract a buyer. The children looked over the wall and saw a small boy, a black child, sitting on his haunches amidst the pile of rotting fruit and pawing through it in search of edible portions.

Sharif saw the black boy eating the oranges, some of which were purple-blue with mould, and made a sound of distaste.

He said: 'Look at him eating those old oranges.'

Shahida said: 'Perhaps he's hungry.'

'He's not hungry. He likes eating old oranges.' He made a face. 'Yech. I wouldn't eat them.'

Shahida said: 'I think he's hungry.'

'He's not.' Sharif looked around and picked up a stone. He threw the stone, but his arm was powerful enough to send it only over the wall and halfway across the street. Its clattering fall made the boy look up from his pile of oranges, and his bemused expression as he looked around to determine the source of the unexpected noise caused them to giggle and then duck out of sight behind the parapet, snorting with suppressed laughter.

It was only after Sharif had thrown two more stones that the black child realized where they were coming from. He retaliated with one of the bad oranges but his aim was no better than Sharif's and the fruit burst on the side of the pavement. Emboldened, the black boy, carrying an orange in each hand, crossed the street.

Shahida had not taken part in the miniature battle, except to laugh when Sharif threw the stones. But the black child's hostile look frightened her and now she also picked up a stone and hurled it. Perhaps fear gave her extra strength, perhaps it was only a fluke, but the stone flew accurately and struck the black boy below the eye, cutting open his cheek. He dropped the oranges and began to cry, and a thin wash of blood ran down the side of his face.

They looked down at him in wordless dismay. He stood in the middle of the street, weeping. At that moment the noon gun sounded and pigeons flew above the distant city buildings in their daily alarm.

Sharif took off his coat and dropped it over the wall.

What prompted him she could never afterwards determine. A peace offering? A bribe, in the hope that the black boy would go away? There would be trouble if the urchin went to Sharif's mother to complain, but it would be nothing compared to the loss of his coat.

She would always remember the wheeling pigeons and the black child running at the end of the street, carrying the red coat, and Sharif looking after him, his face already registering the solemnity of what he had done. She wondered: was she still, after all this time, looking for someone to whom she could give a coat?

The tedious job of checking hundreds of culture bottles stewing away in the blood-heat cosiness of the incubator was usually left to an assistant. Because of Dr Hauge's particular interest, however, Fissher had taken over the morning and evening routine. He had examined each bottle, then tipped it to reseed the growth medium with the broth of blood.

Inside the bottles was nutrient agar, mixed into a rich broth with penicillinase and para-amine-benzoic acid and liquid, all in an antiseptic, oxygen-free concoction which protected whatever might grow in there, even as it was fed and encouraged and pampered.

This morning, for the first time, he had seen a change. Shiny round glistening colonies of bacilli had developed in a number of cultures.

There was nothing dramatic about it, no more so than about any other process of procreation and growth, and yet Fissher always found a curious satisfaction in seeing the equation of life work out once more.

He showed no excitement, however, as he went about the complicated process of identifying the particular microscopic bit of matter which had probably caused Nurse Jakavula's death. There could be no wild guesses in a laboratory. You went on doing the same things routinely, for it was only by routine, by an orderly arrangement of standard procedures, that your work had any meaning.

Some samples were set aside for Gram stain tests. Others were put up on plates in an anaerobic jar to determine whether they grew best in oxygen-free conditions. Their antibiotic sensitivity was tested by means of a range of antibiotic discs.

Other colonies were seeded again in tubes of broth and allowed to grow for a few hours. Then small, precise quantities were introduced into pre-prepared test tubes containing various sugar solutions – glucose, lactose, mannite, mannitol, sucrose. The reaction of these sugars and the drops of living matter would give him a lead to what he was dealing with.

The results of the biochemical tests were extremely puzzling. It took him a while to work out an answer.

Russell Hamilton stared around him with an expression of hauteur and made a show of looking at his watch. He had a band-aid strip over the palm of his left hand.

'Can we start?' he asked loudly. 'I'm running late as it is.'

'We're waiting for Dr Hauge,' Brand said.

'He's always late,' Hamilton snapped.

'This meeting is at Dr Hauge's request.' Brand was determined not to be intimidated. 'We'll wait until he comes.'

There was an awkward silence. Shahida Karim sat with her head bowed, examining her fingernails. Helmut Fissher, seated beside her, was toying with his cane. His expression was enigmatic. Brand

56

wondered if he knew what was coming. He had been helping Hauge in the laboratory and must surely have some knowledge of whatever it was the old man had found.

A moment later Hauge, characteristically dishevelled, unbuttoned white coat flying behind him, came in breathlessly. He made no apologies and abruptly took a seat, immediately opening a bulging file he had brought with him and starting to rearrange the papers inside.

It took time and patience to get him started. He was more woolly-headed even than usual and kept scrabbling among his papers, so that Brand could not help secretly sympathizing when Hamilton again consulted his watch significantly. He sat tight, however, starting to suspect that the old man's performance was less ingenuous than it seemed.

'Our purpose was to try to demonstrate the presence of salmonella typhii in the blood or the stool of the young woman, Nurse . . . Nurse . . .' Hauge shuffled his reports and triumphantly came up with the name: 'Nurse Jakavula. We were fortunate to have a full range of haemotological investigations both before and after death. Interestingly enough, the Vidal turned out to be positive. As you know, the test is designed to show the existence of typhoid antibodies. However, it is not conclusive.' He pulled his reading glasses down to the bridge of his nose. 'Serological tests are designed to determine the reaction of blood serum to various microbes. When we do a culture, on the other hand – '

Hamilton threw up his hands dramatically. 'Could we be spared a lecture on microbiology, please?' His voice was biting. 'I'm sure we would all like to get to the point.'

Hauge looked more flustered and crestfallen than the interruption warranted. It took him several floundering minutes to get back into stride. Brand's suspicions hardened into certainty. Hauge was spinning a web and Hamilton was the self-important fly buzzing ever closer.

Brand said firmly: 'I think we should allow Dr Hauge to continue in his own way.'

Hamilton gave him a poisonous look but subsided into mutinous silence.

'Thank you,' Hauge said with ironic emphasis. He began to

57

speak more rapidly and methodically now, as if tiring of the role of pedagogue. 'Let us consider the findings. There was significant bacterial growth only in the case of one culture from the blood taken before death. We found the presence of a Gram-negative bacillus. But only in that single culture. However, in the culture from the blood taken at the autopsy we found the identical bacillus in every case.'

Hamilton sat up with a jerk.

'Salmonella typhii is Gram-negative, isn't it? That's what I said all along. Typhoid.'

He received a distant nod and a chilly smile.

'Dr Hamilton is partly right. The bacteria which cause typhoid fever are indeed Gram-negative. But that isn't what we found. What we did find was nothing more than our old friend E. coli. Escherichia coli,' Hauge added, as if this further identification made everything clear.

'But that's absurd. What are you suggesting? Septicaemia due to E. coli?'

'That was the trap I almost walked into, and one which even a medical student would have avoided. Like all of us I had been staring too hard at the obvious.' The old man pointedly avoided looking at Hamilton. 'Because of the preconception that we were dealing with typhoid we were determined to find a bacillus. So when I found E. coli in two sets of cultures the temptation was to say: ah, this must be it. What I had briefly forgotten, and what every student knows, is that, although E. coli is a common organism of the digestive tract, after death it also invades the bloodstream. That accounted for the second set of results.'

'And what about the first?'

Hauge looked suddenly bored. 'Fissher will tell you about that.' Without warning he turned away and began to page through the papers in his file. They were caught unprepared.

Brand said encouragingly: 'Mr Fissher?'

Fissher spoke so softly that they had to strain to hear.

'It was contaminated,' he said.

'What's that?' Hamilton asked sharply. 'What's he saying?'

'The culture was contaminated. The first one. There was no connection between it and the others.'

'Well, for Christ's sake, why have we been put through this

58

rigmarole? We're no further than when we started. All we know is that the lab has made a foul-up.'

Fissher coloured slightly. 'Even under the most sterile conditions it is impossible to exclude all contaminants.'

'We'll have to take your word for it,' the surgeon said sarcastically. 'But so what? What does all this prove?'

Hauge looked up from his papers. 'It goes to show that Mr Fissher here is perhaps a better scientist than the rest of us. He works on what he finds in the laboratory and isn't led astray by clinical observations. It was his suggestion which put me on the right track. We have not been able to isolate salmonella typhii or any other form of bacteria. Perhaps we now have to concede that we have been looking in the wrong direction. Where should we look instead?' His voice was suddenly ominous. 'Among the viruses perhaps. And then among those which cause haemorrhagic fever of a fatal nature. I can give you the names of two of them. Lassa fever and Marburg disease. I'm sure I need not tell anyone here what the implications are.'

5

From the moment Hauge had suggested that the hospital might be faced with an outbreak of a deadly viral disease, Brand's life took on the quality of a nightmare. There was the same dread he sometimes experienced in dreams: that of being hemmed in by ponderous forces which somehow remained always out of sight and beyond reach. He struggled, solitary and afraid, and yet the things around him were untouched.

He had read little medical literature on West African diseases, for knowledge of them was sparse, but he knew enough to make him afraid. Marburg disease had been named after the German city where five laboratory workers had died after being in contact with the blood of vervet monkeys shipped from Uganda. There had been further outbreaks in Frankfurt, where two people had died, and in Belgrade. Lassa, too, was a place-name; in fact there was a whole string of names of remote places – Rift Valley fever, St Louis

59

encephalitis – but the romantic names could not disguise the cruel reality of sickness and misery and death.

Although he had been kept furiously busy, he seemed to get nowhere. What had occupied him had been routine isolation and prevention. People who had been in close contact with the dead nurse and the child would now, because of these encounters, have to serve a virtually indeterminate sentence in an isolation ward until the dangers had been assessed. He and the other doctors who had treated one or both of the dead patients should strictly speaking have joined the group in detention. It had been decided, however, that this would hamstring the normal workings of the hospital and that a daily physical examination would suffice. There were so many things to do and oversee: endless lists of supplies and equipment, plans for coping with further possible outbreaks, for this or that emergency. He was kept busy, but that was not enough. He wanted answers and these would only be provided in time.

Hauge's laboratory was inadequate for the specialized and very hazardous work of isolating dangerous viruses. The specimens he had taken from Nurse Jakavula and the Moremi boy had been sent to a virology unit in South Africa which was equipped with a high-security laboratory. There whatever it was that had caused the two deaths would be detected and analysed. But until then all they could do was wait.

One hope they held to was that the Moremi family might provide a lead, no matter how slender, to the source of the disease. The search for the mother changed from an academic exercise to a problem of the utmost urgency.

But it was a search which led, literally, to a blind alley. The old man and woman who had brought the child to hospital could not be found. Either the address they had given was false, or the clerk who had taken it down had been careless. Shahida spent a whole day in a mean street in the township while scores of old people were produced from huts and shanties in the neighbourhood for her scrutiny and possible identification. In the end, near tears, she confessed herself at a loss.

The Moremi family had vanished.

Brand and Russell Hamilton met inside the foyer, at the main entrance. Brand nodded a polite greeting and made to go past, but the surgeon detained him.

'James. I've been wanting to speak to you.'

You knew where to find me, Brand thought. It was childish to resent the surgeon's high-handed manner, but he could not bring himself to like the man. For this reason he tried to make his voice especially cordial.

'What about, Russ?'

'The drug estimates for my surgical wards. You admin guys have cut my antibiotics allocation again.'

It was a familiar complaint. Hamilton was notorious for his free and easy approach to drug orders.

'You know how expensive the things have become,' Brand said soothingly. 'But I'll speak to Mr Fissher.'

'Huh! That bloody little Kraut. If old Hauge wants fancy stuff for his labs, that's OK. But when it comes to – '

'I'll take it up with Mr Fissher. Was there anything else?'

'Maybe you should cut your fancy Minister of Health's kickbacks. Then we might have some more money for health in this country.'

Brand was genuinely puzzled. 'The minister? Minister Makaza? What does he have to do with it?'

'Drugs, man! He's the most corrupt of the bunch. You want to tell me you haven't heard?'

'Russell, I give you my word I have no idea what you're talking about.'

Hamilton seemed alarmed at what he had said, but he went on staunchly. 'Makaza and the drug suppliers. They're hand in glove. It's a well-known fact.' His expression changed and he added quickly: 'Mind you, don't say I told you.'

'Is there any proof of this?'

'You know, the usual thing. One hears these things. He's supposed to get a percentage of all the drugs that come into the country. Must add up to a tidy amount.' He made a gesture of rubbing together thumb and index finger. But he was clearly less assured, and Brand suspected that his charges were founded, as he had admitted, on nothing more solid than rumour. 'But don't tell anyone I said so,' Hamilton said.

'It's already forgotten,' Brand assured him. He examined the

61

other man more closely. There were beads of sweat on his forehead. 'You don't look well, Russ. You're very pale. Are you OK?'

The surgeon pushed irritably past him. 'It's nothing. Just the heat. Don't forget my drug allocations, now.'

It's only the heat, Russell Hamilton thought. It's too hot in this bloody little country. He had a headache and his eyes felt as though there were grit in them.

He wanted the refuge of his operating rooms. There, within the scrubbed limits of his empire, with the tools of his trade arrayed in glittering, disciplined rows, he was immune from doubts and the betrayal of the body. He had a long slate today. He had to hurry.

Hamilton said sharply: 'Swab here, damn it! Do you think I can work in a bucket of blood?'

His assistant shifted the nozzle of the suction pump. 'Sorry.'

'I didn't ask you to be sorry. All I want is you to use your bloody brain, what there is of it.'

The younger surgeon stared fixedly at the open chest cavity, bordered by a rectangular aperture in the green shroud which concealed the patient on the operating table. The raw wound was festooned with rectractors and clamps like the neck hump of a dying bull in the last stages of corrida. There was a moment of motionless, crystal-hard silence. Then the theatre sister shifted her feet uncomfortably and the moment was ended. Hamilton handed her a pair of scissors and she gave him a curve-pointed forceps, and the intricate rhythm of instrument following instrument was partially restored. Not completely, for it seemed to him that something was out of beat, like an irritating, ragged tune played by an unpractised orchestra. The fault did not lie with his assistant, who had a good pair of hands, or with the instrument nurse, who was the most efficient member of his team, but with himself. He realized that he was working more slowly than usual and finding it more difficult to concentrate.

Annoyed, he tried to speed up. He had cut down to the diseased lung and ligated all around it in preparation for the pneumonectomy, but then he discovered that his hands were trembling. He leaned against the table for a moment to rest his arms, and the assistant looked at him curiously.

'Anything wrong, sir?'

'Nothing's wrong,' Hamilton said irritably. Then, in a softer tone, he admitted: 'Been a bit off colour the last couple of days.'

The assistant stared at him in consternation. Hamilton knew that his juniors had nicknamed him, only half-mockingly, 'Ironman', and he was notoriously proud of his ability to stay on his feet in theatre for hours on end without showing signs of exhaustion. It was unthinkable that he should confess to weakness. He tried to continue the operation in spite of the queer feeling that his body did not belong to him.

But the sight of raw tissue and the bloody organs under his hands made nausea well up into his throat. He fought down the bitter taste and for the moment the shock of almost vomiting at the sight of blood cleared his mind.

But then there was a sensation of soaring, and everything – the operation wound, the cluster of instruments, the invisible patient under the green cloth, his own gloved hands – became incredibly distant and small, as if he was viewing them through the wrong end of a telescope.

He staggered back from the table. As he collapsed he heard a confused clamour of voices like the ringing of shrill bells somewhere deep inside his own head.

'His condition is extremely critical,' Dr Hauge said.

Brand pretended interest at being told the obvious.

'I realize that. We are already making arrangements.'

The old man was concerned only with his own preoccupations.

'I have no doubt that he has contracted the same fever as that nurse. A haemorrhagic fever of unknown origin.'

He sounded as if he were preparing lecture notes, Brand thought irritably. They were standing outside the isolation ward where Russell Hamilton had hurriedly been admitted. He was still in the white singlet and linen trousers he had worn under his theatre gown, with a paper cap covering his hair. Brand had found himself

63

curiously bothered by this dress. A doctor's uniform was out of place, almost indecorous, on a sick man.

Hauge was still lecturing.

'The symptoms are identical. Sudden onset of prostration. Haemorrhagic rash. Tendency to epistaxis. Marked leukopenia on the blood count as well as thrombocytopenia. It's the same disease, and we cannot treat it here.'

'I realize that. We've already made arrangements for him to go to a fever hospital in Johannesburg. The Bapangani health people are making a plane available for us.'

'I shall go with him,' Hauge proclaimed.

Puzzled, Brand asked: 'But why, Erik?'

'He needs constant medical attention.'

'Surely a nurse – '

'Besides, I know how he contracted the disease.'

'How?'

'It occurred when he cut himself. Do you recall? In the autopsy room on Monday. He infected himself through that cut.'

'The thought had occurred to me. But we still don't – '

Hauge was not interested in the possibility of error.

'This confirms that the cause is a blood-borne virus. The researchers have been working on the blood specimens I sent them and it is vital that I discuss my findings with them. I will be able to make an important contribution.'

'Well, OK then,' Brand agreed reluctantly. 'If you feel it is important I guess it's OK.'

'It is extremely important,' Hauge said.

Erik Hauge's sense of mission, however, barely outlasted the flight from Leruarua. The aircraft which brought him and an unconscious Russell Hamilton to Johannesburg late that afternoon was met by a highly efficient medical team and, although he was treated politely enough, it was soon made clear that his presence was an extra, not particularly desirable complication.

Practised and expert hands transferred the unconscious man to an ambulance fitted with an isolator bed, a hermetically sealed canopy of plastic sheeting and perspex and stainless steel inside which he lay motionless like a traveller awaiting dispatch to some distant planet. There was no time, and very little patience, to waste with Hauge.

64

'You've been in contact with him,' a young doctor said thoughtfully. 'We should really put you in isolation too.' He saw Hauge's expression and added hastily: 'I suppose it'll be all right. Provided you keep in touch and let us know at once if you feel ill. You know the routine, don't you?'

'I must speak to the people who are working on this virus,' Hauge told him. 'I have certain information that is vital to the research.'

'It will have to wait, doctor,' the young man said firmly. He had an abstracted air. His mind was already with the medical problems represented by that plastic-shrouded capsule in the ambulance. He turned away. 'We'll give you a lift to a . . . a hotel or something.'

Hauge found himself crammed into the back seat of a small car at the tail end of the swift procession of vehicles which bore Hamilton away from the airport. It was an ignominious start to his great mission. He sat with long legs awkwardly folded, nursing his grievances in silence during the journey to the city.

Tomorrow, he resolved. Tomorrow he would visit the virology laboratory, and then he would make certain of being heard.

Something about the smell of the place troubled Hauge, until he realized that it was in fact an absence of smell, an air-conditioned essence of sterility. It made him feel like a bumbling intruder in a world of pure, inviolate science. He tried, as he followed his guide through the double, electronically controlled doors, to shake off the feeling. The security laboratory, for all its sophistication, was no more than an extension of his own lab back in the hospital at Leruarua.

'We'll have to go through the showers, I'm afraid,' his young companion said apologetically. 'We leave our outside clothes here. OK?'

Hauge nodded curtly, as if this was routine to him. But, standing naked and conscious of the paleness and flabbiness of his big body, the feeling of inadequacy returned more sharply. On the outer door of the shower partition there was a warning sign in luminous red open circles in a clover design denoting an area of biological hazard. He stared at it defiantly, as if it was also a warning that his skills were out of date in this world of space-age medicine.

They came to another set of sealed doors. Through the glass panels he could see half a dozen technicians at a long row of protective canisters.

Hauge asked aggressively. 'What results have you obtained from the specimens I sent you? I made a provisional diagnosis of Lassa fever. Am I correct?'

An eyebrow was half raised. Then the virologist said mildly: 'We're not quite there yet. Come, let me introduce you to Mr Rosenthal. He's working on it.'

The technician was handling a suckling mouse inside a container, his hands encased in gloves built into the perspex box. A dozen other mice struggled feebly on the floor of the container.

Names were exchanged.

'We've had problems with this thing,' Rosenthal said. 'Has Dr Louw told you?'

The virologist shook his head. 'No. You explain to him.'

'Well, we tried to incubate it in eggs first. We did a variety of inoculations, yolk sac, amniotic, allantoic and choric-allantoic.' An expression of polite inquiry came to the technician's face. 'Are you familiar with the techniques?'

'Yes, yes,' Hauge said testily. 'Go on.'

'We had no luck. Nothing would grow. Of course some viruses won't grow in embryonated eggs, so we'd also inoculated a batch of these little fellows.' He indicated the mice. 'But unfortunately we had to put the mother in with them and she turned cannibal on us. Cleaned out the whole nest.'

'She ate all her young?'

'That's right.'

'Then they must have shown symptoms. The mother would not have eaten them if they were healthy.'

Rosenthal's voice hardened a little; he was making it clear that he did not appreciate instruction in his own field. 'Sure, but that's a long way from being scientific proof.'

'Naturally.'

'Well, that's by the way. What's interesting is that we had another go with monkey cell cultures and that didn't work either. The cultures all died off, for some reason we still haven't fathomed. But at least we've finally got it going on a HeLa cell line. And the results are certainly very interesting. . . .'

Portions of the organs Hauge had sent here had been ground, suspended in a growth medium, then centrifuged to produce a supernatant, a concentration of whatever had invaded the bodies of Nurse Jakavula and the Moremi child. This in turn had been inoculated into culture bottles seeded with the living cells. Viruses killed these off, creating a ragged effect on the cell sheets, as when moths had been at an old coat. This cytopathic effect, which the researchers called CPE, was one of their tests, an aid to identification. A virus was known by the nature of the harm it caused.

Hauge looked round at the large room with its handful of intent, silent workers. Strange to think that this complex and costly structure, earthquake-proof, equipped with the most elaborate safety devices and backup systems, all designed to make it as impregnable as the vaults of Fort Knox, owed its existence to an inert, parasitic bit of matter.

The smallest known living creatures; though in fact scientists hotly disputed whether viruses could properly be called living. He thought about the many electron-microphotographs of the minuscule things he had seen. Most of them resembled nothing one could think of to compare, except perhaps a vaguely geometric design, like a child's attempt at drawing a hexagon.

It drained the imagination sometimes to conceive that something so small that even light waves passed it by, so apparently inactive that it could not feed, grow or multiply on its own, could yet be so deadly. Basically the thing was no more than a speck of nucleic acid; the stuff of life and yet not alive. It was only when a virus invaded living matter that it took on a vicious life of its own, twisting the host cell to its own purpose, which was the millionfold re-creation of itself.

Viruses carried within them the seeds of their own destruction. Somehow, in a way science had not yet determined, they produced in their host a capacity to oppose them. Antibodies were formed, bits of protein, and these were precisely structured to lock on to the invaders and destroy them.

The battle for survival was endless.

'So that's our conclusion,' the young virologist said. 'We haven't been able to class this bug of yours with any others we know. Not clinically, not histologically, not by ATKTM.' He saw Hauge's mystified look and explained good-naturedly: 'All Tests Known to Man.'

'Do you wish to tell me', Hauge said excitedly, 'that we have here a virus presently unknown to science?'

Dr Louw flinched slightly at the dramatic phrase.

'Well . . . yes, I guess you could call it that. Of course there are lots of bugs we don't really know much about.'

'Not so many which cause fatalities.'

'I suppose that's true.'

'Would it assist to trace the origin of the disease?'

'It wouldn't do any harm.'

'We could set up an investigation in Leruarua. There might have been other cases.'

'There might.' The young man looked dubious.

'At least there is a possibility.'

'A possibility.'

'And if such cases could be traced and antibodies found to be present. . . .'

'That's a hell of a lot of "if"s, doctor.'

'If you are unable to do the necessary fieldwork, I am prepared to undertake it for you.'

Dr Louw's startled reaction showed that he had realized only now, too late, in which direction he was being steered.

'Well, sir, that's very kind. . . .'

Erik Hauge returned to Leruarua at the end of the week. The wearying journey (he had missed the twice-weekly direct flight from Johannesburg and had had to make a hop-and-step journey by unscheduled aircraft across the Kalahari Desert) had failed to damp his enthusiasm. He sought out Brand immediately he got back to the hospital.

'They are prepared to put their facilities at my disposal,' he announced proudly. 'Equipment . . . any equipment we need, respirators and so forth to protect the investigators . . . anything else we require.'

Brand sighed wearily.

'They have actually confirmed this to be a new virus?'

'Yes. In fact it already had been provisionally named. They were

68

kind enough, the people in Johannesburg, to accept my suggestion.' The old man reached for the scratch pad on Brand's desk. 'May I . . . ?'

'Go ahead.'

'We found that other researchers had already laid claim to the names Alpha and Beta and so forth, right down to Epsilon. It would perhaps have been fitting to name it for Mr Fissher, who first suggested that I look among the viruses, but unfortunately the Greek alphabet is deficient in the letter F. So we went one further and named it Virus Eta.' He had taken out a pen and now he firmly wrote the symbol H on the scratch pad. He pushed it towards Brand and sat back to gauge reaction. His attitude, that of someone who had prepared a practical joke but was uncertain whether it would succeed, gave Brand the clue.

Not Virus Eta, but Virus H. The Hauge Virus.

6

Shahida went back to night duty that Sunday, two weeks after Nurse Jakavula's illness and death. She did so almost with reluctance. There was an air of gloom about the dilapidated old buildings. Night duty, particularly after the imposition of a curfew, was a period of boredom and frustration. Now the quarantine had brought the normal workings of the hospital virtually to a standstill.

She had never been quite clear in her mind what she really thought about the AID unit and her involvement with it. Even before she had come to this country, while still waiting to hear if her application for a post had been approved, there had been a minor scandal. It had started with a television exposé of AID's recruitment of foreign medical staff. There had been a fierce interview on NBC, subsequently rebroadcast by the BBC, with a group of medical hotheads who implied that anyone volunteering to work in South Africa must be a secret fascist.

Fortunately the shouting had died down. The organization seemed obviously altruistic in its work in Africa. And then there was the hard fact which had to be faced, no matter how reluctantly:

medical organization in South Africa was advanced and effective, compared with the chaos elsewhere on the continent.

She had been offered the job and she had accepted, putting her doubts aside. There had been a certain excitement about going near a country where her race made her a target and perhaps even the object of dark desires.

The sullen black nurse who had worked in the Emergency Unit a fortnight ago was again on duty. She was friendlier tonight and her attitude, Shahida was amused to note, was more deferential. The quarantine had caused a scare among the local staff; some of the more frightened had to be fetched from home where they had fled. But the curious consequence was more faith in the doctors and what they said and did.

There were no new admissions, because of the quarantine, and they disposed of a few routine matters before Shahida got ready to continue her round through the other wards.

'Some of these people . . . I don't know how they think,' the nurse said.

Shahida, not really listening, took up her stethoscope from the table where they had been working.

'They seem to think a hospital is just there for their convenience. Those old people were here today – on a Sunday – wanting their child's clothes. I asked them what do they think this is, a laundry open every day of the week?'

Shahida turned back to her, alerted now.

'What old people?'

'That old man and woman who brought the child. I said where did they expect me to find old clothes on a Sunday? They must come back tomorrow when Matron is here, or else we'll send the clothes to them through the post.'

'What child are you talking about? The Moremi child?'

'That's the one. Those stupid old – '

'But you utter idiot, what have you done? Did you send them away?'

The nurse stared resentfully. 'Of course. How must I know where to look for old clothes on a Sunday?'

'Don't you realize we have been trying to find that old couple for more than a week now?'

The woman muttered: 'No one told me.'

70

'When did this happen? Where did they go?'

'They came this afternoon. On a Sunday afternoon, how was I supposed to know?'

'Oh, damn your Sunday afternoon! Is there a chance they might not have gone?'

Vague understanding seemed at last to penetrate the woman's sulky defensiveness. She said, shaken: 'I don't know, doctor. I didn't see them go.'

'Well, go and see if you can. . . . No. Wait. Did you say something about posting the clothes?'

'I said Matron would probably put a parcel in the post for them.'

'But then you must have found out where they live. Or did you take the address from the file? It was not correct.'

'They told me where to send the parcel.' The nurse began to scrabble among the untidy assortment of loose papers on the table, while Shahida waited impatiently.

At last the nurse produced a slip of paper, jaggedly torn from a prescription pad, from the bottom of the pile. 'This is the address they told me.'

'Dumela Street 31B. Where is this? In the townships?'

'I think it is in the Old Town. Where the Matetwa people live.'

'Go and find a hospital driver. At once. And a car. Tell him to get ready at once to take me to this place.'

The car's windscreen was dusty and smeared with grease, so that the lights of oncoming vehicles became a splintered blur through the glass and caused the driver to swear and jerk at his steering wheel as if in fear of imminent collision. He made no attempt, however, to clean the windscreen, and Shahida did not have the courage to suggest it. She had brought this on herself, she thought, and therefore she had to endure the frightening journey with as much good grace as possible.

Enough time had gone by for her to start questioning her own decision. To go into the townships after dark without proper escort was foolhardy. True, it was essential that the parents of the dead child should be found without delay. But had she not perhaps been too impulsive because she was angry with the nurse? She hoped forlornly that they would not run into trouble.

71

Presently the car turned off the main road and went for a distance along a rutted track. Then there were scattered lights on the left and they turned again, towards these. She did not know where they were, only that these were the squatter camps west of the city. She had been here before, but only in daytime and with the security of an ambulance crew in attendance.

They were among the houses before she realized it, for most of them were low to the ground and darkened. The lights which had shown from a distance became curiously diffused when you were close by, an occasional cooking fire here, an oil lamp behind an open doorway, no more than sparks in the encircling night.

The driver had slowed to a crawl and was peering out, muttering to himself. Figures appeared in the headlights, a group of youths outside a tin shanty, curiously watching the passing car. The driver stopped, turning so that the lights were full on the youngsters, but as he did so they vanished, so swiftly that the effect was that of a conjuring trick. Shahida found herself blinking involuntarily.

After a moment of fiddling irresolutely with the gear shift the driver switched off the engine, mumbled something and climbed out. He moved away and disappeared from sight as quickly and thoroughly as the youths a moment before. She was alone and a little frightened.

The driver returned with two of the youths. They were talking and one was pointing. The driver started the car up again. They drove on, round a corner and then another, moving slowly while the young men ran alongside, laughing and chattering to the driver through his open window. Far from being threatened, she was being assisted.

The car stopped again. The driver said brusquely: 'You must come.'

She stumbled blindly after him, her eyes unaccustomed to the dark sky, conscious of the movements of the two youths behind her. Down an alleyway with soft soil underneath. (She hoped it was only soil.) Past dark hovels and the stench of rotted vegetation and wood smoke and human excrement and that other, the thin, bitter smell of abject poverty. Something moved and scampered away: a dog, a goat, a man on all fours? The driver was walking too fast and the two black youths followed every move she made.

Then a shanty identical to the others, with a door made of nailed wooden slats. A lamp, smoking in spite of being turned low, on a bare table. People, four or five of them, in the shadows. The smell again, but heightened tenfold. They were all crowded together in the single room, she and the driver and the two young men, and the room was full to bursting point and still she could not make out the faces in the shadows.

The driver asked questions, tensely, his voice demanding. The answers were soft, placatory. He asked again, becoming impatient. The voices that answered him became even softer.

'She has gone,' he told her in disgust.

'Who?'

But he had already turned away and was again addressing the others. He singled out one man with a skeletal face and close-cropped scalp. He stood threateningly over him and spoke with such brutal force that she feared he might hit the man. She wanted to catch his arm and shout: No! No! But she was afraid too, as afraid as the thin-faced man.

'It's no good,' he told her abruptly, turning his hands outwards in a gesture of defeat. 'The woman has gone.'

'Where has she gone?'

'She lived here with the two children and the child who died,' he said, ignoring her question. 'Then she became frightened so she took the children and went away.'

'But where?'

He spoke to the thin man.

'To where she came from.'

'Where is this place?'

'Far away. Far.'

'Ask them about the sickness. Has anyone else been sick? Any of the children?'

'They do not know. They took the house when the woman left. They are not her people.'

'But surely they must know something about her.'

Indifferently: 'They know nothing. These are Matetwa people, all those who live in this camp. They are stupid.'

But something in the air of that place, something in the attitude of the people, alerted her in spite of her feeling of being alien. They knew the answers to her questions, but would not give them.

73

'Ask them how the child became sick. Was he sick for a long time?'

The shutters were closing even as she battered despairingly against them.

'They know nothing about the child. The woman was not of their people.'

'I think they're lying. It's not likely that the woman would be taken in by strangers, or that she would give her house to strangers.'

'That is what they say.'

On sudden impulse she moved to the table and picked up the lamp. She was not sure what she intended doing with it, so she held it high and moved it in a circle to light up the room, shining it on the faces of the other occupants, one by one. The people shrank away from the searching light.

She said excitedly: 'That one! That old man!'

The old man had been sitting motionless in a corner, on his haunches. His peppercorn hair was smudged with grey and his wrinkled face was drawn in between his shoulders, poking out like the head of an aged tortoise. His eyes regarded her with a distant, reptilian stare.

The others, including the driver, watched her too.

'He brought the child to the hospital,' she said. 'He and a woman. She wasn't as old as he, but she was too old to be the mother. She did most of the talking, but he was there too. Ask him if he went there today to fetch the dead child's clothes?'

The driver, enthusiastic again, started to question the old man. The old man sat impassively and did not reply. He looked as if he could sit there, silent, for ever. The driver became angry. There was not a flicker of expression on the old man's face. The thin man intervened, his voice querulous. He and the driver argued.

'They say you have made a mistake,' the driver said sulkily. 'This old man has never been to the hospital. His legs are bad and he cannot walk.'

'I'm sure it was him.' But in saying this certainty left her. Old people all come to look alike. And to her shame she had to admit that African faces sometimes confused her. The trouble was that one didn't really look. She thought she had seen the old man with the woman and the child that night, but now she could no longer be sure.

74

'They say he has not been away from this house.'

'But a moment ago they were saying they've only lived here for a couple of days.'

He shrugged. 'All these Matetwa tell lies.'

The weight of apathy, of nothing-can-ever-change, pressed heavily on her shoulders. But she had to resist it.

'They're coming with us,' she said determinedly. 'I don't care what they say, but I'm not leaving it here. Tell them that. They're coming with us. The whole lot of them.'

She had expected further protests and denials but, strangely, the people in the shack accepted her instructions with impassive resignation. She went to the door, waiting for them to follow.

There were loud voices outside, then shouts and sounds of what might be a struggle. Something heavy was violently overturned. She retreated until her back was to the table. She stared wordlessly at the driver. He looked puzzled rather than afraid. The others in the room were utterly silent. The two young men who had accompanied them from the street moved away from the doorway.

The door was flung open. A short, squat, powerfully built African stood there. He was furiously, fearsomely drunk. He shouted at the thin-faced man and then at the driver. The driver replied soothingly, but the drunk man continued to shout. Then he saw her. He asked a question, obviously about her presence. Both the driver and the man with the thin face replied together. She caught the word 'doctor'. She could not back away any further, but she put her hands on the table behind her.

The newcomer continued to stare at her. Her hands were shaking. She knew that she must conceal her fear. The driver and the man of the house were still talking, still explaining, while the drunk stranger watched her without paying attention to them.

Suddenly he said to her, in a truculent voice, speaking English: 'The people shall be free.' He raised an arm in a clenched-fist salute. 'The people shall be free.'

She did not know whether she was intended to respond to the slogan. She could only look back at him, breathlessly.

He said again, in the same hostile chant: 'The people shall be free.' Then, his voice conspiratorial: 'The doctors, they are our friends. Have you come from Shinyana?'

The driver spoke very rapidly and angrily, using the same word, or name, whatever it meant – Shinyana. He waved the drunk man away with an imperious gesture, and then said gruffly to the others in the hut: 'Come.' She was amazed that the drunk man made no attempt to stop any of them.

Only much later, back in the car and on the road to the hospital, with the five black people from the hut wedged into the back seat, did she remember to ask: 'What did that man mean, asking if I was from . . . what was it? Shinyana?'

'Nothing,' he said brusquely. 'He meant nothing. He was drunk.'

The passengers jam-packed in the back seat sat there silently, uncomplaining. None of them spoke a word throughout the journey.

Brand found out about Shahida's night-time journey only when he came to the hospital in the morning. He was both dismayed and angry.

'Do you realize how dangerous it might have been?'

'Might have been,' she retorted. 'But it wasn't.'

'That makes no odds. It's idiotic to go into the black areas after dark.'

'Why black areas, particularly? Isn't that a rather racist attitude?'

'It's a practical attitude. One doesn't have to be . . . uh . . . anti-lion to realize it's not clever to put your head in its mouth.'

She was prepared to continue the argument – who the hell did he think he was anyway? – but she decided there were more important things to think about. She was also not a little intrigued by his concern for her safety.

The story they got from the occupants of the house in Dumela Street continued to be confusing and contradictory. It was only after Brand called in the aid of the hospital security officer that the truth began to emerge. The sight of the black uniform and silver buttons was intimidating enough to put an end to further fabrication.

The old man with the supposedly bad legs was the Moremi woman's uncle. He admitted that he and his wife had taken the child to hospital. His niece had another child, the dead child's brother. The boy had been sick too, very sick. It was because of his

76

illness that the mother had travelled to the city, but he had recovered on the journey, so she had never taken him to hospital. Then the second child had become sick as well, the one who had died.

'Is this the truth now?' Brand asked sternly of the security officer. The black man shrugged. 'Who can tell?'

The reason for the lies and denials became more clear. It was difficult to find a house in the Matetwa township. They had feared eviction because of the woman and her sick children. They had told her to go away.

It was a likely enough story, although Brand suspected that it was not the whole truth. But he was not concerned with motives for past deeds and he let it go.

The old man was asked the name of her home village and his reply confused the issue even further. He said 'Seroromo', and they could find no such place on the maps. Then it became clear that he was using a dialect word and that *seroromo* meant 'the mud land', the marshes for which the Sesangani phrase was *lehatshe ya letlhaka*, 'the country of reeds'.

The misunderstanding brought home to Brand the hopelessness of the task; how was the woman to be found in that wilderness when even black men used different words to describe it?

Hauge remained fiercely insistent.

'She must be found. The other child must be found. He is a potential suspect. If we are to contain the disease he must be found.'

'Do you realize what you are asking?' Brand asked him tiredly. 'It's a no man's land out there. She could be anywhere within two thousand square miles.'

'I am not concerned about figures,' Hauge retorted grandly. 'She must be found somewhere.'

But more questions at last produced an identifiable name. There was a place called Sekhong, the old man said. It was a village on the river, far away, and he gestured vaguely towards the north. His niece's husband had lived at Sekhong, so perhaps she had gone back there.

It was a lead, no matter how slender. The Health Bureau, however, was less than enthusiastic that it should be followed up by Hauge or any other member of the AID unit. Brand travelled into

77

town to present the idea to Dr Van Jaarsveld, but the Health Director was unreceptive. There were a dozen reasons why a visit to the northern border was out of the question. This town Sekhong lay inside the M T D, Van Jaarsveld said. Seeing Brand's mystified look, he explained: the Matetwa Tribal District. And the M T D lay within the security area. The army did not like civilians stumbling around in restricted areas. Sekhong itself was in fact an advanced military base. The army provided medical services for the local population. What would Dr Hauge achieve that the army couldn't?

No, Dr Van Jaarsveld said acidly, he did not care for the idea that the Minister of Health should be asked to intercede with the army.

Obviously he saw the shrug with which Brand received this interdict as an admission of defeat. He cleared his throat in a conciliatory way.

'Sorry I can't help you people. But it's really in the army's hands. And I'm afraid my minister hasn't much push when it comes to defence matters.'

'I see,' Brand said noncommittally.

The director laughed as if at some joke they shared. 'Our . . . uh . . . black brethren sometimes get a bit carried away with their own importance.'

The message was clear. RESOLVED: upon a resolution moved by Member Van Jaarsveld and seconded by Member Brand THAT it behoves white men in a black country to stand together for the common good.

It was easy enough to write off that kind of thinking by mocking it. More difficult, because it went counter to one's own style, to appear to agree and then change it by slow pressure. Most difficult of all, because one did not know where this might lead, to oppose it frankly and openly. One had, after all, to live and work with people. Hadn't he learned that lesson?

'I think I'll see the minister after all,' Brand said. 'Perhaps he has more influence than we believe.'

There was total bewilderment among Michael Makaza's clerks when Brand arrived unheralded and announced his intention of seeing the minister immediately. He was reminded of the behaviour of a flock of birds around a snake: a great deal of noise and protest, subsiding, when the intruder refused to withdraw, to fatalistic resentment.

Brand almost surprised himself by his own high-handedness. Was there an element of racism, of contempt and impatience for the way of blacks, about his insistence? Had he already grown weary of this country?

He would think about it. But right now there was no time.

The minister's anteroom to which he was finally ushered might have been the waiting room of a reasonably prosperous, fairly trend-conscious physician. There was an abundance of glass and chrome and polished surfaces. On one wall hung the obligatory colour photograph of the Chief Minister. The other pictures were Impressionist. Stacked on a low table among the generously padded chairs were copies of *Time* and *Reader's Digest* and *Paris Match*, no more than a month out of date. There were no South African magazines. In a vase in a corner stood a large arrangement of dry grasses and driftwood and pebbles. The grasses were plumed like soldiers in an army of long ago.

A glass door slid aside on oiled rollers and Makaza came in, hand outstretched in greeting. Brand was led through to the inner office, which was furnished in direct contrast to the sleek look of the outer rooms. Here everything was grained wood and worked leather, simulating age although it was brand new. The effect was that of a stage or a movie set.

Brand took the proffered chair, but did not allow himself to appear at ease in it. He sat on the edge of the seat and held his back stiffly.

'Mr Makaza, I assume you've been told about this . . .' – he hesitated before using the loaded word – '. . . this epidemic of possible viral fever. It's a very alarming situation.'

Makaza looked both grave and gratified, as if to show his appreciation of being invited to share the concerns of the medical profession.

'Dr Van Jaarsveld assures me – '

Brand interrupted him brusquely.

'Mr Makaza, we want action, not reassurances. We need to trace this family from which the primary case came. The Health Bureau is not co-operating. I want to ask you to allow us to find the mother.'

A conflict of desires showed in Makaza's expression. On the one hand was the natural resentment he would feel, as parliamentary head of the department, at having his followers and his policies criticized by an outsider. But perhaps there was something to be gained by appearing to side with the critic, particularly when he was also a member of a usually inviolate profession. When doctors disagreed, laymen took sides with the most argumentative.

Makaza fell to temptation.

'Perhaps the problem is that Dr Van Jaarsveld would prefer to handle the matter himself. He likes to be in the saddle, you know.'

'We don't dispute his authority for one moment. All we ask is that something should be done.'

Makaza looked away, towards the window, through which sounds from outside filtered distantly, like a slow hiss of surf. He did not say anything.

Brand leaned forward. 'Minister, it's in your power to give us the permission we need. Allow us to go and find this woman and her family.'

The black man tapped his fingers agitatedly on his desk blotter. 'How can I go against the advice of my own chief executive?'

In his fidgeting Makaza had managed to brush several letters and papers off the corner of his desk. He leaned over to pick them up.

'After all, he is a medical man. He should know.'

One bit of paper had sailed in under the desk, where Makaza could not see it. It caught Brand's eye. It was a narrow slip with machine-printed numbers in a row of ruled boxes. In one corner was a neat monogram made of the letters G and S enclosed in a stylized Z. Beneath it was a name. He could not help seeing that it was the name of a bank. Genossenschaft Staedtler Zentralbank Aktiengesellschaft. Repeated in French: Banque Centrale Staedtler Société Anonyme, and again in a language he did not know but which might have been Spanish. The address was Zurich.

He tried to avert his eyes, but they kept coming back to that innocent-looking scrap of paper. There was a typed name in one of the boxes: Michael B. Makaza. The other boxes all contained rows of figures. He could not make out which of them gave the balance of the account, but all the figures were impressively long.

He remembered Russell Hamilton's hints about Makaza and the drug industry. Well, if the minister chose to maintain a Swiss bank account, that was his own business.

'You're his boss,' he said.

Makaza pretended to weigh the statement. His fingers ceased their nervous play and he put them together in a judicial pose.

'That's true.'

'I can't help thinking that Dr Van Jaarsveld sees this more as a political matter than as a medical problem. He seems more concerned with military security than with medicine.'

Makaza's face became secretive. 'Politics, security. Who is to know the difference?'

'I believe I can reassure you on that score. We would be sending in a small team to find this woman and to take some blood samples among the local inhabitants. That would be all. There's no political involvement.'

'Conditions are very primitive in the border area.' Makaza's eyes had shifted again.

'Meaning?'

'That unrest is not entirely unknown. There would be some danger.'

'Do you mean there's fighting going on?'

'Just the occasional incident,' Makaza said hastily. 'There are one or two small bands of Matetwa, no more than brigands really, who break into a trading store now and then, or get involved in a skirmish. That kind of thing. Nothing serious.'

Brand decided to use the tactic of seeking innocent and apparently unrelated information.

'By the way, one of my doctors had an odd experience while she was out investigating the child's background. There was confusion about who she was and some talk about her being from someone or something by the name of Shinyana. Have you any idea what could have been meant?'

Makaza's face stiffened and his eyes seemed to glaze.

'I cannot say.'

Brand tried to compensate for an obvious, though inexplicable, blunder.

'She believes it was some kind of superstitious association. A tribal god, or something. These people are Matetwa, aren't they?'

Makaza was still staring at him suspiciously.

'Superstition? I'm not sure. Probably.' Had he seized on the

81

explanation with too much alacrity? 'Very probably. The Matetwa are very superstitious.'

Better to steer clear of the subject.

'Frankly, minister, judging by what you've told me, I can see no objection to our people going to this Matetwa district. Especially since we already have the support of the South African health authorities.'

Brand noticed that the reference to South Africa had not made Makaza's expression appreciably more friendly. Perhaps, he thought, that was the line to follow.

'As I see it, Dr Van Jaarsveld is overcautious. Perhaps he doesn't want to offend the South Africans. It is their forces that operate in the security areas, not so?'

Makaza nodded briskly.

'He even suggested that you . . . I mean, your government . . . might not have sufficient influence to bring to bear on the army.'

For a moment, watching the other man's face, he feared that his tactics might have been too crude. But then Makaza's eyebrows came together in an angry frown.

'He suggested . . . ? Dr Van Jaarsveld said . . . ?'

'I'm sure he meant nothing personal. But it seems almost as if he is a little anxious not to cause the South Africans displeasure.'

Makaza's face had become impassive again. Only the rigid tattoo of his fingers betrayed him. He rose to show that the interview was over.

'Thank you for coming to see me, *Monsieur le Directeur*. I shall consider your request.'

'Thank you,' Brand said.

Travel documents for a journey to the military zone of the northern border area were issued that same afternoon. The party should consist of not more than two people, who would be transported by air force helicopter. The flight would commence at 08h00 the next day.

The papers came from the Defence Department. There was no mention of Dr Van Jaarsveld or the Health Bureau.

PART TWO

The destination

7

She had imagined, watching the helicopter from the ground, that inside she would have the sensation of being able to skim or hover as effortlessly as a dragonfly among the rushes at the edge of a stream. Instead, Shahida found to her disappointment, it was little different from a flight in any other light aircraft, noisy and uncomfortable and prone to stomach-hollowing rises and plunges.

They had left the river and were flying over a monotonous vista of swampland, reed-choked channels winding around numberless islands of scrub bush fringed with trees, with nothing to distinguish one from the other. The solid shoulders of the pilot and his navigator obscured the forward view through the bubble, and the side ports were badly placed for comfortable vision. In any case there was little to see except the blue haze of distance over the drowned African plain. Eventually, she had turned to sly observation of her fellow passenger.

She and Brand had given up any attempt at conversation soon after takeoff, for nothing more than the exchange of shouted inanities was possible above the clattering roar of the whirling blade and its engine. Brand sat with his head resting against the bare metal bulkhead. His eyes were closed and she wondered whether he was asleep. There was an open briefcase on his knees, threatening at any moment to slip to the deck and spill its contents. She was tempted to reach across and retrieve it but reluctant to intrude. A sudden violent lurch resolved her predicament. Brand sat up with a grunt, clutched the case and shifted it to safety on the empty bucket seat at his side. He smiled at her and silently mouthed a question.

'You OK?'

She smiled back and nodded vigorously. Then she turned away from the examining eyes and went back to contemplating the slow passing of the sky.

She had been surprised and flattered when Brand had requested that she accompany him on this journey. Dr Hauge had expected to make the trip and it had cost Brand considerable time and tact to persuade the old man that he could contribute more by staying at home. No further Virus H cases had been detected, but there was still a grave risk of a secondary outbreak at Leruarua. The hospital was still under quarantine, for they were all in the dark about the duration of the virus's incubation period. It was vital, Brand had stressed, that Dr Hauge should be on hand where the real action might be. Routine investigation in the field, he implied, could well be left to less experienced people like himself and Dr Karim. Brand had been very convincing, but she was not certain that Dr Hauge had fallen completely for the subterfuge. However, it had achieved its purpose. Dr Hauge was really too old to go traipsing around in the bush.

Shahida allowed her thoughts to drift a little, into a warm contemplation of James Brand as a man, but then caught herself up abruptly. That way lay danger. Forget it, she told the betraying, soft part of her mind. He's hardly aware you exist. And it's better so.

The helicopter had changed without warning from straight and level flight and was descending, canted over at an angle. She looked down, pleased that they were arriving early at their destination. The terrain had changed and what appeared to be a single broad river curled below them in coils like a long and lazy snake. A solid-seeming mass of vegetation stretched away from either bank. Only when the helicopter sank lower did she see the glint of water among the reed beds. A wind was blowing and waves of shifting colour, now green, now silver, went sliding across the blown reeds on the flood plain.

Clumps of trees and the seared yellow of high ground showed in the distance, and the helicopter flew towards it. Then they were over a town, or at least a human settlement of some kind. She saw the beehive shapes of scattered huts, a patchwork of fields beside the river, and people looking up and waving. Then the scorched-looking earth came up with a rush and they were down.

There were sheds and a windsock at the edge of the landing strip. Vehicles were drawn up in a tidy row. Two army officers and a detachment of white soldiers in camouflage dress had come to meet them. The officers introduced themselves stiffly. They looked at

Shahida curiously, but without surprise. They had obviously been forewarned. Behind them, on the trucks, the young soldiers sat staring unabashedly.

Baggage and equipment were sorted out and distributed among the vehicles. The soldiers worked swiftly and efficiently, like a practised drill team. The truck drivers were black men. They sat in their vehicles while the white soldiers did the loading.

Shahida and Brand were seated in a Land-Rover with the officers. The helicopter crew travelled in a second Land-Rover. Two open lorries followed. The soldiers, armed with automatic rifles, sat in the lorries. An armed personnel carrier went at the head of the convoy.

The junior officer was behind the wheel. The other, who was the base CO and who had introduced himself as Commandant De Waal, sat beside him. He leaned back over his seat and looked at his passengers.

'Accommodation is a problem,' he said. He was middle-aged with grey hair and a stern but not unkind look. 'I think it would be best if you stay at my quarters.'

Shahida thought that he had almost added: 'Where I can keep an eye on you.'

They had reached a patch of heavy sand and for a moment both the officers concentrated on the road ahead. The unpleasant thought occurred to Shahida that they seemed to be on the watch for something. An ambush? Land mines?

The commandant spoke again. 'Of course we'll give you whatever help we can.'

Brand said: 'The most urgent need is to find this woman and her child. You have been informed?'

De Waal nodded. 'I had a signal about it from HQ and we made inquiries at once. But there is definitely no such woman in the village here. She must have come in from the bush.' He gave a bleak smile. 'And as you see there's a lot of bush out there. You don't have any more definite information?'

'No.'

'She might even be from the other side, you see.' The officer made a sketchy gesture towards the river. 'In which case. . . .' He left the sentence significantly uncompleted.

'The river is the border?'

87

'In a way, yes. Some of the territory on that side is ours and some of it isn't and no one is quite sure which is which.'

'There are people living there?' Shahida asked.

The man's air was reticent, almost apologetic. 'People? Yes, there are people. But they're not our people. They're not our responsibility.'

'Then whose responsibility are they?'

'We do patrols on that side to keep the terries out ... the terrorists, you know? That's all we can do for them. The people have to look after themselves.'

There was a flat, defeated silence.

De Waal said, as if from a distance: 'They're not our people, you see.' And then, as if by a show of enthusiasm he could throw off latent feelings of guilt: 'Tell me what we can do to help you.'

Brand said: 'Finding this woman is the big problem. But we shall also need to take as many blood samples as possible. We'll need your co-operation.'

'I'll see to that.'

'And working space, of course.'

'We have a clinic for the LPs. The local population.'

'Is it staffed?'

'My wife is in charge. She's a nurse. She has four black nurses working for her.'

'You don't have doctors?'

'Oh, yes. Our army doctors visit the clinic.' A hint of the propagandist came to the soldier's voice. 'It is part of our social action programme. We have a school too, for the black children. We are here not so much to fight as to lead these people to a better way of life.'

'Where do the patients come from?' Shahida asked. 'Are they also people from out in the bush?'

De Waal became watchful, as if he feared she might be an enemy. 'From around here, mostly. From Sekhong village itself.'

'And the bush people?'

'It is not easy to help them. The terrorists keep them away. They raid the villages and if they hear the people have been to white doctors they shoot them. They do this to their own people. We come to offer help to them and then they are shot by their own people.'

88

She did not say anything. In a conflict between two forms of authoritarianism, she was thinking, there could be only one loser: the people.

'We'll make use of your clinic,' Brand interrupted. 'And we'll need an interpreter to help with the inquiries. Can you supply someone suitable?'

Da Waal turned back to him with obvious relief. They were soon lost in the pleasures of logistical planning. Shahida, half listening, became occupied with her own thoughts. She was not sure what she had expected to find at the end of the journey; perhaps a village like those of the Malayan jungle, where people clustered together within the confines of a clearing, or like the shantytown slums that festered at the edges of most African cities. She had come unprepared for this far-spreading land of reed and water and people living with barriers of emptiness between them.

The military compound was foreign to this untidy landscape: square buildings set out in straight lines, all enclosed within a fenced and sandbagged rectangle. A guard at the gate presented arms as they drove past. Soldiers were drilling on a distant parade ground. There were anti-aircraft and machine-gun posts on the perimeter.

The commandant's bungalow stood in a corner of the compound, facing the river. It had its own high fence with more sandbags and shrapnel alleys between them, and there were security lights at the corners of the building.

A woman stood waiting for them on the veranda, which was meshed against night insects. She wore a uniform with nursing epaulettes. She was a tall, angular person and she smiled and talked brightly, but her eyes were sharp. Shahida was taken off to a bedroom at the end of the passage. It was small and ultrafeminine, predominantly pink and with frills and flounces on the furniture. It was altogether unbelievable in these warlike surroundings.

'It's very nice.' Shahida was at a loss for anything else to say.

The commandant's wife said: 'Make yourself at home.' She leaned closer, confidingly. 'We had the Chief Minister and his wife staying with us not long ago, when he was on a tour here. He's a good old man. Always so . . .' – she hunted for a word – '. . . polite.'

Shahida realized, with mixed feelings of amusement and indignation, that she was being reassured of her welcome, despite being a person of colour in this white house. Other black people had slept here before her.

The tall black man got rapidly to his feet as they came into the room. He remained standing, his expression attentive and deferential.

'This is Mr Kgosana,' Commandant De Waal said. 'But we all call him William around here.' He smiled, and the black man smiled too. 'He's the headmaster of our local school. He works for the administration, but we've borrowed him to be your interpreter.'

The African glanced at the army officer from the corner of his eyes.

'Just call me William,' he said.

He spoke very precisely, without the singsong cadence of most African voices. Shahida noticed that his clothes were ordinary civilian khakis. The shirt sleeves were rolled up to the elbows and the collar was open. He was powerfully built.

'William will help you handle arrangements,' De Waal said. 'Just tell him what you need.' He stood at the door, making it clear that he wished to leave. 'If there's anything else I can do for you, just ask.'

'Thank you,' Brand said.

De Waal nodded, drew himself up to attention and left them.

Brand cleared his throat. 'Now, Mr . . . ah. . . .'

The black man had a quick, arresting smile. 'My surname is Kgosana, doctor. But' – he made a mock-conspiratorial motion of the head towards the doorway – 'it's easier for people to call me William.'

Shahida sensed that the man named William was examining her, but pretended not to notice. She would not allow herself to be drawn into his private joke.

Brand explained the background to their quest, translating medical details into lay language without talking down to his listener. The black man was quick to understand, interrupting to ask sensible questions.

'These random blood samples you wish to take . . . is that the word? Random?'

'Correct.'

90

'You cannot predict what they will show, not so? It would be better to find this woman, I think. The Moremi woman and her child.'

'That is what we hope. But your Commandant De Waal is not optimistic. He says she might be anywhere in the bush. Or even across the border.'

'News travels quickly, even in the bush. When the people hear there are doctors here they will come. Perhaps the woman will come also.'

'I doubt it. She's running away from us.'

'Then perhaps the chief will have her found. The people here are very respectful towards their chief. Perhaps if you were to take him a small present. . . .' Again there was that note of secret irony, as if the knowing suggestion of bribery of a chieftain concealed a further hidden meaning.

Shahida noted that he had said 'the people', not 'my people'.

'Is Kgosana a Bapanga name?' she asked suddenly.

The black man turned to her, puzzled and wary.

'Doctor?'

'Is your name Bapanga? Or . . . what is the tribe that lives here? Matetwa?'

'No, doctor, it is neither. It is Setswana. I am a Tswana.'

'I see.'

'Why do you ask?'

'I was curious, that's all.'

He seemed to withdraw a little, to become unaccountably hostile.

'Yes,' he said. 'I am not from these parts. I am a Tswana.'

Brand said impatiently: 'Then the first thing is to see this chief. When can it be arranged?'

William turned back to him, attentive and businesslike once more.

'I will see to it right away, doctor. There will be no delay. We have no time to waste.'

The sight of the unfamiliar array of equipment, all glass and polished steel, with its mysterious and probably sinister purpose, was enough to start the small black girl trembling with fear.

91

The nurse watched indifferently, and Shahida's eyebrows tightened.

'Nurse!' she said sharply. Then, soothingly to the child, hoping her tone of voice would convey a reassurance the foreign words could not: 'Come, little one. I won't hurt you. It'll only take a minute. Come on, now. Be brave.'

Propelled by the nurse's plump arm, the child moved unwillingly towards her. She dabbed expertly with cotton wool and cleansing fluid, flexed the stiffly held black elbow, flicked a forefinger against the vein to bring it up and slipped home the needle.

The child flinched and automatically she tightened her grip, murmuring: 'All right. All right now.' Blood flowed into the clear container and the little black girl started a sad, wailing noise. 'All right. Almost done. Don't cry.' The child tried to wrench away from the double fearfulness of the brown woman who mouthed strange words and the glittering instrument she wielded, but the container was already filled and Shahida pulled the needle free, stopping the flow of blood at the same time with a thumb.

The nurse handed her a plaster strip and she pressed it down over the tiny puncture wound. At the same time she became aware of another presence in the room, and turned, faintly annoyed, to find William Kgosana behind her.

His smile was overtly friendly. 'Afternoon, doctor. Is everything in order? It is going well?'

She worked quickly and deftly to transfer the blood from the hypodermic syringe to a sample bottle. 'So far, so good.' She wrote on the label the nurse presented. Name. Age. Serial number. 'But the people seem reluctant to tell us anything. They come to us because the army tells them to, but they don't volunteer any information.'

'They don't understand. They are superstitious.'

'About what?'

'Things like blood. The taking of blood. It offends their customs.'

'Why didn't you tell us this?'

He looked evasive. 'Sometimes the Matetwa people act strangely. One can't predict.'

'And the Moremi woman? Will she stay in hiding? Is she also superstitious about blood?'

'No one knows a woman by that name.'

Shahida pushed her hair back in a gesture of despair and weariness.

'Perhaps it's all lies about her name too. That's all we get in this country. Lies and lies.'

He did not appear offended. He said reassuringly: 'Doctor, these people sometimes have more than one name. There's a paternal line but often a maternal line too. It's a matter of knowing the right questions to ask.'

'Then why have you been asking the wrong questions, Mr Kgosana?'

He smiled gently. 'William. That's what they call me.'

'All right. William. How would it be if you start asking the right questions?'

The shield of his amiability was impenetrable.

'Surely, doctor.'

The moon was a sliver of silver in the black night and the only light was that of the stars. The man known as William Kgosana moved swiftly and without hesitation in the darkness, following the hardly discernible path which wound in and out between the trees. Occasionally he stopped to listen.

He came to the river bank, through the last dense patch of trees and undergrowth, and here he paused for some time, standing motionless in the deeper shade of the bush, watching the crescent moon's reflection on the dark water. A splash among the reeds on the far bank startled him and he withdrew further into the shadows. The splash came again, and with it the harsh cry of a heron. Relieved, he continued on his way.

A single hut stood on a wide bend of the river, divided from it by a patch of field where withered maize plants grew. He stopped again at the edge of the field. A faint breeze had sprung up and he could hear the dry rustle of the mealie stalks. There was no other sound.

By stooping he could make out the silhouette of the building against the sky. No lights showed. He moved forward with care over the clod-strewn soil between the stands of whispering maize. There was a smell of wood smoke, not recent. A cooking pot stood between the stone outlines of a fireplace, and he walked around it. Chickens in a pen stirred restlessly and there was a sudden squawk from a startled hen. He stopped at once, listening intently. From behind the darkened doorway came a faint clink of metal against metal.

He said urgently: 'Friend. It is Nqhawa.'

Nqhawa was the Xhosa name for the African lynx, which stalks in the night-time. It was a *nom de guerre*, no more his real name than William or Kgosana.

The square of hessian that covered the door was drawn aside. Voices spoke, mumbling, and then someone said more loudly: 'Come, Nqhawa.'

A flashlight gleamed briefly, playing over his body, fixing on his face so that he blinked in its glare.

He said gruffly: 'Don't play with lights outside, brother,' and the flashlight was switched off. He went forward, into the darkness of the hut, conscious of people around him but unable to see them.

'Close the door,' he said. And then: 'Now you can put on your torch.'

In the restless light he could see there were three other men in the room. One wore faded and torn denim overalls, the other two were in equally tattered grey-green uniforms, with peaked forage caps and bandoliers strapped across their bodies. Both carried firearms, the familiar squat Russian-made AK47 assault rifles which were the indispensable adjunct, almost as inevitable as a stage prop, to every revolutionary army in the modern world.

He drew in his breath with an angry hiss.

'Who the hell are you? What are you doing here?' He turned furiously on the man in labourer's dress. 'Are you insane? Who are these people? Get them out of here.'

The other man stammered a confused apology, but William ignored it. 'Be quiet. Let me think.' He looked scornfully at the uniformed men. 'Don't you know better than to come here with guns and dressed like that? Do you think you're playing a game?'

The soldiers flinched back from his anger. Then one said mutinously: 'It is dangerous for us, here. Do you expect us to lie down and be shot?'

'You'll get shot lying down or standing up or waving your arses in the air if someone catches you carrying those things,' William said.

94

The two men looked away. The one who had spoken toyed with his rifle, pretending to adjust the shoulder sling, but there was no threat in the gesture. William glared at them for a moment longer. They were both very young, hardly more than boys. His expression became more kindly, but his voice remained stern.

'It's too late now to do anything about this stupidity.'

The man in overalls coughed nervously.

'But listen well,' William said. 'Forget anything you hear here. Forget that you have seen me. Do you understand that?' The soldiers nodded and he went on: 'You have never seen me. You don't know who I am. Is that clear?'

Again they nodded, and he examined their faces by the wavering light. Satisfied, he turned to the other man. His voice became harsh again.

'And you, brother, what do you say for yourself? What have you done to persuade the people to come and take the needle? Only a few came today, and most were those the white soldiers rounded up.'

The man in the worn overalls said agitatedly: 'What could I do? People are afraid. The old man was to have called them together, but he has been lying drunk all day.'

'That was as it was intended, to show that the old man has no power over the people. You and your men should be instructing them, showing them who are the real leaders. Are you too stupid or too afraid to take advantage of your chances?'

The other did not reply. William waited, with a conscious sense of the dramatic, until the silence became oppressive.

'Tomorrow things will be different,' he said at last. 'You will see that people come to the doctors. I don't care how you do this. Tell them it is what Shinyana wants them to do. And if they don't do it his brave soldiers' – he looked disdainfully at the young men with their guns – 'will come out of the *seroromo* and shoot them. Understand?'

'Yes.'

'There is another thing. There was a woman who went from here to the town, who called herself Moremi. She had two children who were sick and one died and then she returned here. I want that woman found. The soldiers say there is no one of that name, but I think she gave the wrong name because she was afraid. You are

95

to find her, or her man or her uncles or her brothers or whatever.'

This time he did not wait for an answer. He went to the door and pulled aside its sackcloth covering. He listened. There were frogs among the reeds down at the river.

'Wait for ten minutes after I have left,' he instructed the two young men. 'And when you go, go quickly.'

He was gone, swallowed by the darkness.

8

On the Thursday, their third day in Sekhong, Brand came to the clinic where Shahida Karim was working and stood in the doorway, silently watching her.

She turned away from her patient. 'Have you any news?'

He nodded. His bulk was dark against the sharp sunlight outside and she could not make out his expression.

'The Moremi woman? She's been found?'

He came into the room and now she could see his face.

'I've spoken to Mr Fissher on the radio.' His voice was flat, defeated. 'He tells me that Dr Hamilton died last night.'

'No!'

'Yes. It is all' – he made a savage gesture which encompassed both of them, her patient, the clinic building, the African landscape – 'all useless.'

They went on working nevertheless. To Shahida's surprise there was a long queue of waiting patients when she and the major's wife opened the clinic on the Friday morning. She had expected no better attendance than on the first days; probably worse, for the willing had already presented themselves and the remainder were presumably those who could not be persuaded, even by their chief or by the white soldiers. But the number of people who came to surrender their small libations of blood increased during the morning.

She and the commandant's wife spoke about it as they drank a hurried cup of tea in the cramped, hot office adjoining the clinic.

'Where do all these people come from? What health services are there for them?'

'We try our best,' the white woman said. 'But you can't keep track of them. They're always moving around.'

'Do they come from across the border? Your husband mentioned that a lot of people live out in the swamps.'

Sister de Waal seemed to perceive the need for caution, or to sense that her work here was a target for criticism. 'Some are from over the border,' she said stiffly.

'There are no medical services there?'

'No. Some come to us. But we can't go to them. Not into another country.'

'But surely if there were doctors here more people would come?'

'The terrorists keep them from coming to hospital. It's a shame.'

'Who are they?' Shahida asked, her curiosity aroused. 'What are they? Refugees?'

The barrier went up. 'These are military matters,' the commandant's wife said. 'We're not allowed to talk about them.'

She tried to question William Kgosana. He had been in his element today, organizing the queues, bullying the reluctant, humouring the fearful.

'These are only a few,' he told her. 'There are many more in the bush. Many of them hide, like this woman you're looking for.'

He saw her doubting look and said vehemently: 'You do not know of this because no one speaks about it. The people have been chased into the bush. I could show them to you, but we are both prisoners here. You also, although you do not know it.'

'What do you mean?'

But he, too, became suddenly withdrawn. 'I can't talk about these things. Look around you.'

She and Brand were invited to the officers' mess that evening. It was a building with a rough exterior of wooden slabs, on a stone foundation, but the inside, long bar included, had been lovingly finished by the soldiers themselves, as she was immediately informed. The setting was lovely: there was a stone-paved terrace and a view down the river bank framed by great wild fig trees. They were served drinks outside and watched monkeys playing in the gnarled limbs of the trees. The young officers were very polite and very formal under Commandant De Waal's watchful eye. The sun went down behind the trees across the river. Mosquitoes made their appearance, and they went inside.

Three black men sat among the white officers at the bar. Two of them were sergeants, the third was William Kgosana. They were introduced. The sergeants had been seconded from the army to teach at the school of which William Kgosana was the principal. She wondered if their presence was a token, offered to the presumed liberal sympathies of foreign visitors. The black men drank beer and kept themselves a little apart. The white officers talked longingly of South Africa, which they referred to as 'the States'.

William came across while she and Brand were talking to De Waal and his wife.

'I have good news. The Moremi woman has been traced. She and the child have been living in this village in the marshes.'

'What is the name of the place?' the white officer asked.

'It is not a name I know.'

De Waal gave the black man an ambiguous glance.

'Can she be brought here?'

'It is not a long journey. Three or four hours, perhaps.' William added, apparently innocently, although Shahida thought she caught an ironic inflection: 'Three hours by boat, that is. There are no roads, so it is impossible to travel any other way.'

'Why can't the woman be brought here?'

Brand interrupted. 'It would be advisable that we go there ourselves. It may be necessary to do tests on other inhabitants besides the woman.'

Finally, reluctantly, De Waal gave his consent. They would be provided with a launch and a military patrol vessel as escort.

'You must remember that there is always danger from the terrorists,' he warned darkly. 'We cannot guarantee your safety down in the swamps.' His bearing, as he turned away to order another round of drinks from the corporal behind the bar, was aloof, as if he suspected someone had made a fool of him. And Shahida believed that she, alone, had detected the faint smile which came and went on William Kgosana's lips.

Conversation in the mess had grown louder, like the rumble of surf all around, but for a moment Brand and Shahida were isolated within an island of relative silence at its centre. He smiled and lifted his glass in an ironic toast to the noisy soldiers. Then he made a quick sideways motion of the head. 'This way. Come over here.'

Wondering, she followed him to the windows where, their backs to the others in the room, they could look out over the river. A crescent moon's light lay on the dark water. The stars were brilliant in the African night. The scent of some night-blooming flower hung in the humid air. The setting, Shahida thought, was impossibly romantic. She felt uncomfortable. There had been a secretive air about their tiptoe move away from the party.

Brand's first words did not help dispel the unease.

'Difficult to speak to you alone. These young officers are very attentive.'

'It's nothing. They're lonely.'

'Aren't we all?'

She toyed with her drink.

'You know, you intrigue me.'

'I don't know why I should.'

'You always look so remote. So wrapped up in your own mystery.'

'I'm a very ordinary person.'

'I doubt that.'

'It's true, however.'

'You know . . . this kind of party. . . .' He gestured around them. 'One is forced to speak such rubbish.'

He seemed anxious to be understood. She wondered if he'd had too much to drink. Or had the moon and the stars gone to his head?

'You intrigue me,' he said again.

How long could she keep up her noncommittal smile? It was already beginning to fray at the edges.

'I've often wondered about your background. I know you worked in Malaya and England and that you were trained at Edinburgh, but that's about all. Were you born in Malaya?'

She seized on the promised change of subject with relief. 'On the contrary. I was born in Cape Town.'

He stared at her in astonishment. 'Cape Town? You mean in South Africa?'

That's the only Cape Town I know of.'

'But, good Lord, that's . . . that's incredible. You mean you're a South African too?'

'Too?'

'So am I. I was born in Johannesburg.'

It was her turn to be surprised. 'But I thought you were Canadian. And your accent isn't – '

'Just protective coloration. I have Canadian papers. But I was born right here. Not exactly right here, but you know what I mean.'

'I do.'

They laughed together in happy acceptance of the coincidence, at the same time acknowledging that it was not really a coincidence. He put the thought into words.

'So you came back too. Had to come back.'

'Yes.'

'After how long?'

'Oh, a long time. I was quite small when my family left. Five years old.'

'But when you were small you lived in . . . District Six?'

'The Malay Quarter,' she corrected him.

'Oh. Sorry.' He was not sure why he was apologizing. 'I don't really know the Cape all that well. I'm an ignorant Transvaaler. So your family left South Africa. Why?'

She eyed him steadily. 'That was in 1956. The year the Coloured people lost the vote. Remember?'

'Yes, of course.' Again he felt an obscure need to apologize.

'My father was quite a wealthy man. He wanted my brother and me to grow up in a different kind of world. I think he was wise.'

'Probably.' He was embarrassed because of his white skin and the fact that he had been born an Afrikaner. 'Not that we all think the way the Nats did in 1956, of course. I mean, some of us didn't agree with what they were doing.'

She sipped her drink quietly.

He tried again. 'We are a weird society really. I mean, take my names, for example. I was named James Barry, after General Hertzog. Not so unusual because we were distantly related on my mother's side. But do you know where those names originated? From Dr James Barry at the Cape.'

She said with interest: 'The woman doctor who – '

'That's right. Who was *said* to have been a woman. Although the

100

truth is probably that he was bisexual. But the point I'm trying to make is this: unless you can understand these odd little twists in our make-up – a Boer general named after a British queer, for example – how can you understand South Africa? So much for the visitors who see the Kruger National Park and Soweto and the Voortrekker Monument and leave here as instant experts.'

Her contrived smile made it clear that she did not agree.

'Not that there isn't a hell of a lot wrong, of course. Don't think for one moment I'm defending the damn country.'

She said, not looking at him: 'I understand how you feel.'

He was concerned that he had taken the wrong turning and this made him reckless. He reached out and gently turned her face towards him. 'I told you once that you have a beautiful name.' He felt the resistance, but was not sufficiently forewarned. 'You are as lovely as your name.'

She froze. He noticed now and looked at her in dismay. He wanted to say something, was searching for the words.

'Leave me alone,' she snapped at him. She turned and fled.

She found tears of resentment coming to her eyes as she hurried to the ridiculous pink bedroom. I suppose he felt himself free to take liberties, she thought viciously. He'd just heard that I was only a Cape Malay slut, hadn't he? And he's a true-born white South African. So what more natural than that he should make a play for the little piece of dark skin? She sat on her bed, dry-eyed now, but quivering and furious.

Why did he do it? Why?

And, equally: why did I do it?

Why couldn't I have turned him off with a light laugh and a cool look? Why did I have to overreact?

As anger began to fade she had to admit in all fairness that its source lay as much with herself as with Brand's clumsy gesture. She had been angry and she had lost control. She hated it when men tried to force their attentions on her.

She got up from the bed and went to the dressing table to examine her narrow, high-boned face. How could anyone see beauty in that? She started to repair the damage caused by anger and tears.

She should have made it clear who and what she was. Her surname should have given him the clue, if he had not been an ignorant Transvaaler (she smiled to herself at that thought; it was what he had termed himself), that she was of high caste, a Brahmin. Of course she would not have said exactly that, it would have been too blatant. But no doubt he would have been interested to know that her ancestor had been a prince, exiled from Java by the Dutch. That was what her father had always told her. He had clung fiercely to the legend of royal blood, although it made little difference in the alien land where all people of dark skin colour were classed as inferior.

In a way Brand reminded her of her brother. Both had a very earnest, searching look. Why had she made such a fool of herself?

The blood rushed to her face again and she turned abruptly away from the mirror.

Brand had been clever at detecting her secret. What was it he had said? 'So you had to come back.' And he added 'too', which implied that he had been driven by the same compulsion.

He had understood. That was it exactly. She had *had* to come back.

The launch was an aged spluttering vessel. Commandant De Waal, seeing them off early in the morning, apologized for its inadequacies.

'It's all we have that's big enough to carry you and your equipment.' He was still a little stiff with them, although he said nothing about Shahida's early departure from the party. 'We're army here, not navy. But at least you'll be safer and more comfortable than on a patrol boat.'

They sailed all morning on the sluggish stream, between the high banks which obscured all vision of the land beyond the river. There were crocodiles on the mud flats, and the occasional band of hippo, and many birds. It should have been a fascinating voyage, sailing on a lazy tropical river, but the troops manning the launch insisted that the passengers, Shahida, Brand and William, sit down low inside the cramped cabin, so that there was nothing to see except the tops of the trees and the sky.

William told her consolingly that there would be little of interest to see in any case, with the river being so low. The great game herds put in their appearance only during the rainy season.

Shahida listened impatiently to his explanations. She was bored with this interminable journey. She suspected that the soldiers were exaggerating the dangers in order to underline the distinction between themselves and mere civilians. She was cross with Brand, who sat inside the cabin like a dummy, saying nothing. Was he angry about last night's scene? Was he embarrassed? So he should be. Why didn't he say something?

It was already long past noon when they reached their destination. The description William had given of the place had been as vague as its location. Now she realized why. To call the squalid sprawl of huts and shacks a village or a town was to lend it false dignity. It was no more than an encampment, a temporary halt in a journey without destination. The nearest huts, those they could see from the river, seemed already to have been abandoned.

She stood up, in spite of the disapproving soldiers, and stared across the narrowing stretch of water as the launch approached. She was filled with doubt, reinforced by the neglected air of the place. Had the people been forcibly removed from here or had they fled further into the wilderness where even those intent only on healing and restoring could not reach them?

It was only when the launch, engine stopped, went gliding towards the bank that there were signs of life. A handful of women came from behind the huts and stood silently watching. They made no move to approach.

William was standing beside her.

'This is a place of fear,' he said. 'First we shall have to overcome this fear.'

His observation reflected her own feelings.

'What is this place?' she asked. 'What is it called?'

There again was the faint smile with which he met many questions.

'It has no name. Or, rather, it has many names.'

'What do you mean?'

'It does not appear on maps, but the people who come here and who have to live here call it Motloboga, the Place without Hope. Or Tlhobosega, Place of Despair.'

'Who *have* to live here? What does that mean?'

103

'This is where they have been put. For the time being.'

'What are they? Refugees of some kind?'

'You would call them that.'

'Mr Kgosana, did you bring us here deliberately? Is this what you wanted to show me?'

'How could that be, doctor? The woman and child you are seeking are here.'

'Are you sure of that? Is that not just an excuse for coming here?'

'You came to find the woman. And if you find other things then that is simply a question of luck, isn't it?'

'Was it luck that brought her here?'

William did not reply.

He irritates me, Shahida thought.

No. That was not the precise word. He makes me uneasy. That's better. Beneath the man's obsequious air she felt something harder and colder, something that did not fit.

William's gaze had strayed from her towards the escorting patrol boat. All morning the smaller boat had hovered about the lumbering launch, keeping station astern most of the time, but occasionally skimming past arrogantly to make a sweep into some small inlet or narrow channel, with the lookouts searching the bush and the machine gunners hunched over their weapons. Now, as if the skipper had finally tired of playing tag with his clumsy charge, it had increased speed and was cutting across the launch's bows, running full tilt for the beach.

The boat hit the sand with a thump and went skidding a dozen paces beyond the water's edge. The soldiers tumbled out, dropping to the ground and taking cover, going through the motions of routine infantry drill, but with no special urgency. A command came echoing flatly across the water and the young men rose, dusting themselves, laughing, jostling one another with youthful energy.

Shahida looked towards the rise above the huts where the black women had stood watching. They had gone.

William saw her expression and this time his smile was definitely ironic.

'Yes,' he said. 'That is one way of overcoming fear.'

*

Whether or not it was because of the untimely military display, gaining the confidence of the people who had fled the riverside proved a lengthy and frustrating task. The women and the children had gone deep in the marshes, beyond the tracking abilities of the army patrol. Some of the men had stayed (there were no young men among them, Shahida noticed), but they were unwilling to talk about the whereabouts of the others.

It was William who, with patient persistence, persuaded the old men that the strangers, the soldiers and the people on the launch, intended no harm.

And finally, towards evening, William in triumph produced the Moremi woman and her child.

Brand said in bitter frustration: 'Here we have the key. But it's a key that won't turn any lock.'

He glared exasperatedly at the frail African woman who stood before them, like the accused in a dock, shrinking away from his inexplicable anger.

'Ask her again,' he instructed William. 'Was anyone else sick? Did the child have anything to do with sick people?'

William spoke to the woman, his voice gentle. She kept her eyes averted; her replies came in monosyllables.

'No. She sticks to her story. The child was healthy but he became sick on the journey. When she got to the town she had someone take him to hospital. That is all she knows.'

It had been a strange moment of anticlimax when the gaunt, frightened woman had been brought to the doctors. They knew almost at once that the search was not yet over.

With the woman was her other child, the brother of the one who had died. He had been sick also, that much had been true. However, it had not been from the disease that had killed his brother. Shahida had taken a history, routinely, but it had hardly been necessary. The diagnosis was clear from the start. The boy had all the symptoms and signs of chronic malaria.

'Why did she give a false name at the hospital?' Brand asked.

'She was afraid.'

'Afraid of what?'

'She did not have the right papers.'

105

'Who ever has the right papers?'

'Also there was no work for her and her uncle would not keep her. Her relatives were angry with her because the child had died.'

Brand's attention sharpened. 'Why was that? Because they feared infection? Do they know about this disease?'

The woman gave him a brief, scared look from under her brows. She mumbled.

William translated. 'The child was bitten by a monkey.'

'By *what*?'

'By a monkey.' William consulted again. 'Yes. She says the child had caught a monkey and it bit him.'

'I remember that,' Shahida said. 'There was a bite mark on the side of the child's neck. And his hands were lacerated. Dr Hauge noted it in the postmortem report.'

'But why should her relatives be angry because a monkey bit the child?'

'I think there is a religious significance,' the black man said. 'She says they called it an omen and the work of angry spirits. They would not have her in the house.'

Brand threw up his hands. 'Superstitious nonsense. I don't believe a word of this. She's lying.'

'I think she's just ignorant. She does not understand what it is you want from her. Life and death are very simple here. The child is dead and as far as she is concerned that's all there is to it. She is frightened because you ask questions about it.'

Brand eyed him queerly, taken aback by the unsought lecture.

'Why did she leave here in the first place?'

'The child was sick.'

'But she told us the child became sick on the journey.'

'She meant this child.' William indicated the boy who clung to his mother's skirt, his fever-wasted face hidden in the folds. 'She wanted her relatives to look after him. She has no money because her husband died.'

'I thought the child who died was not in contact with any other sick person.'

'Her husband was not sick. He died.'

'What on earth does she mean?'

William, frowning, questioned the woman. Her answers came with renewed reluctance.

106

'She says he was killed. It was a long time ago. She doesn't want to tell me how, but probably he was shot. Probably he had joined the terrorists.'

'That might explain why she is afraid,' Shahida said.

William looked at her gratefully. 'That would explain her fear,' he said. 'It is not good to be the wife of a dead terrorist.'

It was too late to return to the Sekhong base, so they slept there that night, making their beds in the launch's small cabin. The soldiers stood guard along the riverside, and the patrol boat lay anchored in midstream with its machine guns manned.

During the night, somehow, the word went back to the people in their refuges in the marshes: there were white doctors who had come to treat the sick at the settlement called the Place of Despair. By daybreak patients were already waiting by the riverside.

Shahida and Brand worked side by side. The sense of constraint between them was still there, but it faded as the day progressed. One could not place much importance on petty personal emotions in the face of so much mass misery.

Shahida was appalled by the condition of the people, the children especially. The basic problem was malnutrition. She had not seen such widespread evidence of the diseases of under-nourishment – vitamin deficiencies, electrolyte disturbance, the ricketsial diseases, marasmus, kwashiorkor – since she was in Malaya.

'We're only scratching the wound, doing what we're doing,' she said to Brand. 'We should have full-scale services here – clinics, nurses, a hospital.'

'In these marshes, with nothing but miles of bush and no roads?'

'These people should not be here in the first place.'

'No. I hadn't realized this kind of monstrosity existed in this country. It reminds me. . . .' He hesitated and she looked at him questioningly.

'There was once a place called Rietfontein.' He paused again. He had not spoken about this for years.

'Yes?'

'It's not a pleasant memory. I thought about it when you spoke about doing refugee work in Malaya. It's curious we should both

107

have had dealings with this kind of thing. You had your camp at whatever it was. . . .'

'Kuala Trenganu.'

'Was it a place like this?'

'Much like this.'

His encounter with Rietfontein had come shortly after he had qualified, when he had taken a job as medical officer for a peri-urban board.

'It was a squatter camp, out in the country beyond the city lines. I ran into a lot of trouble there.'

Rietfontein had been a dump, in every sense. It lay within a small, treeless valley which had been turned into a rubbish tip. The black people who lived there made their homes in the rusty remains of motor cars, in old water tanks, inside boilers and even in broken asbestos pipes discarded during the construction of the city's water pipeline.

'We – my health staff and I – tried at least to provide the essentials of life: water, sanitation, a soup kitchen. But the authorities resisted every move we made. As far as they were concerned those blacks didn't exist, for they were supposed to be back in the Bantustans, you see. Therefore, by their extraordinary logic, Rietfontein didn't exist and there was no need to do anything about it.'

She shook her head. They looked at the sad huddle of huts alongside the river.

'And this place? Will they believe it when we tell them about this?'

'Perhaps. Times have changed.'

'Have they really? What happened to Rietfontein in the end?'

'It was razed. Bulldozed. And I suppose it was my fault really.'

He had made the strategic error of consenting to appear in a television documentary. The director had been a young man from England who claimed he wanted to depict South Africa whole and unvarnished, the good and the bad. The film about Rietfontein would be one of a series. Brand agreed to read a commentary. Later he had been astounded to find himself actually in the film too.

Where or how the camera had been hidden he could never work out. It had caught him in the midst of Rietfontein's poor, moving in symbolic white dress among the black bodies and against the sombre-hued background like a self-chosen Christ ministering to the multitude.

The films were not shown on BBC television until the New Year. The first of the series, which was a more or less routine indictment of the migratory labour system, passed without much attention. It was not until the showing of 'The Dumping Ground' on a freezing night in mid-February, when the plight of cold and hungry souls living in a rubbish dump was given extra vividness, that the storm broke.

Brand found himself at the centre of it all, instant hero to some, instant villain to a great many more. Much was made of his Afrikaans background, his reputed descent from President Brand of the Orange Free State. (The press had it wrong. His mother was distantly related to General Hertzog.)

Was he a man of mercy, a saint, a charlatan, a traitor to his country, a victim of forces beyond his control, a dupe, a symbol of humanity, a communist conspirator?

The offer from the Canadian university came opportunely. There was a post for him in the Faculty of Medicine and a research grant which would enable him to continue his studies, with the prospect of bigger things to come. It was a splendid opportunity and under any circumstances he would have been a fool not to grasp it.

Then why did he feel, always afterwards, that he had run away?

Brand made no mention of departure, and the young commander of the patrol boat became disturbed by the continued delay.

'I don't like this, doctor. How do you know who these people are?'

'They are patients. People who are sick.'

'I understand you came here to check up on some kind of tropical fever and not to treat patients.'

'It's all part of the same thing.'

'Can you tell me when you'll be finished?'

'Impossible to say. All kinds of factors involved.'

'I understand, but I will have to radio my base and get new orders. The longer we stick around here the better chance of the terries hearing about us.'

'No one will harm us,' Brand told him.

Shahida was less confident. She believed that they had been manoeuvred here, for a purpose she could not guess. But she kept her doubts to herself and went on with her work.

Throughout the day the patrol boat kept constantly on the move, ranging far up and down the river. The skipper no longer ran boldly ashore, but instead kept his vessel out in the stream, while his troops suspiciously surveyed the bustle on the river banks.

In the afternoon he received his orders. They were to return to base. Permission for the doctors to remain in the operational area had been withdrawn. Shahida and Brand would be transported to the capital in the morning.

PART THREE

The ship

9

'We have to go back,' Shahida Karim said.

They were in Dr Hauge's laboratory, where they had tracked him down that morning after their return from Sekhong. Shahida was still in her travelling clothes, tan-coloured slacks and top, and with her hair bound in a scarf. The severely practical dress curiously made her look younger and more vulnerable. Brand thought again what a remarkably attractive young woman she was.

'Of course I agree in principle,' he said. 'But the problem is the means.'

Her voice was unexpectedly sharp. 'It's up to us to find a way. We have an obligation towards those people. We can't just abandon them.' She added, with a neat stroke directed at a potential ally: 'And we mustn't forget about the work on Virus H. There's still a lot to be done.'

'Precisely,' Dr Hauge said. 'It would be criminal to leave it at this stage. This woman you found is our best lead so far.'

Brand felt himself cornered.

'Isn't it really a question of laboratory work from now on?'

'Tracing contacts is equally important. That's the only way we can get to the root of the disease.'

'I understand that. But I can also understand why the army is troubled about the responsibility for civilians in a military area.'

'Is it the army, or is it Van Jaarsveld?'

'I dare say Dr Van Jaarsveld felt slighted when we went over his head.'

'He is a pompous fool,' the old man snorted. 'Forget his feelings. Put more pressure on him. Telephone him right now and ask him why you were sent back. You're entitled to know that, aren't you?'

Dr Van Jaarsveld was hostile.

'It is a security matter,' he said. 'I cannot discuss it.'

'But we were up there for the better part of a week,' Brand pointed out. 'There were no problems.'

'We are quite capable of handling the matter ourselves. We can't have independent groups interfering.'

'I can't agree that vital research can be described as interference.'

'My department will provide you with any data you might need. But it would be quite irregular to allow you people to drift in and out of a security area. You found the woman you wanted. What more do you want there anyway?'

Brand dodged the question.

'Then there's another matter. We feel AID could be of use in the border areas in a more permanent capacity.'

'In what way?'

'We could extend our services up there. Perhaps we could consider establishing a hospital.'

'Present services are perfectly adequate.'

'We found the contrary.'

'You should have been minding your own business.'

'Health is a doctor's business, wouldn't you say?'

The Health Director was ominously silent. Brand decided it was time to be more tactful.

'I do believe we should at least do a feasibility study. We might well find that there's no need for a hospital, or that some other form of service would be better suited. But let's have a look at the problem at least.'

'We know what is happening in the border areas,' Van Jaarsveld told him haughtily. 'You don't have to involve yourself.'

At the end of the week Hauge received a cablegram from the virology research laboratory. At least three, perhaps more, of the samples of blood which Brand and Shahida had brought back from the northern border contained antibodies which reacted specifically with Virus H.

The implications were fairly straightforward. Somewhere in the bush there were people alive who had once (how recently was one of the factors to be determined before the scientific equation would

114

be complete) contracted the haemorrhagic fever that had killed three people here in the capital.

News of the discovery drove Hauge to new extremes. Every day brought a note, scribbled in his atrocious handwriting, as if he was either too filled with urgency or too secretive to allow them to be typed by his secretary. They were in turn bombastic, wheedling, visionary or exhortative. They set up plans for an enlarged expedition, contained lists of the staff and equipment needed, sought immediate explanations for the continued delay, requested a detailed report on transport facilities to and in the border area, so that the build-up could be maintained after the assault team had gone in.

The military metaphor was unavoidable; for Hauge it had become an operation against a stubborn enemy, to be conquered for the greater glory of the general, and only by the expenditure of the maximum in manpower and armaments.

Shahida Karim's approach was, perhaps not unexpectedly, more subtle and disconcertingly more direct. She listened with apparent equanimity as Brand explained that the Health Bureau had continued to veto Hauge's plans as well as her own proposal for a hospital or a clinic run by AID.

Then she said: 'There's something that puzzles me.'

He waited politely.

'You remember my telling you about this name Shinyana? The night I was looking for the Moremi child in the township. The drunk man came in and said something about Shinyana.'

'Oh, of course. Did I tell you that I asked the minister about it?' Uneasily, he remembered Makaza's frozen response. What was coming now? 'He had no idea what it could have meant.'

'I don't think he was telling the truth. You see, I've found out that there's a man named Shinyana who is a leader of the Matetwa people. Hauge is right when he says that the whole thing is political.'

'I don't understand.'

'Alfred Shinyana is his name. He was one of the leaders of the People's Democratic Party.'

'The organization that was banned?'

'Yes. In fact it was a political party. But Shinyana had also formed something called the Matetwa National Union, which was

115

anti-independence and which caused the PDP to be banned. People were arrested, but Shinyana got away.'

He shook his head slowly. 'Seems very complicated to me. Doesn't it prove my point that we should stay out of local politics?'

'Don't you find it curious?'

'What?'

'Why should that man have thought . . . what possible reason did he have to think that I had anything to do with Alfred Shinyana? And why should the minister lie about it?'

Brand was silenced.

'They are trying to hide things,' she said. 'All we have to do is threaten to expose these things and force them to give us what we want.'

He laughed. 'That sounds like blackmail.'

'Yes,' she said calmly.

It was the jocular remark Brand made then that triggered the idea in Shahida's imagination. He had seen her disappointment and said: 'You have to keep faith.' And then, trying to turn it into a joke, 'Like Captain Da Costa.'

She was puzzled until she remembered his story about the derisive renaming of *Three Gay Ladies*. Then it came to her.

The paddle steamer (perhaps *Faith* was not so inappropriate a name after all) was too large and its running costs too high for it to be used merely as a ferry to the hospital. But if it could not be a ferry, could it not take the place of a hospital instead? A floating hospital to voyage up the river and into the swamps?

She had no idea how far the river might be navigable. There might be narrows around the first bend. The waterway was probably choked with floating plants and papyrus. She remembered the far-stretching plains of papyrus she had seen from the helicopter. The launch and the patrol boat had navigated it with difficulty. A large vessel might well be bogged down altogether. Possibly, too, there were rapids on the river to forbid the passage of anything bigger than a raft.

She could imagine a whole set of difficulties and problems. Nevertheless it would do no harm to find out whether they existed. And, if they did, how they could be overcome.

She had the afternoon off duty and had planned a shopping expedition in town. Instead she paid a visit to Captain Da Costa on his river boat.

The master of *Three Gay Ladies* was far more friendly this time. Perhaps he'd had time to consider and the scent of money had become more alluring. His estimate of the cost of operating his vessel had dropped dramatically. It would be possible, he said, to run a ferry service out to the hospital for very little more than the old rate the boatmen charged before they became greedy. Provided only that the boat kept to a schedule which assured a minimum of twenty passengers both ways. He had worked it all out, he said, and showed her the scraps of paper with greasy fingermarks all over them on which he had scribbled his calculations.

The lady doctor was contemplating a longer voyage? Where to?

Told, he blinked in astonishment and a sly look came to his face. He obviously did not believe Shahida's explanation, but he was willing to play along with her game, provided credulity was not stretched too far.

The river was navigable for most of its length, far into the marshes, he told her. Now, during the dry season, it needed care and expert knowledge, of course. Captain Da Costa made it clear that he was the only person with the required skill. There were many shoals and sandbars but the paddle steamer, with its shallow draught, had been designed to be worked under such conditions. Naturally the river changed from time to time because of the floods, and the floating weed sometimes choked a channel and caused it to silt. But if it was possible to get through his ship could do it.

There were no charts for the northern reaches, or if there were they were available only to the military. But he had prepared a chart from his own knowledge. He took her to the pilot house behind the bridge and showed where, fastened sheet to sheet with adhesive tape, he had thumb-tacked a series of 50,000:1 survey maps issued by the South African Government Printer. On the blank spaces left for whatever was beyond the river he had drawn his own interpretation of how the land lay. It was done neatly enough, with fair skill, and Shahida's hopes rose. She noticed, as if it were an omen, that the name Sekhong had been marked in next to a black dot and a circle in the far north of the map.

*

117

The next move, she realized, was to persuade Dr Brand. But she delayed approaching him, wanting to be sure of her ground. And in addition she was still a little afraid of him, afraid he would refuse. What arguments would he use against her? That they had problems enough running the hospital here. That the marshes to the north were a military zone. That they had an obligation to stay clear of politics. She rehearsed her own answers: that the old mission was inadequate; that there was a need for outlying clinics; that a floating hospital would overcome the transportation problem; that the marsh people were dependent on the river. And, most convincing of all, in her mind: those people in the bush were a reality; ideology would not cause them to vanish. Among them were many who were sick and suffering, and her aim was to help them by any means, orthodox or not.

She had all her counter-arguments neatly arranged, but still she delayed. And then suddenly there was no time for further delay. She came into the children's ward that morning and was surprised to find the nurses at the window, chattering and laughing. One of them held a small boy up against the sill so that he could look out. She turned to put down the child, saw Shahida frowning at them, and cried out excitedly:

'Look, doctor, look! A ship!'

Disbelievingly, she joined them at the window. She could see a narrow strip of the river, bordered by wild palms. On the river, beating slowly but bravely against the yellow stream, sailed the long-derelict paddle steamer. She stared at it in astonishment while the black people around her applauded noisily.

The *Faith* (there could now be no other name for it) made a slow turn to port and headed in towards a spur of headland behind which it presently disappeared. Only a long column of tarry smoke marked its further progress. A rag-tag line of patients and hospital staff was straggling across the bare space between the buildings and the river and crowding on to the banks. After a moment's hesitation she went outside to join the throng.

By the time she reached the waterside the steamer had already anchored in the shelter of the headland, out of the stream. A dinghy (she remembered having seen it upside down on the afterdeck) was being rowed rapidly and expertly ashore. A black man sat on the stern thwart and Captain Da Costa was at the oars. Women in the waiting crowd began a rhythmic clapping and stamped around in an impromptu dance of joy. The oarsman back-watered to turn the dinghy, and the black man jumped out to hold the bows. Da Costa came dry-footed ashore. He waved indulgently at the dancing, chanting women. Then he saw Shahida and came towards her.

'Doctor-missy,' he said triumphantly, 'there is your hospital. We are on our way.'

Disconcerted, she looked around. But it was unlikely that anyone within earshot would have understood.

'What on earth are you doing here?'

He stared at her. 'Bring boat. What else?'

'But why? What for? No one told you to bring that thing here.'

She looked at the ungainly, top-heavy vessel floating out at the edge of the stream.

'It's a wonder your engines didn't blow up.'

He seemed to think she was joking. He laughed heartily.

'Boilers OK too. Lots of rust, but hell they don't blow up. Engine old but very good. Come from stateside, I tell you.'

She was hovering between apprehension and doubt and a frightening devil-may-care kind of joy. The clapping of the women around her sounded like drumbeats.

'Do you really believe you could sail into the marshes with that?'

'Fine boat. Sail anywhere with that boat.' He reconsidered and added astutely: 'Not on sea. Not fit for sea. Sail on any river with that boat.'

Dr Brand had come up to them unnoticed and overheard the boast.

'So where were you thinking of sailing your leaking sieve, captain?' he asked with forced light-heartedness. There could be only one reason for the Portuguese to have brought his steamer here: an attempt to put on pressure over the ferry service. He did not care much for the prospect of telling the fellow that it was all off.

There was an awkward silence. His joke had not gone down well. Da Costa, scowling, was examining the muddy ground at his feet. Shahida Karim appeared to find something engrossing about the wavelets lapping at the shore.

Brand cleared his throat.

'I take it you've come to talk about the idea of using your boat as a ferry. I'm sorry to say – '

119

'No,' Da Costa said abruptly. 'Hospital.'

'That's what I mean. A ferry service to the hospital.'

A suspicious look. 'You don't know about the hospital?'

'I'm sorry, I . . . .'

Da Costa gestured towards the girl. 'She no tell you?'

'Tell me what?'

'About the hospital?'

'I don't understand.'

'This doctor-missy ask me: can my boat sail up the river? I say: yes, why? She say she want to make a hospital. She no tell you?'

Brand turned to Shahida. She was biting her lower lip. She turned her face away. It was the first oriental gesture he had ever seen her make and it was strangely moving.

He asked mildly: 'What is this about?'

She said, not looking at him: 'It's just an idea I had.'

He waited and she went on with more resolution: 'I thought the steamer might be used as a floating hospital for the people on the border. Captain Da Costa says it's feasible. As far as navigation is concerned, at any rate.'

'My boat go anywhere,' Da Costa told him enthusiastically. 'Upriver, downriver, anywhere.'

Brand laughed disbelievingly. 'You must be kidding.'

Shahida's eyes flashed at him. Her chin rose.

'Why didn't you tell me about this?'

'I wasn't sure it would work.'

'It won't work, you know.'

She faced him squarely. 'Perhaps that was what I was unsure of too. What your reaction would be.'

'That I might disapprove?'

'Yes.'

'It's not even a question of my approval or disapproval. It simply isn't practicable.'

'Why not?'

He lifted his hands helplessly. 'If you can't see that . . . .'

'What I see is a large number of people without medical care. And I also see an opportunity to help them.'

'You don't understand. I haven't made the rules.'

She flared at him. 'But because there are rules you'll obey them, whether they're bad or not.'

120

It was close enough to hurt. He became angry too. 'Look, doctor, let's keep this impersonal. I believe your idea is completely impractical. It wouldn't be approved either by AID, who would have to pay for it, or by the Bapangani government, which has the right to say what happens in its territory. And it has nothing to do with my opinion about rules, good or bad.'

Her lips tightened mutinously, but she kept silent. Brand tried to speak reasonably.

'Look. I understand your concern. I'm prepared to put up a fight to get a hospital established up on the border. In fact' – he looked at his watch – 'I'm due to see the minister this morning to put our case to him. But one has to do it on a proper basis. This' – he gestured towards the steamer – 'this kind of thing, trying to force their hand, is sheer melodrama. Romantic notions won't get us anywhere.'

Da Costa asked morosely: 'Now you not want my boat?'

'I'm afraid we don't want your boat, captain,' Brand told him.

The Portuguese became indignant. 'Then who pay, eh? Who pay for me to bring boat here? Cost me. . . .' He made an angry tally on his fingers.' Ten dollars for wood to make steam, eight dollars to pay black men for crew.'

'Come with me,' Brand said. 'We'll sort out something.'

They walked away, leaving Shahida Karim on the river bank, looking across the water at the anchored vessel.

Michael Makaza's lips were curled in an unhappy pout and his gaze kept straying distractedly towards the electric clock against the wall.

'I see,' he said. 'You want to go back to the Matetwa district. I see.'

'And to establish health services there,' Brand said boldly.

Makaza shook his head. 'I don't know if this is possible.'

'It was possible previously. Why not now?'

'There are reasons.'

'What are they? Military? Political?'

'Military and political and other reasons.'

'We believe that many sick people in the border area don't get medical treatment.'

'Who told you this? The army doctors have clinics.'

121

'Nevertheless that is what we found. Once the word got around we were there, people started coming in from everywhere.'

Makaza gave a derisive snort. 'Agitators. Troublemakers.'

Brand looked at him blankly.

'What?'

'The people were forced to go to you. By agitators. We have information about this.' Makaza was becoming heated. 'They are communists. We know who they are.'

'They must be very humanitarian at any rate. Agitators who drive people to receive medical attention. We could use more of them.'

The minister's eyes narrowed, but he did not say anything. He looked at the clock again.

'I want to discuss the possibility of AID establishing a hospital in the Matetwa district.'

Makaza's gaze wavered. 'There would be no point to it.'

'Why not?'

'For you to build a hospital . . . it would be pointless. The Matetwa people are being . . .' – Makaza searched for the word which would be least damaging – '. . . rehoused.'

'What does that mean?'

'Certain Matetwa villages are being relocated because of military considerations.'

'You mean the army is simply uprooting entire villages? But why only Matetwa?'

Michael Makaza got up from his desk and retreated to the fireplace, panelled like the rest of the room and with a fine copper hood below the mantelpiece. Brand wondered whether the fire had ever been lit. He could not imagine it ever growing cold enough in this country. The chimney draught was very good. Makaza, leaning against the mantelpiece, had lit a cigarette, and the twist of smoke was drawn unerringly into the fireplace.

Makaza said in a troubled voice: 'You mustn't misunderstand me.'

Brand waited.

'The problem is . . . I'll tell you what the problem is.' The sound of his own voice seemed to reassure him and he went on more confidently. 'It's a problem in all these homelands the South Africans are forcing on us. We're nations within a nation. And in Bapangani we have nations within the nation within the nation.

122

Like the Matetwa.' Makaza tapped his fingertips against the copper hood, as if to indicate mounting impatience. The metal rang under his fingers. 'There are ethnic differences. They are Amatetwa, an offshoot of the Amazimba nation, the same root as the Zulu. The Bapa'hanga people come from Makaranga stock. It is an accident of history which put the Matetwa here among us.'

'And this is why you have taken their land from them?'

'The Matetwa are rebellious. Born troublemakers. There has been constant unrest, schools being burnt down, faction fights, police patrols being stoned and so forth.' Makaza put up his hands in a gesture of resignation. 'They co-operate with our enemies too, with the terrorists from across the border. There are agitators who go among them, stirring up more trouble. I ask you: how can we allow such a situation?'

'And your solution is to put them in concentration camps?'

Quickly: 'Oh, no, no, no. Nothing like that. They're going to resettlement areas. They will get very good land.'

Memory brought an odd little picture into Brand's mind: half a dozen hens and a rooster squawking and flapping as they were chased in and out among great churning lorry wheels.

The picture appropriately was coloured in the faded sepia tones of the mud at Rietfontein camp. The television film had been the spur: the authorities had ordered the removal of the squatters. No one knew exactly where they were going: orders were given and changed as each new set of officials arrived on the scene. Bulldozers were sent to raze the shanties but after they had gone the people collected their bits of corrugated iron and planks and sacking and stood them on end and their town grew again in the mud. Here and there a sheet of iron might have been bent after a caterpillar track had run over it, but it would still be good enough to keep off the rain. A Catholic priest had sought a court order to restrain the demolition. But even before the hearing the bulldozers returned and this time there had been lorries too, to load the people and their last possessions. One of the items had been a chicken coop, which burst as it was being loaded. Children had given exuberant chase as the chickens scattered and the old woman to whom they belonged sat wailing on top of the truck. Two of the chickens were run over before the rest were caught. The chase had been vastly entertaining, except perhaps to the chickens and their

123

owner. It had established a note of goodwill and humour between the officials and the people they were moving. Even the police who were there to ensure order and prevent news photographers coming near had enjoyed the joke.

Brand remembered that he, too, had laughed to see the chicken chase. Should one laugh also to see the insanity spread even further afield, transferred to this new country?

He was angry now, but there was no target for his anger.

Makaza said: 'You understand how difficult it is for us. We have to keep this thing quiet or our enemies will say that we ill-treat our people. Worse things happen all over this continent, but do you think people consider this? Do they remember Biafra or Idi Amin? No. We are the scapegoats, no matter what we do, because our freedom comes from South Africa and not England or France.'

'I understand your problem,' Brand said.

He was filled with the need to strike out at the formless things around him, at the spectres of apathy and prejudice and callous disregard, at the dull weight of history which held no lessons for those who would not learn, at politics without insight and policies without compassion. He had to do something, demonstrate something, and yet he had no plan of where to start.

So, in that quixotic moment (he recognized this, even as the anger filled him), he grasped at someone else's vision.

'I understand very well. You need not be concerned. We will keep your secret. But of course. . . .'

Makaza looked at him.

'Of course you recognize the needs of these people. I can see,' Brand said with heavy irony, 'you are troubled by this. Fortunately we can help you. At least we can alleviate the problem of medical care for the Matetwa refugees.'

'I don't see how. Out in the bush . . . there are problems of infrastructure . . . logistical problems . . . I don't see how these can be overcome.'

'Don't be concerned, minister. We'll beat your problems. We have a ship.'

'A . . . ship?'

'Yes, minister,' Brand said firmly. 'A ship.'

*

It had rained heavily in the night and a grey drizzle was still falling in the morning. Shahida ran, head ducked against the rain, across the open space between the hospital's main building and the children's ward.

There was an unaccustomed flurry of activity in the ward. A row of empty cots stood in the passage outside, nurses were stacking piles of folded blankets, spare drip units were being dismantled and packed into their containers. She looked on, puzzled, then stopped a passing sister.

'What's all this about? It looks as if we're being evacuated.'

The nurse laughed. 'I really don't know, doctor. It's Dr Brand's orders. He wants equipment not in use to be made ready for transfer somewhere else. Perhaps he can tell you.'

A breathtaking possibility began to take form. She found Brand supervising the packing of crates of medicine in the dispensary.

He said exuberantly: 'Good morning. Have you come to join the fun?'

'Where on earth are you going with all this stuff?'

'Not on earth. On water.' He laughed. 'We're taking a little boat ride up the river.' And to her confusion he winked at her.

'The steamer?'

'Precisely. Are you coming?'

'What made you change your mind? Only yesterday – '

'Never mind why. Are you coming?'

'All right,' she said. 'Where do we start?'

The steamer sailed into anchorage off the south bank of the river in mid-morning.

Shahida watched from the window of the children's ward as the vessel turned out of the channel and manoeuvred at extreme slow speed across the shallows. The paddle wheels stopped. The anchor chain went down.

'The *Faith*,' she said aloud to herself.

James Brand's voice came from behind her, amused and puzzled: 'The what?'

She turned with a start: 'Oh!' She found herself blushing foolishly. 'I didn't know you . . . I didn't hear you come in.'

125

He smiled at her. 'Came to see how you're getting on. What did you call that thing?'

'I . . . it's just a name I. . . .'

'The what?'

'The *Faith*,' she said, blushing again.

'That was just a joke, you know.'

'I know, but it seems . . .'

'Appropriate. Yes, it does rather. It's very good. It's a good name for her.'

Throughout the day they laboured to transport equipment aboard and to convert the steamer into at least a semblance of a miniature hospital.

There were obvious shortcomings: the passenger cabins were cramped, with bunks too low for nursing needs. The main saloon, on the other hand, was too large for any practical purpose. Plyboard partitions screwed to the wooden pillars made the saloon more functional, against Captain Da Costa's strongly voiced objections. Eventually the Portuguese retired sulkily to his bridge, where he spent the afternoon brooding and drinking red wine. The work went on without him.

It was already evening before Brand declared himself satisfied. His last accomplishment of the day was to supervise the hospital carpenter as he fastened two large boards to the paddle-housings. The boards were big enough to obliterate the gothic lettering which spelled out 'Three Gay Ladies'. Each bore, instead, a large red-painted cross and, below it, the word 'Faith'.

They went ashore for the last time. Shahida looked back and saw that the steamer's riding lights had been lit. They shone reassuringly in the quickly gathering darkness. She could just make out the starboard-side paddle-house with its red cross and new name.

The *Faith* looked absurdly, touchingly frail and out of place. It was difficult to imagine her even starting on the voyage they were contemplating. The rain, which had held off for most of the afternoon, came down again in a solid rush and the steamer disappeared from view, all except the dim loom of the lights burning on either side of the tall funnel.

Shahida, soaked through in an instant, felt intensely cold and knew that the feeling was not entirely physical. Could she do it? Brand, ignoring the rain, was busily instructing the boatmen who had brought them ashore. He, at least, no longer knew doubts.

It was still raining in the morning when the *Faith* sailed north, upriver.

10

Water and watery sky. Reeds and river. The tall reeds concealed the banks on either side and closed in on the imagination so that it became imprisoned by the monotony of the passing scenery. Was there a world beyond the confines of the papyrus walls? To Shahida, standing on the boat deck, only a few feet above the water line, there seemed no way out except upwards, into the pale, rain-washed sky.

Ahead of the *Faith* the river curved endlessly, one slow loop opening on the next.

Habitation had dwindled as they had voyaged northwards. At first there had been villages and the people had come running to stare and cheer at the passing of the strange craft with its smoke-spewing funnel and churning paddles. There had been other traffic on the river, dugouts and the occasional raft. They had passed fishermen working their nets and on one occasion drovers fording the channel with a herd of cattle. But signs of human life grew more and more sparse, to make way for animals and birds. Da Costa lectured importantly on the varieties and habits of the game they could expect to encounter in the marshes. Shahida suspected he was reciting from the tour guide prepared for the abortive game-spotting cruises of long ago, but she found him interesting nevertheless.

Towards evening of the first day they came to a locality where the river broadened and the flood plain was split into a maze of small wooded islands. The channel that Da Costa chose proved to be blocked. Even the *Faith* with her shallow draught could not pass the massed mat of vegetation which choked the waterway. Da Costa stopped the engine and its beat grew muffled and ceased. The monotonous slapping of the wooden paddles faded away. They drifted in silence.

'The river, she is bad this time of year,' Da Costa said. 'Much rubbish on the water when she is low.'

Shahida had been allowed a turn at the wheel and was still up on the bridge. She said: 'This must be the start of the rain season, not so? It will be better once the river floods, won't it?'

Da Costa shook his head gloomily. 'This is not proper rain. This rain don't last. River stay low.'

She thought he had become less enthusiastic about the voyage now that it had started. Was he still annoyed about the alterations Brand had ordered, or were there other reasons?

'I think I go look for a way round this stuff,' the Portuguese said. 'I take the skiff.' He looked at her. 'You like to come also? See what it's like on land?'

She hesitated for a moment. The invitation was not unwelcome, for she was becoming bored, cooped up on the boat. She liked Da Costa, in spite of his unprepossessing appearance. He reminded her of simple, rough materials, things like rope and leather.

'All right,' she said. 'Let's go.'

Two of the African crewmen launched the dinghy from the stern and the Portuguese climbed in to fiddle with its battered outboard motor. He got it running to his satisfaction at last and stood up to help her aboard. There was a long, scuffed leather bag on the bottom boards of the dinghy. Seeing her questioning look he grinned faintly, then explained: 'Maybe we shoot something, a bird or something for the pot.' He looked more serious. 'Also there are bad peoples in the bush. I don't like not to have gun.'

A great flock of birds – egrets, pelican, ibis – took off from the sandbar as the little boat went noisily down the channel and round the next bend. They reconnoitred two blind channels, winding in and out between the islands, before finding a third which seemed to present a clear way through.

Da Costa steered the dinghy inshore towards a clearing in the reeds. There was a high bank with a single palm tree. Water lilies grew thickly at the edge of the bank. The propeller chopped into the floating lily pads and the stiff-petalled blossoms. The silence, after Da Costa had killed the engine, seemed absolute. Then, gradually, the evening sounds of the bush came back to them. A dove made liquid notes somewhere up ahead. Guinea fowl were clack-clacking to one another.

The sun was almost down behind the line of trees, but there was still bright light on the piled masses of cloud far to the west. Shahida listened to the river and the bush and felt more at peace with herself than for a long time. The decision had been made, the voyage had begun; now she was content to be carried along on its unpredictable course.

She did not notice, at first, that Da Costa had stood up in the bows and was listening intently. It was only when he reached down for the worn old gunbag that she realized something had changed. The guinea fowl had fallen silent. And as she listened the dove cut off in mid-note. Now there was only the sound of the wind in the reeds.

She turned, frowning. 'What – '

He silenced her with a peremptory gesture. He opened the leather bag very quickly and deftly and slid out the pump shotgun it held. He loaded shells out of his jacket pocket, barely glancing at the weapon as he did so, all his concentration on the bush.

A sable antelope stepped hesitantly into the clearing. It stopped at the water's edge and shook its head challengingly, like the curt, cold salute of a swordsman to his opponent. Then it turned and stood looking back at the dark bush.

The shotgun was at Da Costa's shoulder even as Shahida moved to stop him. The gun roared hideously in the silence. The dinghy rocked perilously. She clung to its sides to prevent it tipping. Bitter words of recrimination formed in her mind. But before they were spoken she registered the fact that Da Costa had fired into the air and that the animal had vanished from the clearing. The shotgun sounded again, and immediately, as if in a series of separate echoes, there was the spattering sound of fire from an automatic weapon, two short bursts and then a long one.

Shahida cowered in the bilges, but the unseen marksman was firing at some other target, for no bullets went by. Da Costa pulled off two shots in quick succession, but this time there was no answering fire. He loaded again, replacing the four spent shells. Then he stood listening. There was no sound in the rapidly darkening bush. After a long time the dove started to call again, repeating its plaintive three-note song. Da Costa said something brief and violent in what she assumed was Portuguese. Then he put the gun back into its case.

'We go.'

He started up the motor. Shahida looked into the bush from where the antelope had emerged. It was quite dark now, and anonymous.

'What was all that about?'

'Poachers,' Da Costa said. He spat into the water. 'Bastards.'

For a while they were silent. Then Da Costa said, in the same murderous voice, 'They would shoot a sable. What for? Because it is *nyama*, meat, and they cannot comprehend that sables are already as rare in this country as polar bears or honest men.'

It took a moment for her to recognize that what she had perceived as a subtle change in the Portuguese was in reality an alteration in his speech. The accent was still heavy, but the aggressively simplistic style had changed. She stared at him, intrigued, but it was already so dark that she could make out little more than a silhouette against the steely glint of fading light on the water.

'Is there a lot of poaching?' she asked encouragingly.

His laugh was bitter. 'What do you call a lot? To wipe out zebra or rhino or elephant in a whole district, is that a lot? Wherever the black bastards. . . .' He stopped himself. 'No. I cannot say that. All are killers – white, black, yellow. But they cannot see it is beauty they are killing. I understand why they do it. It's only *nyama*. When you go into a new country to hunt then you ask in Swahili: "*Ike nyama hapa*? Is there meat here?" That's how they see game. An elephant means one thing only: lots of meat. And the tusks. They can sell the tusks. Do you know how many elephants are killed in Africa each year? One hundred thousand. Can you imagine?'

'You seem to know a lot about it.'

'I know about it. I was once a conservator, yes? What you would call a game ranger. So I know about it.'

'Are many animals killed with automatic guns?'

'A lot. We have wars, revolutions, and so a lot of people get guns, learn to shoot guns. Or else a poison arrow. That's better because it's quiet. Snares, too, are quiet. They're the worst. Long lines, we call them. You know how tunny-boat fishermen use long lines? No?

130

'That's so much . . . I nearly used an ugly word. I can't stand that kind of thinking. To see people like so many insects, like rats in a sewer. I hate that.'

They were silent for a while. The noise of the paddles had lessened and the *Faith* was slowing down, as Captain Da Costa searched for an anchorage.

'You're worried we might fail?' she asked.

'Very.'

'Will someone try to stop us?'

'Probably. This voyage is a test of some kind. And someone is bound to disapprove of noble experiments.'

The two helicopters flew over the steamer for the first time early in the morning. They were small reconnaissance aircraft, with camouflage paint and South African Air Force markings. Both made several low-level passes, and it was possible to see the pilot and the navigator staring down at the *Faith* as she ploughed steadily ahead.

Captain Da Costa made a rude gesture at the machine.

'Like wasps. Buzz buzz buzz all round people's heads. Why they not leave us alone?'

Shahida noticed that he had reverted to his old way of speech.

'Do you think they might try to stop us?'

Da Costa shrugged. 'How? They up there, we down here. They not drop a bomb on a hospital, no?'

She gave a nervous laugh. 'I just hope they realize that this is a hospital. Could it have anything to do with the poachers last night?'

Da Costa shrugged. 'Perhaps they hunt poachers. Perhaps they hunt terrorists. Perhaps they hunt us. Who can tell?'

He turned on the bridge radio and tried several times to call the aircraft, switching from channel to channel. There was no response.

'They use different . . . what do you say? . . . frequencies. Army frequencies. Top secret.'

The helicopters came in on a formation run and then flew off, low over the trees. But they returned in mid-morning and after that persistently shadowed the steamer. It was impossible to ignore their presence. Tension grew on board, showing itself in the reluctance of the black crew or the nursing staff to venture on to the exposed outer decks, in the way people stared speculatively at the sky, in short tempers and long silences.

'What are they doing?' Shahida asked. 'Why don't they go away?'

'They watch,' Da Costa told her. 'They tell others where to find us.'

'What others?'

Da Costa looked back at the hovering aircraft.

'I guess we find out soon enough.'

His prediction was accurate. Half an hour later a launch swept round a bend up ahead, circled the *Faith* once at a respectful distance and then, by gestures from the helmsman, indicated that it intended coming alongside.

They looked down at the small craft in apprehensive silence. It was a military patrol vessel like the one that had escorted Shahida and Brand to the refugee camp, manned by half a dozen soldiers in steel helmets and camouflage battledress. Twin machine guns were mounted amidships, beside the lightly armoured steering console. Both barrels pointed ominously towards the steamer's bridge.

'What do we do now?' Shahida asked.

Da Costa laughed shortly and pushed the engine control lever firmly down.

'We stop.'

The patrol boat circled away in a flurry of foam, then came up on the starboard beam, manoeuvring with impressive precision. One of the crew, rope in hand, jumped the gap between the two vessels, then, disdaining assistance, fastened the rope to a bollard. Bow against bow, the oddly mismatched craft lay head-on to the stream.

Two more of the soldiers boarded the *Faith*, leaving their companions to man the machine guns. They stood on deck watchful and yet inquisitive, looking around with an air of bemusement. One said something and the other laughed. Then they made for the companion ladder which led to the bridge. The young man who had first come on board remained on the boat deck.

The helicopters hung in the sky above the river, engines clattering, the down draft of the spinning rotors causing a continuous swirl of water.

134

Neither of the soldiers wore rank marks on their uniforms, but one was older, with a lean, quizzical look, and his attitude of assurance indicated that he was the leader. He had a holstered pistol strapped at his waist. His companion carried an automatic rifle with a stripped-down butt. Both of them silently inspected the bridge and the people on it. Then the young man with the pistol on his belt said, almost diffidently: 'Good morning. Which is Dr Brand, please?'

Brand said: 'I am.'

The soldier turned respectfully to him.

'I am sorry to stop you, sir, but I have orders.'

'What are they?'

'I have to ask you to turn back your vessel. This is a military zone. Civilian boats are not permitted here.'

'We have the permission of the Bapangani Minister of Health. He has given express authority for this ship to sail on this river.'

The soldier did not lose his air of detached courtesy. 'I have orders to turn you back, sir. It's dangerous to travel the river so far north.' He turned to Da Costa and his voice was sharper. 'Are you the captain?'

Da Costa nodded unwillingly.

'You should have known it is not safe here. This is where the terries come across.'

The Portuguese shrugged and looked away. Clearly he had decided to allow others the responsibility and blame, if there was to be any.

'This is a hospital ship,' Shahida said aggressively.

The young man measured her coolly. 'Those are my orders.'

'And if we do not choose to obey them?'

The soldier surveyed the vessel, which, with her tall topsides and derelict look, resembled nothing more warlike than a floating tenement building. Shahida believed she saw a recognition of the unreality of the situation in the young man's expression, which was half curious, half derisive. A band of raggle-taggle gypsies wandering into the deadly serious world of men at war would have evoked the same reaction.

'Then we shall have no alternative but to force you,' the soldier said, still with the utmost courtesy. He turned to his companion and gave a crisp command.

135

The man with the automatic rifle slung his weapon and went swiftly from the bridge. His boots made a ringing sound on the bridge ladder as he climbed down.

The other soldier turned back to Brand. 'I am calling in my CO, sir. Perhaps he can persuade you that we mean what we say.'

There was no good humour today on the face of the Sekhong base commander, but his first question was also, in a way, an admission of the absurdity of the situation.

'What do you people think you're playing at?' Commandant De Waal asked with cold anger. 'Don't you realize we're fighting a war here?'

His party had arrived in one of the helicopters. The patrol boat had ferried them from the landing place on the river bank and De Waal had come stamping up to the bridge. With him, to Shahida's surprise, was William Kgosana. Why had the black headmaster been brought here? To make the point that this was not entirely a military exercise?

The polite young officer brought up the rear. Commandant De Waal was less than polite, for reasons he soon made clear.

'I've had signals flying round my head ever since yesterday,' he said resentfully. 'Down at Command they seem to think I encouraged this damn-fool outing of yours.'

Brand said in a cool voice: 'You have no right to stop us. As I've already pointed out to your subordinate, this expedition has the full sanction of the Minister of Health.'

'Dr Brand, if you had the sanction of the good Lord himself I still wouldn't allow you to come joy-riding inside a war zone in this . . . this. . . .' Words failed him and he made a contemptuous gesture which took in all of the decrepit paddle-wheel steamer and its crew.

'This vessel has been fitted out as a hospital. You surely don't object to our bringing a hospital here?'

De Waal gave him a pitying look. 'Doctor, you're lucky your hospital is still afloat and that someone hasn't taken a pot shot at it.'

'The point remains that we have permission from the Health Ministry.'

'You haven't got permission from the army and it's the army that's in charge here. It's as simple as that.'

'I don't believe it's simple at all. You're saying that a cabinet minister in the elected government of this country can be overruled merely because you and your army say so?'

'We're here to protect his country. And we decide how it's done.'

'Is it your job to "protect" the people of the country from medical attention?'

They faced one another, bristling. Shahida had never seen Brand so angry. She was afraid he might come to blows with the officer, and she feared for him among these soldiers and their guns.

'Commandant,' she said, 'even if you are fighting a war, there are still ordinary people who have nothing to do with it. It's only those we're concerned about.' Use sweet reason, she told herself. Don't antagonize the man.

'You're in my way. We've wasted enough time already chasing after you.'

'We didn't ask you to.'

'It's for your own protection.'

'Are you suggesting anyone would deliberately fire on this ship? We carry Red Cross markings, as you must have seen.'

He laughed brusquely. 'Doctor, you could carry a swastika or a hammer and sickle for all the difference it would make. It's part of terrorist tactics to go for civilians. You're sitting ducks on this thing.'

With a sense of chill she remembered the sound of gunfire in the dark bush last night. She said nothing.

'I'm sorry,' De Waal said. 'I'm not risking my men to protect you while you play at being angels of mercy.' He gestured towards William. 'You tell them.'

The black man seemed nonplussed. 'Commandant?'

'Tell them about the nuns. And about that little boy.'

'Oh. Yes.' William's expression was conciliatory, as if he were pleading for their understanding. 'The nuns, yes.' He began in the chanting tones of a tribal storyteller. 'There was a mission station at a town called Nova Braga, just across the border. It was in the days before the trouble started. There were nuns there and one white Father and they were very good to the people.'

'Is this going to be an atrocity story?' Brand asked De Waal. 'Because I can assure you we've all heard our share of those.'

Shahida remembered that at their last meeting William had said

137

to her: we are prisoners. He had been right, but James Brand had not yet realized it.

'OK, then,' the officer said. 'Forget about the nuns. Tell them about the kid.'

'There was a raid on a village the other day,' William said. He addressed himself to Brand and Shahida as if he had a message for them alone, something hidden, which lay beyond words. 'The villagers got away, but a boy eight years old was caught by the terrorists. They were angry that the others had escaped so they shot him in both knees. And then they emptied paraffin out of an oil lamp over him and they set him alight.'

They looked at him in cold horror. Neither of them spoke.

'Tell them,' Commandant De Waal said. 'Tell them what happened then.'

'One of our patrols came to the village and found the child,' William said. 'He was still alive. He was taken to base hospital and then casevac'd out. He's in hospital in Pretoria now. He's had operations and skin grafts.'

'What William is saying is that we can cope with this kind of thing ourselves,' De Waal said. 'We don't need your help. The army can cope.'

'But what about the others?' Shahida said. 'What about that camp? Those people need help, and that's why we've come.'

Commandant De Waal's voice was implacably hostile. 'Doctor, we don't need your kind of help. We don't need you here and we don't want you here.'

There was silence. None of them could think of anything else to say.

Chugging back downriver, they had the stream behind them and they made better time. On the afternoon of the third day the *Faith* was back on her moorings.

11

Brand had been uncertain how Michael Makaza would react to the news of the *Faith*'s aborted voyage. The Minister of Health had, after all, virtually been blackmailed into authorizing the mission; probably he would be secretly happy it had failed. So he was surprised to find Makaza in a towering rage.

'It is what these Boers always do,' Makaza stormed at him. 'They come to us and pretend to be so wise and so polite.' He mimicked savagely: ' "*Meneer die Minister*" this and "*Meneer die Minister*" that. "This is your country, *Meneer die Minister*, so you've got to say what's to be done!" But when the crunch comes, who's got the final say? The bloody Boers, that's who. Then it's we who're supposed to say: "*Ja baas, nee baas*, three bags full, *baas*." '

'If it has to come to a showdown, which side would you support?' Brand asked.

Makaza became cautious as quickly as he had become incensed.

'Now wait. Wait a minute. We can't create an international incident here.'

'I could think of worse reasons,' Brand said promptly.

Makaza stared at him and then, surprisingly, laughed.

'What do you want me to do?'

'It's up to you.'

'I could try to get the backing of the Chief Minister. They could hardly. . . . I think I could persuade him to. . . . And if he approves, then the approval of the cabinet is merely a formality.'

'If you could do that . . . if the Chief Minister says it's on, then there's no way they can turn us back again.'

'There is an official function at the Assembly this evening and he will be there. It's a cocktail party. I'll get an invitation sent to you. I'm sure we'll find a few free moments to discuss the matter with him.'

'And I'll see that A I D headquarters brings pressure to bear. Our people in Paris, I mean. In fact, I might even go over in person to speak to our directors. I've been asked to read a paper at a seminar in Copenhagen. If I decide to go I'll make a detour through Paris.'

The invitation, although several months old, was still open. It was a consequence of his work at the Canadian university, but it was still flattering that the Danes should wish to hear him speak on the problems of medical services in Third World countries. He had been hesitant about accepting, for time and distance were obstacles. But the cost of the air ticket was thrown in with the invitation.

'You would go to Paris yourself?'

'I might well do that.'

Makaza laughed again. 'You should get your people to speak to Interpharmacor. That would really – ' He stopped abruptly.

'Speak to whom?'

'No. It's nothing.'

'Interfarm something?'

The minister looked agitated. He seemed about to say something. Then he shook his head.

'Nothing.'

Sounds like a pharmaceutical company, Brand thought. Again he remembered the story about Makaza's link with drugs purchases and corruption. He rose.

'Thank you for your time, minister,' he said. 'If you can help us on the lines you've suggested, then I believe we can achieve something well worth while.'

The flashlights from a number of cameras played like distant lightning at the far end of the room, where the Chief Minister and his wife were being photographed.

All light and no sound. The spectacle without the danger. He remembered an electric storm he had seen one night years ago, during a holiday at the coast. An Indian waiter he had befriended had asked him up to the hotel roof, where there was an unhindered view. He had watched the unending flashes and zigzags darting among ponderous cloud formations and there had been no sound at all, not even a distant mutter of thunder. It was uncanny and discomforting. The waiter had explained that the storm was very far out at sea, at the edge of the blue water twenty miles offshore.

It was weird to experience the same feeling of unease here, safely indoors amidst the cheerful uproar of a cocktail party. He was only one among a hundred others and yet he felt isolated and vulnerable, as if lightning might strike at any moment.

He edged away to the back of the room. The picture taking had stopped, but the Chief Minister was now in conversation with two young men carrying notebooks. Brand had no desire to attract the attention of the press.

He took a drink from a passing waiter and stood with it, back to the wall, while he looked around. Most of the guests were black, with a sprinkling of white officialdom. He saw no one he felt like talking to. Minister Makaza had not yet appeared. He did not even know the reason for the party, for his invitation had come by way of a hurried phone call. Perhaps if there were speeches he might learn.

Brand had the uneasy feeling of being watched. He looked towards the Chief Minister, but the old man was still holding forth to the reporters and they were taking notes. Would he be able to introduce himself if Makaza did not arrive to prepare the ground?

Someone was watching him. He turned quickly. Shahida Karim was standing near the buffet table, talking to a tall black woman in a flamboyant caftan with a foot-high turban wound round her head. By comparison Shahida looked like a slender child. She did not seem to notice his glance, but he was sure she had been watching him a moment earlier.

He pushed determinedly through the crowd. She was picking a canapé from a plate.

'Hullo,' he said. 'Didn't realize you'd be at this bun fight.'

She gave him her grave smile.

'Have you met Mrs Lokosho?'

Wife of the Minister of Education, he remembered. They made social noises. Mrs Lokosho was less interested in talking to him than to Shahida. Someone else drew her attention and she turned away from them.

'If I'd known you were coming I would have offered you a lift.'

'I came here with Mrs Lokosho and the minister.'

He knew nothing about her private life. She existed for him only in a medical setting. He wanted to change that but did not know how to go about it.

'I didn't realize you knew them.'

141

She said, with a touch of reproof: 'Mrs Lokosho is chairman of the hospital's Board of Aid. She asked me to the party.'

'Of course.'

Her dress was severely simple but she still managed, among the bright colours of the other women, to look exotic and fragile, like a bird of paradise in a cage of parrots.

'Anyway it's nice to see someone I know. I was starting to feel like Ishmael.'

She laughed and said in mock sympathy: 'Poor man.'

He surveyed the plates of biscuits primped with bits of olive and anchovy and cold meat.

'Wish there was something more substantial. I'm starving.'

She whispered conspiratorially: 'There will probably be fried chicken bits later, if you can bear to wait.'

'I'll have to fill up on olives meanwhile.'

They laughed together, more at ease. He felt encouraged. At least they were off to a better start than at the last party they had attended together.

'How do you know about the chicken bits? Do you come to a lot of these functions?'

'I'm guessing. It might be stewed meatballs.'

The banter restored his humour. It was a relief to find that Shahida could be flippant. She was a pleasure to look at and talk to, even if the conversation was mere froth. This was what they needed: a reprieve from seriousness. Life for him was always so serious. And, come to think of it, so dull.

'If you're as near starvation as I am, how about dinner when this is over?' he ventured.

'I'm not sure if I. . . .'

He was preparing to overcome her hesitation with a display of firmness when, to his chagrin, he felt a hand on his shoulder.

Michael Makaza said: 'Forgive me, *Monsieur le Directeur*, for interrupting.'

Brand made reluctant introductions, conscious of the other man's knowing look.

'I have heard much about Dr Karim,' Makaza said. 'It is indeed a pleasure.' He turned back to Brand. 'The Chief Minister is ready for us. Perhaps Dr Karim would care to join in our little meeting. I'm sure she can be most persuasive.'

As they made their way through the crush to where the old man and his wife had been placed in seats of honour, Brand wondered if Shahida's presence here was solely coincidence. There were stories that the Chief Minister was susceptible to attractive young women. Shahida had come as the guest of another minister. He would not put it past Makaza to be working a bit of inter-cabinet intrigue. But perhaps he was being too suspicious.

The Chief Minister was affable but cautious.

'We have great admiration for your work among our people.'

'You know that we have encountered certain obstacles?'

'Good works are often misunderstood.'

'Then one has to remove the misunderstanding together with the obstacle.'

The old man had a habitual look of weary patience, as if he was tired of the weight of office. His lined face and grizzled hair came across well on television, when he pleaded the case of his small land in the midst of southern African turmoil. But there was no doubt about his political acumen.

'Sometimes obstacles are best overcome by going around them.'

'That's what we're trying to do right now,' Brand said audaciously.

The Chief Minister laughed. His shrewd eyes rested on Shahida for a moment. 'We'll have to consider ways to smooth your passage. Can you come to see me. . . .' He stopped to consider. 'Not tomorrow, I regret, for I have a full day. Perhaps the day after, if that will suit you.'

'Most certainly.'

'And perhaps. . . .' He looked at Shahida again. 'Perhaps Dr Karim will be there too? My secretary will telephone you to fix a time.'

Brand suspected that the old man already knew all the arguments for and against. He and Shahida left together. He repeated his dinner invitation but she declined. She had promised to return with Mrs Lokosho. However, she would be happy to go with him to the Chief Minister.

He saw her to the car already waiting under the porte-cochère, then went to his own car and a lonely meal at the hotel.

*

143

The telephone call from Dr Van Jaarsveld came in mid-morning. The Director of Health did not waste time on social exchange.

'Have you seen the local rag this week?'

The *Bapangani Times* was a weekly newspaper with a chequered history. Once a staid recorder of the capital's equally unlively social scene, it had been acquired by an editor with a chip on his shoulder and a dislike for authority, large and small. It was now in a constant turmoil of scandalmongering, libel actions and threatened suspension.

'We don't get the paper out here till late in – ' Brand started to explain.

'Then you don't know how large you feature in today's collection of claptrap.' Van Jaarsveld read in a sneering voice: ' "Mercy ship given thumbs down by army." You know nothing about this? "Authoritarian military officers this week ham-handedly squashed plans for a floating hospital. . . ." There's much more of it. Do you want me to read it all?'

'I have said nothing to any journalist about this – '

But Van Jaarsveld was in no mood for explanations. 'I believe you have also had discussions behind my back with my minister and with the Chief Minister.'

Brand became annoyed. 'I am not aware of any restriction on my rights to speak to people.'

'Including the press?'

'I've already told you I have not even seen – '

'You seem to like becoming involved in this kind of public controversy, doctor.'

The jolt of memory was as unexpected and unpleasant as an electric shock. Rietfontein. It could be nothing else.

'What are you talking about?'

'Some years ago you made certain statements to the overseas media, didn't you? When you were working in South Africa.' Contempt was evident in the man's voice. Unspoken, but solid as a wall between them, was the accusation: renegade.

It was a chilling example of how widely the net was spread. Where had the information about his past come from? How long had Van Jaarsveld known? He had never tried to hide his background but also had never made a display of it. His acquired Canadian twang served further to conceal his origin. Then how had

144

Van Jaarsveld known? He realized, with foreboding, that this was a declaration of war.

The hell with it, he thought. He ended the conversation equally coldly.

But the full realization of the extent of Dr Van Jaarsveld's resourcefulness and influence did not come until the afternoon, when there was a call from Paris. Monsignor Pauchet came on the line, and he did not waste time coming to the point.

'I understand you are experiencing difficulties with the press and with the local health authorities.'

'No, not particularly. The Minister of Health is very helpful. And I believe the Chief Minister is also on our side.'

Some electronic quirk in the international connection caused his words to echo back to him as they were spoken.

Pauchet clearly disliked being more explicit. His voice rose a tone. 'Have you not been engaged on some project in a military security area? I understand the authorities are not happy about it.'

Brand wondered whether the priest was experiencing the same distortion at the other end. 'The Health Minister has been most co-operative,' he said again, but this time with a change of stress.

Pauchet caught the implication. He was silent for a moment. 'I see,' he said thoughtfully. Then: 'Will you explain the situation briefly?'

At the end of Brand's account there was silence. At length Pauchet said: 'It entails travelling in a hazardous area?'

'Who told you that?'

'We have been approached by an interested party.'

Bapangani had no diplomatic relations with other countries outside South Africa.

'Is this on orders from the army? Or is it political?'

'Doctor, I cannot speak about this matter over the telephone.'

'Are you instructing me to abandon our project?'

'We would prefer you not to proceed at this stage. Not until the situation is clearer.'

There was a significant pause. Then Pauchet continued and even across the thousands of miles and the electronic disturbance Brand could hear that the unctuous tones had returned to the priest's voice. 'We trust you, doctor, to find a tactful way out. I would rather not say too much over the telephone.'

145

'Perhaps I should prepare a report for you.'

'An excellent idea,' the priest said eagerly. 'By all means do that.'

'I might even deliver it in person.'

Another moment of silence, followed by a puzzled: 'Yes?'

'I have been invited to address a symposium in Denmark.' No harm in letting Pauchet know he was in demand elsewhere. 'It's being held in Copenhagen. I can go via Paris.'

'That would be useful.' Pauchet's voice was discouraging.

'I'll let you know,' Brand said.

He was angry and hurt and felt betrayed, but there was no one he could tell. Had there ever been anyone? He had long ago grown accustomed to keeping his miseries to himself. Was he guilty of taking a perverse pride in his own loneliness?

He toyed briefly with the idea of speaking to Shahida Karim. It was a beguiling thought and it could be justified, for she was involved. Then why did he hold back? He knew that he would receive the comfort he needed and yet he could not bring himself to seek it, from an old habit of reserve, coupled with a faint mistrust of women. Somewhere in his mind was a scratchy feeling that it was unmanly to admit to frailty. He knew that it was illogical, even childish, but the hesitation persisted. He could not show himself fallible before Dr Karim. Already, unreasonable as the belief might be, he felt that, by not defying Monsignor Pauchet, he had somehow betrayed her trust and faith.

To go to Paris or to stay away? Brand could not make up his mind. A confrontation with the AID directorate would at least force the issue into the open. To resort to long-distance phone calls and letters and reports would allow time and delay to obscure the essential simplicity of the issue. But the point was: did he have any kind of case to present?

He twisted the chair sideways and pulled out the bottom desk drawer to serve as a footrest. In the drawer was one of the AID brochures he had studied long ago in Montreal. He picked it up and turned the pages. It was well put together, with photographs in colour and an uncluttered design. Bouncing black babies and beaming black nurses. X-ray machines and children getting their shots. A mobile clinic at a black village somewhere in Central Africa. (If it's OK in Gabon, why not in Bapangani, he thought crossly.) There was a tear-out sheet for donations and, on the last two pages, the officially certified statement of accounts for last year.

He never could work out balance sheets. Rows of figures produced an instant mental block. He shut the booklet. Then opened it again. *Maybe*, he thought, *just maybe it's time you learn*.

The accounts in the brochure, it was soon evident, were presented in summary form, the bare bones of income and expenditure, without details. Sufficient, presumably, for a would-be donor wanting to know that his gifts were subject to audit and would not be misspent. But there was nothing in there about where the money came from and where, eventually, it went.

Surely more detailed accounts must exist. Surely legal requirements would demand more than this neat and bland summary of dealings in (and this he noted with interest; he had not realized AID was so well endowed) very large sums of money.

He wandered irresolutely into the corridor. Two doors away was a sign reading 'Secretary'. Helmut Fissher was at his desk, grey head bowed over a mound of papers. He looked up as Brand came in and made a sketchy gesture of rising.

'There was a call from Paris. Did they find you?'

Brand was reminded again that in spite of the secretary's diffident air nothing much slipped his notice. Told of the conversation with Pauchet, Fissher was wryly sympathetic.

'Dr Hauge will be disappointed.'

'We all are.'

'Monsignor Pauchet is not known for his liking to . . . what is the phrase? . . . "buck the system". Is that correct?'

'How well do you know him?'

'Not at all well, I fear. Not well.'

'What is his real job with AID?'

'I am not certain. He is a director, beyond that I do not know.'

'Has he an official post?' Brand pressed. 'Or is it merely honorary?'

'He has considerable control over financial matters. Beyond that. . . .' Fissher changed the subject. 'Have you plans to pursue the matter of the boat?'

'I haven't really decided.'

'This is important to you? That the steamer should return?'

'It's become a question of principle.'

'I see.' The quiet phrase was comment enough. Brand was nettled.

'Look, I'm tired of bending my convictions to suit other people's fears. I believe that a hospital on board the steamer can serve a purpose and that it can be achieved without bringing anarchy and ruin in its wake. Maybe we should stop bending backwards to please the politicians and the generals. Maybe, just maybe, we should start thinking about what we're here for. And that is to serve sick people, by what manner and by what means we can find.'

Fissher nodded solemnly. 'But the problem, of course, is how to circumvent that establishment.'

'Yes.' A thought came to him. 'By the way, Helmut, does the name Interpharmacor mean anything to you?'

Was it his imagination, or had a guarded look come momentarily to the other man's face?

'Should it?'

'It's something Makaza mentioned in connection with AID. But he wouldn't elaborate.'

'I cannot recall,' the secretary said stiffly. 'Was there anything else, doctor?'

'You've got lots of work,' Brand said. 'I'll leave you to it.'

The door between Fissher's office and his own belonged to the accounts department. He went in on impulse.

Miss Barclay, hospital accountant, was fiftyish, of British descent (although she had lived in various African countries for most of her life), uncommunicative, always dressed in grey no matter what the weather, dedicated to her work and utterly devoid of curiosity.

Brand greeted her and thought up a hurried excuse.

'There are some aspects of our accounts that I have to take up with the minister. The question of refunds and so forth. I'm a bit hazy about how it works.'

'Mr Fissher normally handles all that.'

'I know. But I'd like you to explain, so that I don't feel altogether a fool next time I speak to the minister.'

The plain, severe face came as close as it could to animation as she unfolded the mysteries of the accounting and filing systems on his behalf. The department, Brand was happy to learn, had so far not advanced to the sophistication of computers, for that would have foiled him. And at the same time he was ashamed of his ignorance. If it produced nothing else at least this exercise would force him to learn something about the workings of his own hospital.

'Was there something particular you wanted to see, doctor?'

Tempting. She would know exactly where to look. It would save a lot of time. But better not. Miss Barclay was anything but a chatterbox; nevertheless she might let something slip.

'Don't bother.' He had seen where the photocopier stood. On top of the machine lay its instruction book. Surely it would not be more difficult to operate than, say, an ECG machine?

He sat in his office for a time and then, feeling rather as if he was really playing truant, drove to town. In a street fronting the river was a row of shops owned by Indians. He went into one where he saw radios and cameras in the window, and bought a pocket calculator. He had never owned one of the damned things and the purchase brought back the feeling of guilt, coupled with an odd excitement, as if he was a boy again, buying condoms in a chemist's shop.

He had reason to work late that evening, to make up for time lost during the day. By the time he had cleared his desk it was already close to seven. The admin block was deserted.

Hesitantly, as if still wondering what had brought him there, he went down the corridor to the accounts department. He let himself in and, feeling faintly foolish, drew the blinds before switching on the light. Then, settling down with the photocopying machine and the calculator with its quick green digits, he set to work.

It was half-past two in the morning by the time he finished. He made the last calculation, put away the last file, closed the last cabinet. Furtively, he worked to remove evidence of his presence, pushing chairs to their former positions, opening the window to let out stale air, picking up stray papers. He raised the blind again and switched off the light.

His first mistake had been to believe that he would find a complete set of accounts covering the operations of the entire AID organization. In fact, as he should have anticipated, these ledgers dealt mainly with the financial affairs of the Bapangani unit. He had made other mistakes, through ignorance and misunderstanding. He had pursued any number of red herrings. When it was all done he still did not have a clear picture. Everything seemed above board. And yet. . . .

There had been an early moment of excitement when he had found the name Interpharmacor listed among the creditors. Interpharmacor Unternehmungs GmbH, with an address in Essen, West Germany. But when he had eventually traced Interpharmacor's involvement with AID he found nothing more illuminating than a series of straightforward transactions involving drugs purchases and shipments.

That was the problem. There seemed to be nothing to excite the curiosity of an auditor. The debits and the credits added up and the balances balanced. And yet. . . .

He could not put his finger on it, but there was a grey area, an obscurity (and he would be the first to admit that this might be due to stupidity on his part) about the movement of some funds; about their sources and the way they were spent. A chartered accountant would find nothing out of the way. But a doctor might note something strange about the priorities given to some aspects of health and the money lavished on these fields, and might start to wonder. Except, of course, that most doctors didn't give a damn, provided the money was there when they needed it and there was a minimum of clerical red tape.

It became clear to Brand from the start of the interview that he was not the only one to have been subjected to pressure during the past forty-eight hours. The Chief Minister was less friendly this afternoon. He had an abstracted air, as if there were weightier matters on his mind.

Shahida and Brand were received cordially enough and even given the honour of a personal conducted tour through the new parliamentary building. It was only when they got down to business, in the old man's austerely furnished office, that the atmosphere cooled.

The Chief Minister told them he shared their concern for the medical care of his people. He would do everything in his power to assist the worthy work undertaken by AID. And of course he would not consider interfering in the policies laid down by the AID directorate.

So the old man knew about Pauchet's telephone call, Brand reflected dispiritedly. Van Jaarsveld again.

It was unfortunate, the Chief Minister continued, that an apparent conflict of interest had arisen between AID and the army, and he reminded Brand that the latter was also a guest in his country. He was certain that an amicable solution could be found. However, nothing could be gained by overhasty action.

The meeting ended with further expressions of goodwill, but no promises. Shahida and Brand found themselves politely but firmly dismissed.

They stood in the glass-walled foyer, looking at one another with identical expressions of bewilderment. Then they both burst out laughing, to the confusion of the uniformed guard who waited to see them out.

'That was a quick freeze if ever I've seen one,' Brand said.

'He hardly let us get a word in edgeways.'

'Would you say someone else got here before us?'

'The thought crossed my mind.'

They laughed again, and the guard, holding the door open for them, smiled tentatively.

Evening had not yet come, but an orange-brown gloom had fallen over the town. Some of the vehicles on Government Avenue had their lights switched on. Thunderclouds obscured the sun. There was a storm approaching.

Brand took Shahida by the arm. She stiffened slightly, but did not resist.

'Where now?'

'Back to the hospital, I suppose.'

He had parked his car at the far end of the parliamentary gardens, and the storm broke over them while they were still in the open. There was a jagged flash of lightning and an almost instantaneous thunderclap and then the rain came pelting down. He had forgotten how fierce a subtropical storm could be and was briefly alarmed. The rain fell solidly, straight down and then at a driving slant into their faces, as a gust of wind followed the thunder. The paved walkway was awash within moments and they were soaked through.

They scrambled into the car and sat there with the rain

151

drumming on the roof and the windscreen misting from their breath. They looked at one another and laughed.

Her hair had come down at the side and as he watched she pushed it back with one hand, giving herself a hoydenish look. Her thin summer dress clung damply to her body. He could see the outline of her underclothing.

'We can't drive out to the hospital like this.'

'No.' She was still watching the falling rain.

'I think we'd best go to my hotel. We'll find some way of getting you dry.'

She nodded. 'All right.'

By the time they reached the hotel the rain had stopped and there was sudden silence, an evening hush over the wet town, broken only by the gurgle of water in gutters and downpipes. They went, wet and dripping, through the foyer past the amused stares of the clerks behind the reception desk.

When he unlocked his room door he stood aside, careful not to touch her. She went in ahead of him, looking around the room as if surprised to be there. He was aware of the sudden constraint and tried to be matter-of-fact. He opened the wardrobe, pulled out drawers, rummaged through his clothing. He found a pair of jeans and a soft shirt.

'Here. They'll be too big for you, but at least they're dry. Use the bathroom. Then we can see about getting your things dried out.'

While she was in the bathroom he changed too, hurriedly. When she came out, after what seemed a long time, he was speaking to the valet service on the phone. He motioned her to a chair. She had rolled back the trouser legs and the sleeves of his shirt, but the baggy clothes had the same effect as her oversized hospital coat, making her appear even smaller and more fragile.

He put down the receiver.

'They're sending a maid to take care of your dress. I think we could have a drink meanwhile, don't you?' He anticipated her wry gesture at her clothing. 'We can have it here. No need to go down.'

The wet clothes were efficiently whipped away and a waiter came with their drinks, and there was the comforting feeling that at least immediate physical problems had been solved, even if larger problems remained.

Shahida went to the window, drink in hand. The storm had

passed, and the last of the sun shone on the river with an unearthly light.

'The river,' she said. 'Look at it.' And after a moment: 'I suppose it's closed to us now.'

'Not if I can help it,' he said staunchly. 'I've decided. I'm going to Paris to fight it out with AID.'

She turned with that reserved smile. 'You must think I'm awfully single-minded.'

'You know what you want.'

'Do I?'

He took a step towards her but stopped, uncertain.

She continued to smile. Then she placed her glass carefully on the windowsill and, still smiling, slowly unbuttoned the front of the borrowed shirt.

12

The pretty, dark-haired air hostess displayed her professional smile. At the same time she leaned against the laden trolley, as if already tired of being on her feet, although they had been in the air for little more than an hour.

'Something to drink, sir?'

Brand's seat companion was a plump, fair-haired young man and was, as he had informed Brand within ten minutes of takeoff, on a business trip which would take him to Hamburg, Stuttgart and Munich. He made a disproportionate fuss over ordering and being served a brandy and soda.

Brand noticed the resigned look which flashed between the hostess and the steward who was helping her with the drinks trolley.

'You, sir?' the stewardess asked him.

'Scotch, please. Ice and water.'

The drink, on a paper coaster emblazoned with the airline's crest, was placed before him.

'I think some wine with dinner, eh?' the travelling businessman said with high good humour. 'You'll join me?'

'Thank you, no.'

'Oh.' He looked disappointed. 'Think I'll have a bottle anyway.' He took a while making his choice from the not overlong wine list, while the two flight attendants waited wearily.

'Just as well to order in good time,' he confided. 'Always a rush once they start serving the meal.'

'I dare say.'

'You're American, eh?'

'Canadian.'

'Is that so? I always say a Canadian passport is the best of the lot. Go anywhere with it. You're not as rich as the Yanks, so people don't try to diddle you. You've never had colonies, so people don't hate you. And when you quarrel it's among yourselves, not with other countries.'

Brand smiled mechanically.

'Not like us,' his newly acquired friend said bitterly. 'South African passport is worth damn all. No one likes us. Black Africa, India, Far East, we can't even get in. I'm thinking of getting a British passport. Father was born in the UK. They allow you to hold double passports for business reasons, you know?'

'I see,' Brand said. Seeking escape, he turned to the porthole, leaning forward to peer through the double layer of curved perspex. Nothing was visible in the blackness. The 747 had reached cruising altitude. He thought they were probably flying over northern Botswana by now, perhaps already over Angola.

'Weather's bad over the continent.' His seat companion tried again. 'I listened to the international forecast over the radio this morning. Raining in Frankfurt.'

'Oh.'

'But I suppose you're travelling on?'

'Yes, to Paris.'

'Wouldn't mind a bit of that myself.'

There was no adequate reply. Brand returned to his contemplation of the night.

An image of Shahida's face came to mind: of that strange withdrawn quality which made her seem almost indifferent to the world, so that it was constantly a surprise to find that she was not like that at all, that she could be passionately involved in other people's lives.

154

His thoughts about her had a dreamlike quality; what had happened the evening after the storm already seemed unreal. What he remembered most clearly was that they talked. He knew himself to be a reserved and in some ways inarticulate man and yet they had talked together with the passion of penitents after the vow of silence had ended.

Yet she had not told him much about herself. He had wanted to know more and had searched the hospital records, but the facts were meagre and somehow disappointing. MB, ChB at Edinburgh, graduated in 1974 at a comparatively youthful twenty-three. Worked at a London hospital, then at hospitals in Jakarta and Singapore. Glowing testimonials from her chiefs. Back in London two years ago and working towards a specialist degree in paediatrics, especially the treatment of mentally handicapped children. Packed it up suddenly in the middle of the year to join AID and come out to Africa. That was all the records told him: an outline drawing rather than a life.

What would happen to her if his mission failed? Would she find it necessary to move on again? Where to, this time?

And where would he go?

He had once lost a job because of the camp at Rietfontein. Now there were more camps for dispossessed people and once more his job was in jeopardy.

He had never tried to hide from himself the knowledge that the political stand he had taken then, long ago, had helped as well as hindered. The offer from Canada had come with too much alacrity, too well timed after the public row and the television publicity to have been coincidence. Even the present job with AID, he was sure, was another product of Rietfontein.

Not that it was such a marvellous job. Running a two-bit mission hospital in the sticks was a decided step down from what he had been doing in Canada, and let them not forget it, Pauchet and his henchman. AID had been lucky to find him, an acknowledged world authority in his field, just at a time when his wife had walked out on him. He had been ripe for a change then and didn't care what it was.

Rietfontein, what did you make of me? The fact is, I'm no longer the person I was then. If I lose this fight, who will come to my rescue? Have I the same reserves, the same endurance? I wonder.

155

He sat, sleepless and filled with feelings of apprehension, as the aircraft made its way along the length of a continent where few lights showed, a continent which seemed to him as dark as his thoughts.

Two young women in dark blue uniforms stood at the head of the escalator, passing out cards as the passengers straggled upwards. He took one, puzzled, trying to read the German script.

'*Bitte?*'

'*Danke schön,*' the ground hostess said automatically, already reaching out past him to someone else.

He flipped the card, relieved to find English on the reverse side.

'Health Notice,' it read. 'You have travelled from a country in which there has been a recent outbreak of cholera. For your own safety you are advised, while in Germany. . . .'

He made to thrust the card into a jacket pocket, then paused, frowning.

'Transit,' he said to the woman.

She looked at him, bothered.

'*Bitte?*'

'But I'm in transit. I'm not staying in Frankfurt.'

'Transit!' She snatched the card from him almost angrily, as if he had affronted her. 'Transit that way.' She pointed back down the escalator and to the left. 'You have wrong stairs. Transit passengers the other way.'

He turned back to the descending escalator, humping a shoulder to keep the flight bag from slipping. He was the only person going down. Other people, being carried upwards past him, looked at him curiously. His seat companion was among them. He called cheerfully: 'Gone the wrong way!'

Brand nodded and smiled.

Cholera, he was thinking. Where would that be? Kinshasa, probably. Just as well no one knows about Virus H yet.

For a moment he hesitated, filled with doubt and vague feelings of guilt. He himself had been a contact. Was the virus lodged somewhere within him, inactive for the moment but ready to resume its deadly progress at some still unknown signal? Might not his visit here, his future travels, bring risk to others? That was one

156

of the fearful dangers which modern communications had created. Obscure diseases, once relatively isolated in their obscure places of origin, could today be transported from continent to continent in a matter of hours.

Hauge *had* to be given the chance to solve the riddle of where Virus H had come from.

He went on down the corridor towards the departure-lounge control points.

No one knew. That was the problem. Nobody knew.

The departure board made its irritating clacking noise and letters and numerals danced within their frames.

LUFT 301 to Hamburg and Copenhagen hung in the balance for a moment, then the spinning letters spelt out their verdict: CANCELLED. Flight 301 joined the half-dozen others, mostly to northern and eastern Europe, which had gone from delay after delay to eventual abandonment. People who had been standing watching the board, absorbed as if its cryptic symbols might at any moment transpose themselves into a revelation, turned away with expressions of resignation or annoyance. Others got up from their seats, collected their luggage, wandered away to seek other consolations, perhaps other destinations.

Brand cocked a wary eye towards the board to make sure that LUFT 260, Paris, London, was still there under DELAY and beckoned to the bartender.

'Cognac, *bitte*.'

'Coming now, sir,' the man said.

'*Danke schön*,' Brand said with emphasis.

The barman merely smiled, and counted out the change. Brand sipped at the drink, his third. He had stretched them out over the three hours he had sat here waiting for his plane. So much for the glamour of international air travel.

The board, behind his back, started its noise again. This time he did not turn and instead watched the television screen mounted over the bar. He knew.

The Paris, London flight was cancelled.

He grimaced, finished the brandy at a gulp and stood up to reach for his bag. He caught the barman's commiserating smile.

He smiled back and shrugged. That was the way the world went.

The woman at the travel desk seemed to find the notion incredible.

'Train?' she said, as if it was inconceivable that she, who worked at an airport, should be expected to know about earthbound transport.

Brand nodded tiredly. 'Train. You know? Chuff-chuff-chuff.'

The woman laughed, and suddenly became more animated.

'Yes, sir. You want to know about a train to Paris. Let me see. . . .'

It seemed to him, in the first bewildered moment of waking, that he had never been asleep. Then he realized, informed by an inner time clock, that he had in fact slept for only a few minutes before being jostled rudely into wakefulness by someone dropping into the seat beside him. He turned to give the intruder, a fat little man with a straggly moustache, an offended glare, then looked out of the window again.

The little man said something to him loudly, in French. He turned again, frowning his annoyance. There was a heavy belt round the ample belly and from it hung a pouch and a device with coin slots such as bus conductors wore.

Ticket collector? He fumbled in his wallet.

'*Non, non!*' The man with the bus conductor's bag waved his hands and spoke explosively.

What the hell, then? Luggage? Passport? But the French immigration officers had already been past, had interrupted his sleep a short while before when the train had crossed over from Germany, to page indifferently through his passport. Besides, they had been in uniform; this little fellow wore a baggy grey suit and a shirt without a tie. He thought: whatever you're selling, old chap, I don't want it. He made a gesture of dismissal.

It only served to provoke even more excitement. The little man gabbled away at him, in German now, pulling at his sleeve with incomprehensible determination. He could only be a religious nut, trying to peddle his pamphlets predicting the end of the world in 1999, and sticking like a leech to his chosen victim.

He looked helplessly at the other people in the compartment – a Latin-looking woman in a red hat, a student huddled in a parka, two elderly women side by side, knitting and conversing in undertones. They looked away as if it had nothing to do with them.

His persecutor burst into a fresh harangue, speaking, from what Brand could make out, Spanish this time. He cut sharply into the tirade.

'Look. I'm not interested. Whatever it is you want, I'm not interested. Comprehend?'

The little man's expression changed suddenly from despair to beaming understanding.

'Ah! You are American, not?'

'Yes,' Brand said shortly. 'But I don't want to buy anything.'

'Not buy. Exchange.'

'What?'

'Exchange. I change your money. You have dollars, yes?'

Brand understood. A mobile money merchant. He laughed.

'No dollars. Travellers' cheques, in Swiss francs only. And a few German marks.'

'I will change for you. Best rates. You need money in Paris, not? Francs, French money. At station, for taxi, not?'

'Oh, all right. One cheque. Fifty francs. And I've got about twenty marks.'

'I change,' the little man said contentedly.

The other passengers watched the transaction with utter disinterest, as if it were taking place behind glass, in a world they did not inhabit. He took a handful of greasy notes, printed with the symbols of the Republic, from the money changer. He realized he did not know the current rate of exchange. He suspected he was being cheated, but it was too late to do anything about it.

He looked at the foreign notes and folded them together.

'All right,' he said sourly. '*C'est bien.*'

The little man leaped to his feet and drew himself up in a sudden renewal of fury. His moustache trembled with emotion.

'*Non!*' he thundered. '*Très bien!*'

The explosion was so unexpected that Brand was momentarily dumbstruck. Then the comic side of it came to him and he began to laugh helplessly. The other passengers watched expressionlessly. The money changer looked baffled, but then he too began to laugh.

'You like to joke, *m'sieur*, yes? Americans are very funny people. They like the amusement.' He settled down beside Brand again and took the notes from him, smoothing them out lovingly. 'You not understand French money? See, this is ten franc. In dollars, US, that is. . . .' He explained patiently, as if to a child, while Brand listened and nodded. They were friends now.

'Yes,' he said. 'Thank you. I see.'

'At your service, *m'sieur*.' The little man produced an old wallet and thumbed inside it for a card which he presented with a show of formality.

'Your first time in Paris, I think. Allow me to be at your service.'

Brand examined the card politely.

'Monsieur Cornelius van der Hove,' he read. 'That is surely not a French name?'

'No.' With a touch of pride: 'I am Dutch. Hollander. But I am living now in Paris twenty-three years.'

'I see. And what is this? *Investigateur privé*. Is that your profession, *m'sieur*?'

'Investigation detective. What you Americans call private eye, not?'

Brand agreed gravely. 'Very interesting. Also a businessman, a money exchanger?'

'Ah, that. . . .' The little man waved his hand disparagingly. 'At times it is necessary to . . . you understand . . . seem something different.'

'Work under cover, in other words.'

'Quite so.' He beamed his appreciation of ready understanding. 'That is it precisely.'

Brand made to return the card but the other waved it away. 'No. I desire that you keep it, *m'sieur*. In memory of our meeting. And if you wish to call me there is a telephonic number.' He added, in significant tones: 'I know Paris ver' well.'

Procurer too, Brand thought. Jack of all trades.

'I am honoured,' he said. He put the card in his pocket.

Monsignor Pauchet was making it clear that he was a pragmatic man and that scientists were, by definition, partly unbalanced.

'It would appear to me, doctor, that your whole venture is

intended essentially as a gesture. This . . . um . . . vessel in which you wish to voyage among the displaced persons, its value is surely symbolic rather than practical?'

'Of as much practical value, let's say, as a fleet of well-equipped and well-staffed mobile clinics. We intend to take along doctors and nurses and – '

'Very well; would such clinics not best answer the need? A steamboat seems needlessly dramatic.'

'I have explained what the terrain is like. A ship of some kind is a very workable solution to that problem.'

'My understanding of a hospital – or a clinic, for that matter – is that a system of support and maintenance is essential. Whereas a river boat three or four days' journey away from supply points – '

'We're working on the question of maintaining supplies,' Brand said. He had not expected Pauchet to be quite so well informed or so quick to pick up weaknesses. 'It's much like a military logistical problem. And perhaps, once the army has been persuaded to co-operate, they might solve it for us.'

'Which leads to a further problem. Why insist on operating in an area which is politically troubled?'

'That is where the need exists. Besides, what is our concern? Politics or health?'

'The answer is obvious. However, when our concern for health begins to touch on other territories which do not concern us. . . .'

'My view is quite simply that we must do what we have to do.'

Pauchet sighed. 'Admirably simple, no doubt. However. . . .' Again the sentence was left significantly unfinished.

The interview, once again, was being conducted in a hotel room, not quite as comfortable this time, in the Rue St Honoré a block behind the luxurious establishment where Brand had been booked on his first visit. He had no doubt that this held a message for him.

Already he felt the weight of defeat. He knew his account was unconvincing. Their hopes and ambitions for the *Faith*, sailing an African river, seemed insignificant in this faraway, civilized city.

There was a long silence which Pauchet eventually filled.

'There will be a meeting of the directorate in the morning. I shall inform you of the decision by tomorrow evening, without fail.'

'Don't you want me to attend? Perhaps I could explain – '

161

The priest smiled gently. 'That will not be necessary. Thanks to your very clear exposition, I will be able to provide the board with all the information needed. Also on the matter of Dr Hauge's research project.'

Brand shrugged. Pauchet noticed the gesture. He said soothingly: 'You will be able to rest, doctor. To tidy up.' He looked a little too pointedly at Brand's travel-crumpled suit. 'You have had a tiring journey. Which reminds me.' He took a leather-bound cheque book from an inside pocket of his own immaculate overcoat and tore off the top cheque. 'You had certain additional expenses in getting here. We must recompense you.'

'Really, it's not necessary.'

Pauchet waved away his protests. 'We cannot allow you to be out of pocket. There was the cost of the train ticket. And other expenses, no doubt. It is only fair that you should be paid.'

He took the cheque. It had already been filled in. A bribe? It was for 200 francs. They valued his acquiescence at a very low price.

The bank's name was printed in the top left-hand corner. Genossenschaft Staedtler Zentralbank AG. He blinked. Where . . . ?

He asked cautiously: 'This bank? The name seems familiar.'

'The Staedtler Bank. Yes, of course. It is a well-known bank. Swiss. Based in Zurich.' Pauchet smiled. 'You have no need for concern, doctor. The cheque is valid.'

Brand mumbled in embarrassment: 'I wasn't . . . that was not at all . . . it's just that. . . . Is this the regular bank used by AID? Our accounts in Bapangani, as I recall, are handled by someone else.'

Pauchet seemed more wary. 'Naturally an organization as large as AID uses several banks. In America, for instance, we use a different bank. In England. Even here in Paris.' His eyes were watchful.

'Naturally. It's not important.' He pocketed the cheque.

Pauchet said expansively: 'Doctor, I realize you are exhausted after your travels, but nevertheless I would greatly esteem your presence at dinner.' The florid invitation was made to sound like a favour, as if to soften the blow of a failed mission.

Brand's mind hardened.

'Thank you. But I think. . . .' He indicated his clothing. 'I'm hardly in a condition – '

162

Pauchet said quickly: 'That is unimportant. You are tired, so it will be an early dinner. I would be distressed if you refuse me. We are to dine with one of the directors, who is most anxious to meet you. Dr Zür Strasse.'

'Is he a medical doctor?' Someone, perhaps, he could talk to and convince.

'An economist, I believe. In fact' – Pauchet smiled – 'he is also a director of the Staedtler Bank. Perhaps he will assure you that your cheque will not . . . how does one say it? . . . bounce.'

The restaurant was furnished and decorated in an extravagant rococo style and its prices were probably equally extravagant. Brand paged forlornly through the menu, the size and thickness of a glossy picture book. He came across a name he recognized and gratefully ordered *filets de sole Georgette*. Dr Zür Strasse, sitting opposite him, stiffly transmitted his request to the head waiter.

The director of the Staedtler Bank was a cadaverously lean man with carefully brushed silver hair and cold undertaker's eyes. He spoke good but heavily accented English and delivered every statement like a pronouncement.

They spoke in generalities.

The fish was excellent.

Pauchet, who had asked for *canard à la Rouennaise*, watched with a bored expression as the maître went through an elaborate performance with a duck press and chafing dish. But when he was served he ate greedily.

They had reached the coffee stage before he produced his poor joke.

'*M'sieur le docteur*, I have given Dr Brand a cheque drawn on the Staedtler Bank and he is a little concerned whether it will be met.'

The chilly eyes were turned on Brand and surveyed him as if he was a postdated promissory note.

'I can personally reassure the doctor.'

Brand bowed his head ironically. 'Thank you.' He decided to fling his stone into the dark.

'I wonder if your bank, doctor, has ever had any dealings with the Bapangani Minister of Health?' He sipped at his coffee.

163

There was no movement behind those eyes. Pauchet looked puzzled.

'The Minister of Health?' Zür Strasse said at last. He inclined his head. In the gilded mirror behind, Brand could see his rear reflection. The glossy hair was as smoothly in place as at the front. 'I do not think so. Why do you ask?'

Brand persisted. 'Makaza is his name. Michael Makaza. Your bank has not dealt with him?'

'The name is not familiar to me,' Zür Strasse said with finality. The subject was done with, the ledger closed.

They talked of other things.

The valet service was prompt. Moments after he had pressed the bell, there was a knock at his door and a young man in a grey uniform with blue facings stood there.

'I wish this suit cleaned and pressed,' Brand said. 'Is it possible?'

A note changed hands.

'Assuredly, *m'sieur.*'

'Good.' Brand went through the pockets. 'I need to wear it in the morning, you understand?'

'It is understood, *m'sieur.* It will be ready by morning.'

He threw the contents of the pockets on to the bed. Wallet. Loose change. Handkerchief. Notebook. Used rail ticket. In one pocket of the jacket in which he had spent three wearying nights was a business card.

M. Cornelius van der Hove. *Investigateur privé.*

'I don't know precisely what it is I want you to find out,' Brand said. 'In fact I don't even know that there is anything to find.'

Cornelius van der Hove waited with an air of benign patience, palms together as if about to pronounce the benediction.

'The only information I have,' Brand told him, 'the only lead suppose you could call it, is that there is a connection between this man Makaza and the Staedtler Bank. But unfortunately half of that lead points somewhere else. Makaza is in Africa and likely to remain there.'

'Difficult,' the little Hollander ventured.

'Impossible, probably.'

'Not impossible. If facts exist they can be discovered. But at times it is more difficult than at other times.'

Brand was more impressed by his surroundings than he cared to admit. He had telephoned the number on Van der Hove's card on impulse and had been surprised to have the call answered by a woman's voice. He had made an appointment and had come to the address in the Avenue de Gothard expecting to find an office as seedy as its owner, tucked away in an odd corner of a ramshackle old house. At least, he believed, M. Cornelius van der Hove, Dutchman turned Parisian, private eye, would be cheap.

He discovered instead that Van der Hove had his rooms in one of the new modern office blocks, on one of the upper floors and served by a fast American elevator. He was received by an efficient young woman, instructed to wait and then shown into an office with big windows and a distant view of the Seine under a backdrop of steel-grey skies.

He made a mental apology to Monsieur Van der Hove for having imagined him a fraud.

'The other link is equally vague. That is the organization Interpharmacor. I have made inquiries and I'm told it's a large pharmaceutical group with its main offices in Essen, but represented in other countries, including countries in Africa. It seems to be completely above board.'

'The Staedtler Bank, too, is above suspicion.'

'I know. It's probably all in my imagination. And yet I have this nagging feeling. I would like to know if there is any sort of link between these organizations and what their connections are with Minister Makaza.'

'Politicians in the countries of the Third World are . . . you know.' The little man rubbed a thumb and forefinger together. 'And not only in the Third World, not?' Brand remembered Russell Hamilton. He had made the same gesture. It had been on the day . . . yes, the day he had become ill.

'I fully realize that. In fact Makaza is said to be taking something on the side from drugs sales to his department. But I have a feeling this is something more than mere corruption.'

'The gentleman is . . . how do you say? . . . intangible.' He saw Brand's baffled look. 'No? What I mean is . . . he is far away. It

165

would be better for you to make the investigation about him when you go back to Africa.'

'If I go back.'

Van der Hove looked at him with polite interest. 'There is doubt?'

'Nothing. It doesn't matter.'

The investigator nodded briskly. 'Further information you do not have at your disposal?'

'That's all I can think of. I really don't know whether it's worth while.'

'It is for you to make the decision. But if . . . this Minister Makaza and the Staedtler Bank, if there is something not right between them, I will try to discover it.'

Brand hesitated. He had made the call on the spur of the moment, urged by anger perhaps, or by an obscure need to seek revenge. He had disliked Dr Zür Strasse at first sight, and was wounded by the knowledge that the aloof mind behind those dead eyes would today be sitting in judgement on him. Zür Strasse would decide not whether a thing was good or bad but whether it was expedient. He wanted to find a way of firing back. But now, faced with the sobering realization that his ammunition consisted of a few rumours and the momentary indiscretion of a black politician, he wavered.

'What would it cost?'

Van der Hove selected a button from a panel on an instrument on his desk and pressed it, then spoke rapidly into a microphone.

'I shall consult my partner,' he explained.

Brand was not sure what he had expected; perhaps the hard-faced cynical private detective of fiction, if only as counter-weight to the little man's bland pomposity. But certainly he was unprepared for the woman, grey-haired, angular, prim as a schoolmarm, who came through the door.

'This is Madame Van der Hove,' the little man said, with a touch of slyness, and Brand guessed he had not been the first client unable to hide his surprise. 'My wife and partner.'

He spoke to her in Dutch, and Brand was able to catch a word here and there. The conversation seemed to be mostly about money. Finally Van der Hove turned back to him.

'We think it is costing 5000 francs. As a preliminary figure.'

Brand whistled. 'That's awfully high.'

The little man shrugged. 'Nothing is cheap, not? An accountant will be hired and he is not cheap. And then, Swiss banks, they do not easily tell their secrets.'

Brand rose. 'Thank you, Mr Van der Hove. I'll let you know what I decide. But I don't know whether I can afford your services. I hope I haven't wasted your time.'

Van der Hove shrugged again. 'No matter. It is a pleasure to meet again.' He looked more attentive. 'I can assist you in some other matter, not? Perhaps to exchange money?'

The message was waiting for Brand at his hotel. He was to call Monsignor Pauchet immediately on his return.

He took his key and the folded message slip from an indifferent clerk and went to his room. It hadn't taken them long, he thought, as he waited for the call to come through. A minor matter, to be disposed of early in the agenda. Where do I go from here? Back to Canada? Just as well that he had not wasted money because of a foolish urge to see Zür Strasse humbled. It would have been a wild-goose chase anyway. He was going to be without a job for a while and he would need all the money he could hold together.

Pauchet's pontifical tones. 'Dr Brand. You are rested after your journey?'

'Thank you.'

'I am glad you were sufficiently well to undertake a little outing. In spite of our inclement weather.'

Get on with it. 'Yes. I went out for a while.'

'The meeting of the directorate was held this morning, doctor. While you were out.'

'I see.'

'Both the matters you placed before us were discussed. On the question of using this steamer you have acquired as a floating hospital, I fear the directors could not agree. There were a number of reasons.'

'I see.' He never really expected anything else.

Pauchet was still speaking. 'This does not mean to say that the directors were not sympathetic to your case.'

Mealy-mouthed bastard.

167

'Yes.'

'The board has directed me to undertake negotiations with the appropriate authorities, directed to the purpose of AID establishing a hospital or other suitable medical facilities in the border areas of Bapangani.'

'That is very good news. But of course it will all take time. A hospital ship would at least bridge the gap.'

'I understand your concern. However, the directors fear the effect of adverse publicity.'

'On the contrary. Publicity would probably be very positive.'

'But such a very visible presence would seem needlessly provocative. It is essential that we maintain good relations with our host nations.'

In other words: don't rock the boat. Literally, in this case.

'I see.'

'On the question of Dr Hauge's research the news is a little more hopeful. Thanks to the information you gave me I was able to place the full scientific facts before the directors and they understand the importance of his work and would like to see him proceed with it.'

'That's splendid. But that too depends on the authorities.'

'It will be part of our negotiations that he be given all possible assistance. When do you leave for Copenhagen?'

'In the morning. Why?'

'Would it be possible to return by way of Paris?'

'I dare say I could arrange it.'

'Dr Zür Strasse feels you should be at hand as a consultant to advise us on the form of our negotiations. Naturally this would involve your spending additional time with us and he is anxious that your labours should not go unrewarded.'

The elaborate circumlocution puzzled Brand. What was the fellow getting at?

'That's all taken care of. It's part of the normal costs. And the lab facilities are provided by South Africa.'

'We are not thinking particularly of Dr Hauge's work. It is your precious time we are occupying.'

There was no mistaking the implication. My God, Brand thought. A real payoff this time.

'It's not necessary. You're paying for my time anyway. AID has better uses for its money.'

'You misunderstand. This is a personal donation from Dr Zür Strasse.'

I wouldn't touch that bastard's money if he handed it to me on his knees.

'It is most kind of him, but. . . .'

'I would think seriously about it, doctor,' the cajoling voice went on. 'Dr Zür Strasse has already let me have his cheque.' A touch of archness. 'It is, naturally, on the Staedtler Bank. And it is for the sum of 5000 francs.'

13

The nurse said with a touch of reproof: 'Doctor, they're calling you.'

Shahida said: 'What? Oh.' She heard her name coming squawkily over the broadcast system. Why did the loudspeaker voices in a hospital always sound so antiseptic?

She answered the telephone in the ward sister's office. A clerk at the admissions office had called her. He sounded affronted.

'Doctor, there's someone to see you, but he won't give his name. He first wanted Dr Brand, but when I told him he was away he insisted he had to see you. He won't go to Mr Fissher. Only Dr Brand or you.'

'What's it about?'

'He won't say that either, doctor. It's a black man.'

'All right. I'll come over.'

She could not say afterwards whether or not she was surprised to find William Kgosana waiting for her. She had been thinking about the Matetwa refugees and the camp up in the marshes, so the black man's appearance seemed almost a continuation of her sombre reflections.

'It's the school holidays,' he explained quickly, as if to reassure her. 'I decided to spend my vacation here in the big city.' He laughed. Shahida suspected he had been rehearsing the greeting.

There were benches inside the foyer. They sat under the

169

inquisitive gaze of the porter inside his glass cage. Shahida searched for something to say.

'Do you have a long holiday?'

'Only a week.' He shifted along the bench towards her. He spoke in an undertone, glancing at the porter from beneath his brows.

'I wanted to see Dr Brand. But they tell me he's away.'

'He's attending a medical congress in Denmark.'

'Denmark.' William sounded impressed.

'He'll be away about a fortnight.'

'That'll be too late.'

'Too late for what?'

He shifted still closer. She felt hemmed in but did not want to move for fear of offending.

'It's about the camp at Motloboga.'

'What about it?'

'There's been an outbreak of fever. Many people have died. believe it's an epidemic of viral fever.'

'Oh no!'

'The authorities aren't doing anything about it. They want the people to die.'

'I can't believe that.'

'It's true, doctor. All the Matetwa people are hearing this story.

'It must be just a story. A vicious rumour.'

'It is true,' he said stubbornly.

'No doctor would stand by and allow that to happen.'

'It's not the doctors. It's the politicians. And the army. I know the army. I have to work with them, don't I?'

She said with less certainty: 'I simply cannot believe it.'

'They are closing down the other camps and moving people to Motloboga where the sickness is. People who try to escape have been shot dead.'

It sounded suspiciously like scaremongering, the standard fare of propaganda.

'It reminds me of that story you told us about the burned child. Was that true? Or was it make-believe too?'

'This isn't make-believe, doctor. Things are bad up at the border. People are dying.'

'Are you sure of this, Mr Kgosana?'

'I believe it, doctor.'

170

'Why did you come here?'

'I wanted to tell Dr Brand.'

'What did you want him to do?'

'He would have thought of something. He's not a government doctor. He's independent. He could have told people about what is happening at Motloboga.'

Shahida remembered the long rows of shacks and mud huts haphazardly ranged beside the river, so that its bank had the appearance of a burrowing ground for a race of giant, crazed moles. She remembered the lines of patients waiting. She remembered the cries of children.

'I'll have to. . . .' She rose. 'Come with me. I'll introduce you to Dr Hauge. He is in charge while Dr Brand is away.'

Hauge and Helmut Fissher were together in the laboratory. The old man was at first annoyed by the interruption, but when Shahida had explained the black stranger's mission he listened closely.

'Here, Fissher. Come here. Listen to this.'

He made William tell his story again, then fired a barrage of questions.

'The symptoms, man? That is vital. What are the symptoms?'

'I have not seen any of the patients myself. But from what people say it sounds like a haemorrhagic fever.'

'And what would you know about that?'

'Dr Brand described the symptoms to me very thoroughly,' William said with dignity. 'When he and Dr Karim were up at the border.'

'You say there have been deaths?' Fissher asked.

William began to hedge. Shahida wondered if he had suddenly spied a potential trap.

'There have been reports that people have died.'

'But none of the cases has been confirmed?'

'Not as far as I know.'

'Why should the authorities move people into an area where there is the risk of an epidemic?'

'I cannot say. That is the news I hear.'

'It sounds very strange.' Fissher said dryly. He turned to Hauge. 'I think we should check with the Health Ministry.'

'Yes. Telephone that man Van Jaarsveld.'

'I think it best if you speak to him, doctor.'

171

They stood around with the strained expressions of people listening to a conversation without wanting to be thought eavesdropping. The increasing acidness in the old man's voice made it clear that the exchange was not going well. He dropped the receiver violently back on the hook.

'That damn fool calls himself a doctor! He is a bureaucrat with the mind of a wall in a public urinal.'

'He denies it?' Fissher asked.

'He refuses all comment. He will not deny or confirm it. He says it is none of our business. Imbecile. I discovered the damned bug, didn't I?'

'He will not allow us to investigate further?'

'I told you. He says to mind our own business. He makes jokes about it. Asks me if we want to make another voyage on the relic from *Showboat*.' He grinned sourly in spite of his anger. 'I'll *Showboat* him.'

'Is there any way we can take it further?' Shahida asked.

'How?'

'Go to the minister.'

'You know how he feels about us these days. No. We are stuck. They control the transport. So we're stuck.' The old man ran his fingers distractedly through his mane of hair. Then he stopped and stood as if listening to something. 'Unless . . .' he said.

'Unless what?'

'*Showboat*,' Dr Hauge said. 'Come with me. I'll show him a showboat. Come, all of you.'

It was sad to see the paddle steamer lying at her old moorings at the town jetty, the life within her stilled, although the river continued to swirl past. Already, Shahida noticed, the *Faith* had reverted to her former abandoned look. There were signs of neglect everywhere: scruffy decks, greasemarks and untidy rope ends, a row of broken portholes. The paint was starting to blister on the boards with the red crosses and the hopeful name. She had become, Shahida thought, a lost dream. A faith forsaken.

There was no one on deck. William ventured across the rickety gangplank and presently emerged from the deckhouse with Captain Da Costa at his heels. The Portuguese had obviously been asleep. He looked morose and more than a little drunk. His expression did not brighten when he saw the group on the quayside. He steadied the gangplank listlessly to allow them to troop on board.

It was Fissher, unexpectedly, who assumed control. Would Captain Da Costa be prepared to undertake another voyage into the marshes?

Da Costa shrugged. What was the use? The army would stop them again.

Perhaps they could arrange matters so that the army did not interfere, Fissher said.

The Portuguese looked sceptical.

'Could you sail at night?' Fissher asked. 'Lie up during the day and move at night only?'

'It is dangerous. We go aground.'

'The rain season is here. The river is higher than it was on the last voyage.'

Da Costa agreed reluctantly. But the rains brought other problems, he pointed out. The river in flood was more difficult to navigate. There was a risk of losing his ship. If there was more money it might be worth trying. . . .

Fissher questioned William again. How high were the floods? Were there blockages on the river? William was uncertain. How then had he travelled to reach here, Fissher demanded. Partly by water, partly by land, William said. He had got lifts on the transport lorries which operated to the edge of the swamps. It had meant a long detour. He had been three days on the road.

'You made this journey specially to see Dr Brand?'

'It is the school holiday now. I came to visit friends here in Leruarua.'

'Where did you get the information about this epidemic?'

'People are talking about it. They are very upset.'

'I find it impossible to believe that the health authorities would simply ignore it.'

'Perhaps they are not acquainted with the disease. I don't know. I can only go by what people say.'

Hauge broke in brusquely. 'You will accompany us on the boat. That is, if we decide to go. Then you will go with us. And if this whole story is rubbish. . . .' His voice was threatening. The black man looked away. Hauge turned to Fissher. 'You will come also. I need you.'

'But – '

'No arguments,' the old man said sternly. 'It is my decision.' He asked Shahida: 'Who else do we need? What about nursing staff? If there is a genuine epidemic we will have to be careful.'

'Sister Cook will go. She was very good when the hospital was in quarantine. She was with us on the last voyage. And perhaps two or three of the black nurses. That should be enough until we know where we stand.'

On the way back to the hospital Dr Hauge issued a string of further orders. Fissher took out a notebook and wrote dutifully. The old man drove erratically and Shahida sat nervously in the front passenger's seat.

William asked to be dropped at the hospital gate. 'I have to let my friends know where I am.'

'You had better be back here,' Hauge warned, 'by this afternoon, or else. . . .'

'I will be back, doctor,' the black man said.

Their way was blocked by an American car of the tall tailfin and flashy chrome era. Hauge had to turn wide, grunting his annoyance. There was a single black man behind the wheel and no passengers. The driver turned his head as they passed and Shahida glanced casually at him. His face was familiar. . . .

It came to her instantly. The man at the shack in the Matetwa township. The night she had found the Moremi relatives. The man who had been drunk and violent and had used the name of Alfred Shinyana, exiled politician.

And as Dr Hauge pulled into his reserved parking bay it occurred to her that the car had come here to pick up William Kgosana.

'How fast can you get a message through?' William Kgosana asked.

The driver was lighting a cigarette with his dashboard lighter. Shreds of tobacco blocked the glowing element and he dabbed it irritably against the end of the cigarette. He exhaled a puff of smoke before replying. 'Depends where it has to go, brother.'

174

'Where the hell do you think?'

'OK.' He considered. 'Maybe a week.'

'That's too long. Haven't you got any kind of emergency procedure?'

The driver gave him a dry look. Then he turned his attention to the road. 'All the messages we send are emergencies, brother.'

'All right. But this must go as fast as possible. All right?'

'OK. What is your message?'

William produced a ballpoint pen from his jacket pocket. 'Give me that cigarette box.'

'We don't like messages in writing,' the driver told him.

'I want to be sure there are no mistakes.'

The driver shrugged. 'OK. You're the boss.'

William was silent, concentrating on what he had to write, trying to compress it all, the urgency as well, into very few words. He was not happy with the situation. He had not anticipated this business of the boat. He thought the army had put a stop to that once and for all. He had come here, risking but not greatly endangering his cover, merely to whisper a few words into receptive ears. He had official leave from the Education Department; it was all clear cut and easy.

Damn these people and their boat, he thought. I should simply drop out of the whole thing right now. But perhaps it might still be possible to salvage something. He hated things to fail, although he knew this to be a fault in himself. A good worker could see his most elaborate long-range plan go to waste and would abandon it without a qualm. But he was not made that way. He would have to stay with this plan to see what would happen.

He was known as William Kgosana and his cover name was Nqhawa, but he had worked under other names at other places at various times. His real name was Sangotsha N'kayi and his mother had given him the European name Samuel. His mother had been a domestic servant in the town where he was born, Adelaide in the eastern Cape Province of South Africa. She worked for a white doctor whose wife had vaguely liberal sympathies, unusual for that time and place. She was a big woman, stout, with arms like a wrestler from hard work. He did not question the need for her to work fourteen hours a day to secure his education or anything else. One did not question what one was born to. That was permanent,

175

unalterable, and one did not question the very foundation of life. Not at first.

He did well at school and was always effortlessly top of his class. He won a bursary to a famous high school for African boys from the eastern Cape. It was decided more or less at this time that he would continue to study to be a doctor. His mother's employers were amused at his choice of career and perhaps the doctor felt flattered by imitation, for he occasionally made Samuel's mother small loans when she was in difficulties because of having to pay for books and school fees.

He did well at high school too. Of course by this time he had started to question and had known for a long time that the foundations of his childhood world were not permanent at all, that in fact they were very shaky indeed. But it did not concern him greatly, for he was going to be a doctor, and that meant hard work from which political and social speculation would merely serve as a distraction.

Late in his third year at medical school he met Joyce Dlukulu. She was a BA student in her final year, the same age as he, and from much the same background, although she had been born in the city and was a Zulu. Her political views were already clearly formed and radical. She was a frank revolutionary. She would not be afraid, when the time came.

Her time came in the summer of 1968, when she was shot dead at his side, in the act of flinging a stone at a black policeman during a pass-laws demonstration in a black township outside Durban.

He was in his fifth year then and she had left university to work for a black labour organization, but they had been lovers for two years, in snatched moments when they could be together.

He did not finish the fifth year. The police had his number by then. His room was searched several times by detectives of the Special Branch. On one occasion he was found in possession of banned literature and was charged, but found not guilty. He began to work actively in the trade-union movement and as a result was served with a five-year banning order. He found himself in court several times after this, once for going through a traffic 'stop' sign, then for contravening the terms of his banning by being on the premises of an educational institution. (He had started a BA degree in economics and was writing examinations in a hot,

176

dusty, ill-ventilated school hall when the police came for him.)

He went out through the back door at the age of twenty-six. That was what they called it when you fled South Africa by surreptitious means: taking the back door. It was appropriate, for the back door was the servants' entrance.

He received the standard training of a guerrilla at an ANC training camp, but he was obviously not standard material, apart from being older than most of the young men who came in through the door. So he went on, first to Czechoslovakia, where he was allowed to study, and eventually to the mecca, to Moscow. He spent two years studying in Russia. He did not like it. The winters were miserable and the people unfriendly. He wished he could have gone to China instead. Another black student, who came from Tanzania, phrased it succinctly. 'The Chinese walk,' he said. He meant that the Russians, when they went about in the former colonial countries they had since adopted, did so in vehicles. The Russians did not walk, not even (in a figurative sense) in their home country.

At the end of the two years he was allowed to go to France and from there to London. A lecturer's post was arranged for him and he drifted uneasily into the life of an exile, living in a bedsitter in Ealing, drinking in pubs with other exiles, going to meetings and occasional anti-South African rallies. He had acquaintances but no real friends. He had a brief, unsatisfactory affair with a white girl who had studied at the University of Cape Town. She was very bitter, even more bitter than he knew himself to be. It took a while before he realized that she bored him. They all bored him, sitting in their smug London pubs and hating South Africa. He wished he could go to America.

They came to him one bleak November.

'We want you to go back,' they said. 'Are you willing to go?'

It was going to be a dreary winter in England.

'Yes,' he said unhesitatingly. 'I'll go back.'

And to himself he said: I want to go home.

The *Faith* sailed in the evening, without lights and with Captain Da Costa using the big spotlights up on the bridge only sparingly to illuminate the dark river and its shadowy banks. They sailed all

177

night, and with morning the rain came down, so that they were able to continue, hidden behind a grey shroud of rain.

The week in Copenhagen had been to Brand like time spent in another world. It was absorbing again to deal with alert and informed people who thought as he did, to be faced once more with disciplined attitudes towards human and social problems. It was satisfying to his ego to be recognized and find that others wanted to listen to him. The civilized world of the congress was a long way from the savagery and frustrations of a minor and controversial African state. He was almost tempted to put Bapangani behind his back for ever and return to the life that was really his.

Except for Shahida, of course, he thought. But was that mean and makeshift life, working with inadequate facilities among near-savages, really for her? There were wider opportunities. Why not persuade her to seize them?

On the third day of the conference, as he handed his hotel key in at the desk, the porter stopped him.

'A letter for you, doctor.'

A long, bulky envelope, postmarked Paris. He slit it open and read hastily as he stood by the door waiting for a taxi to carry him through the snowbound streets.

The letter and its accompanying report had the appearance of authenticity and sober appraisal. But it left him with the undernourished feeling of a hungry man after an encounter with a candyfloss ball: all wind and spun sugar and, basically, a sticky mess.

Monsieur Cornelius van der Hove, *investigateur privé* of Paris, presented his compliments and his preliminary report. The investigation was continuing and promising avenues of inquiry were to be explored further. The letter included a professionally compiled statement of costs so far (Brand thought he detected Madame Van der Hove's hand in this), which left the account with a balance of a shade over 2000 francs. The records of certain financial transactions which had been obtained were being analysed, in utmost confidence, by a trusted accountant whose report would shortly be sent to the client. There might be a need for a further outlay of moneys and therefore the client should expect to

178

make such payments as were required to bring the inquiry to a satisfactory conclusion.

The report merely confirmed Brand's glum view that he had wasted money and made a fool of himself.

It was concerned principally with the affairs of the group of companies known variously as Interpharmacor Enterprises, Interpharmacor Investment, and a dozen other names. The Interpharmacor group, Monsieur Van der Hove wrote, was a hollow organization. By this he meant that it was primarily a financial holding company with investments in numerous smaller pharmaceutical and chemical firms, particularly in Africa. Interpharmacor had a reputation for not being fussy about its methods. It had used underhand tactics to gain control of some of its interests, even in African states where industry was theoretically nationalized. Concealing financing was its speciality, with investments being covered and covered again to disguise the original source. This was where Staedtler Zentralbank came in. Staedtler Bank had a large, although not controlling interest in Interpharmacor, maintained outside Switzerland, where the stringent banking laws prohibited such dealings. The bank also looked after Interpharmacor's legitimate business, thus buttering its bread on both sides.

The titbit was left for last. Much of the financing for Interpharmacor, it was said in reliable business circles, came from East Germany and possibly sources even further to the east. The head of the beast was situated like an octopus (Van der Hove was strong on metaphors) straddling the Iron Curtain and with its tentacles reaching into strange places. Palestine, for example, where it had a hold on the Black September terrorist movement. Congo, Brazzaville, where it had financed an attempted Marxist coup. The Red Brigade in Italy and the Japanese Red Army. The external wing of Namibia's SWAPO. Hard-core revolutionary movements in Liberia and several Saharan states. All under the guise of pure capitalistic enterprise. Communist money was laundered (Van der Hove had also kept up his reading of current spy-story slang) by Staedtler Bank, then passed down the chain to whoever and whatever was the final beneficiary. It was a highly complex network, spread out in a tangle which was probably intended to defy complete analysis.

There was no mention of a possible connection between the

octopus and Michael Makaza, Minister of Health of an obscure black homeland. Van der Hove had found more interesting things to investigate. Or perhaps, Brand thought, his imagination had flagged.

The whole thing was clearly nonsensical. He tried to imagine upright, uptight Dr Zür Strasse of the Staedtler Bank as a secret terrorist mastermind and all the picture could evoke was a smile. He put the letter and the report back in its envelope and shoved it dismissively into his briefcase. Dr Zür Strasse would not be amused to know how his conscience money had been spent. That was the only joy he'd gained.

14

It was only when the man with the green raincoat reappeared close to him for the third time that Cornelius van der Hove became troubled. He had first noticed the man, with a vague sense of recognition or perhaps only a feeling that he had seen a coat of that colour before, as he waited at a traffic light on the Boulevard Montparnasse. The fellow had been sauntering a little too obviously, examining shop windows, and had suddenly increased speed when the lights changed. Nothing suspicious about that, but then he had put in another appearance on the Metro escalator, and here he was now in the same compartment, three seats to the rear, as the train plunged through its deep tunnels.

Van der Hove shifted in his seat and cupped his eyes with one hand as if in contemplation. The exterior darkness made a bright mirror of the opposite window. By moving his head slightly he could see a reflection of his suspected pursuer, rocking up and down as the train swayed. He examined it covertly.

No. He had never seen the man before. He had a thin, dark face and he wore a moustache which curved down below his mouth. He looked like someone from the south. Or perhaps an Italian or Spaniard. Or even an Arab. He sat with his shoulders hunched, looking straight in front of him. Van der Hove looked away. He did not wish to meet the reflected eye.

It was not the first time he had been followed. His life often touched on the shadowy fringes of the criminal world and there had been previous occasions when individuals or institutions had been curious about his movements. He tried to imagine who it might be this time. One consolation was that Green Coat was obviously an amateur and that he seemed to be working alone. A resentful husband perhaps? There had been that unpleasant divorce investigation a month or two ago. But he knew the man by sight. A friend of the husband? Unlikely.

It occurred to him, disconcertingly, that Green Coat might be deliberately conspicuous and if so this was not an amateur exercise. Hoping to frighten him into doing something by making him aware of a presence at his heels? Or a warning? A means of dissuading him from doing something else?

He made a mental list of the cases he had been working on lately. There were a number of possibilities. One of them was that his green-coated shadow was the result of the questions he had been asking about the Staedtler Zentralbank. He hoped not. Banks, particularly solid and influential banks, made awkward enemies. The last thing he wanted was a powerful enemy. But he could not really believe that it was the Staedtler Bank. His inquiries had been circumspect enough: a few hundred in bribes here and there, which had produced nothing tangible, a few innocent questions among his contacts, and that really was all. He had found the story about the intricate manipulations between the bank and the Interpharmacor Group in a straightforward economic review, the source of many of his best bits of 'confidential' information. He had dressed it up with rumours and speculation because that was the kind of thing that kept clients happy. He had never intended anything more. A few superficial facts to placate the client and seem to justify the account. That was all.

Could he unwittingly have stirred up a hornet's nest? Had the mistake been to ask questions in the first place, no matter how misleading the answers? Ruefully he thought that he would like to explain his basic lack of interest, if only he knew to whom to address the explanation.

He sat up in his seat, suddenly alert. The man looked like an Arab. That was it. Fool that he was to think only of the present and neglect the past. Three years ago he had done work for a Jewish

181

client and it had been obvious, although never openly stated, that the Israelis were interested parties. At the time he had been afraid that the Arabs might become equally interested but nothing had happened and eventually he had forgotten his fears. Now they were revived. Everyone knew that the Arabs did not forget a wrong, even if it did take them a while to avenge it. But when they got round to doing something about it they were implacable enemies; worse than banks. Far worse than banks.

The outer darkness widened and then expanded into dazzling light as the train entered a station. It was still travelling at speed and for a moment he thought it might be going through, but then it slackened off abruptly and came to a long, squealing halt. He caught a passing glimpse of a name board. Two stops before his own station. In a sudden excess of nervous energy he jumped to his feet. Untidy knots of people had gathered on the platform, waiting for the doors. Green Coat was still seated, staring glumly in front of him. He made no sign. Van der Hove hesitated. Green Coat was seemingly oblivious to the imminent disappearance of his quarry. A woman in a greasy fur coat gave him a baleful look and pushed past. He made up his mind and stepped down on to the platform. The door scraped and banged behind him. The train began to move. Green Coat, sitting impassively at the window, slid past him in silhouette. His head did not turn.

Feeling foolish, Van der Hove joined the straggling line of people moving towards the exit tunnel. Could he have been so totally mistaken? The Arab, if he had been an Arab, had shown not the slightest interest. And yet he was sure, with the certainty of instinct, that the man had been following him.

Outside it had started to drizzle. And as if at a signal every taxi had vanished from the streets. He turned up his collar and started the long trudge homewards. Three blocks away from the Metro was a bar. He paused at the invitingly lit entrance as if considering whether to go inside. He looked back the way he had come. A man and a woman who had been close behind him stepped aside and went on down the street. He watched them pass the next corner. There were few other people on the street and no one obviously lingering or hiding in doorways. People were in a hurry to get where they belonged, inside, out of the rain. He had been wrong after all. Nerves. He was getting old.

182

He walked on, wet and footsore, cursing himself for a fool.

The next morning he had the beginnings of a cold. He quarrelled with his wife over breakfast. They left the house together for their office. It was still dark and the day was gloomy. It was going to rain again before long. The trains were late.

A day that had started badly was bound to continue to do so. The office had been burgled during the night. The main safe had been expertly opened: not very difficult to do really, for it was an ancient object. He never left much cash on the premises so the loss was negligible, but what really annoyed him was the mess the burglars had made. Filing cabinets had been wrenched open and the files and their contents strewn over the floor, as if by a prankish whirlwind. It would take days, weeks to sort out.

The police came and went, unsympathetically. He spent the rest of the day picking up papers and flinging them down in exasperation, alternately screaming at his wife and muttering to himself.

It was only towards the end of the afternoon that he remembered the green-coated man on the Metro.

During the days following the burglary Cornelius van der Hove worked harder than he had done for a long time. It was a common mistake of those who opposed him to assume because of his insignificant appearance that he could easily be frightened. He was in fact a very brave and persistent little man and also (as he was always ready to admit to himself and anyone who might be interested) a superb detective.

The burglary had made him very angry. He was now certain that he had been followed that night and he guessed that Green Coat's role had been to check that he was on the way home and would not return unexpectedly to the office. The man was unimportant, however. Merely a hireling, a dog someone had unleashed. Who had held the leash? It was unlikely that Green Coat could provide the answer to that question, even assuming he could be traced among the two and a half million people of Paris. Van der Hove decided he would not waste time on determining which particular client he had to thank for the attention paid to him. His simple solution therefore was to make trouble for as many people as possible.

At the end of the week he was able to post five reports to five clients. One of these went to Dr James Brand at his Copenhagen hotel. But by then Brand had already returned to Paris and the letter missed him.

Brand spent most of the following week closeted with Monsignor Pauchet, working out details of the proposed expansion of AID services in Bapangani. He received a cordial invitation to meet Dr Zür Strasse at the Staedtler Bank. The banker wanted to thank him personally for all he had done.

Zür Strasse received him in an upper-floor office of the towering bank building. The office, although comfortable and with a soaring view over the frosty grey roofs of the city, was not pretentious. Brand found this significant. This was a place of business and appropriately businesslike. The only jarring note, if it could be called that, was the presence of a startlingly attractive secretary in the outer office. Brand was disappointed at his brisk transfer from one room to the next.

The formal business of the meeting did not take long. Zür Strasse inquired about the outcome of the Danish congress and Brand assured him it had been very successful. Zür Strasse expressed appreciation that Brand had been able to spare the time to assist with what was really an administrative matter. Brand told him that thorough planning by the central organization was essential to the smooth operation of AID units in the field.

That was over and they watched one another like boxers in the ring after the first exchange of blows. Then they talked about the need for further research into Virus H and the importance of Eric Hauge's work. The topic shifted to the difficulties of raising money for charitable organizations.

'I am told you are a little concerned about my bank's connection with the AID foundation,' Zür Strasse remarked.

Brand told himself to tread warily. It was true he had asked Pauchet many questions about Staedtler Bank. But had there been an ominous undertone in the banker's voice? Surely he could not know about Van der Hove and his assignment?

'Only in the sense that I found it strange a European bank should be bothered about matters in a faraway little country in Africa.'

'On the contrary. The Third World is a great concern of ours. As it is of yours. I believe that was the theme of your address at the congress, no?'

Another gentle nudge? Was the message: we're keeping an eye on everything you do or say? At the same time Zür Strasse had managed to deflect the question away from where Brand wanted it to lead.

'So many great institutions seem to have interests similar to yours. Interpharmacor, for instance. The pharmaceutical company. They have dealings in Bapangani, don't they?'

Zür Strasse raised his eyebrows. He did not speak. The silence grew uncomfortable.

'You know of the firm?' Brand asked.

A stiff nod. 'Naturally. It is a very large concern.'

'A client of yours, I believe.'

'You will appreciate, Dr Brand, that we do not discuss our clients.'

'Of course.'

'However, it is very possible that Interpharmacor, for instance, has interests in your country. Practical interests, of course, but also those of a charitable nature.'

'Does it support AID?'

'I understand the Interpharmacor group is one of AID's largest donors.'

'That's nice to know.'

'It is very laudable.'

It was unnerving to find your opponent did not respond to your feints but was able to dance round you on his toes, with grace and insolence.

'This rule against discussing your clients. Does it apply to individuals too? Minister Makaza, for instance?'

That irritating silence in response to a question, as if it were not really worth answering.

'You'll remember I asked you about him once before.'

'I recall your mentioning his name.'

'He is also a very staunch supporter of AID. More on the practical than on the charitable side, naturally.'

'One needs practical help.'

'But he is very conscious of the generosity of those who do supply the money. Your bank, for instance.'

'We try to do what we can.' Zür Strasse was more wary now, up on his toes again. He had not been hit, but perhaps one of his antagonist's windmilling blows had come uncomfortably close. He rose to show that the interview was over.

'I understand your stay in Paris is almost at an end?'

'I'll be leaving before the weekend.'

'I wish you godspeed on your return to Africa.'

Dr Zür Strasse's attitude, as he waited for his visitor to leave, was again that of the skilled professional watching the blundering moves of a bar-room brawler. At ease. Disdainful. And yet not quite at ease. He had been forced into exchanging blows, after all, and he was annoyed, for he believed that the rules of bar fighting did not apply to him.

Score it a draw.

The blonde in the outer office looked up from her typewriter when Brand went by and favoured him with a faint, withdrawn smile.

The little Dutch detective's report, readdressed and forwarded from Copenhagen, reached Brand on the morning of his departure for South Africa.

To some extent this report annulled its precursor. Although Van der Hove did not admit it directly, it was clear that he now realized he had been fooled. The investigation he had done previously and much of the information he had been fed had been a red herring. Literally red. Interpharmacor might well be a monstrous organization and its financial arrangements questionable, but its aims and the source of its money were not communist. The links between it and the Staedtler Bank were more complex and more secretive than he had been led to believe.

The rest of the report dealt at length with the history and affairs of a South African entrepreneur by the name of Johannes (commonly known as John) A. Schoeman. Mr Schoeman had visited Europe half a dozen times in the past two years, and had had dealings of an undisclosed nature with the Genossenschaft Staedtler Zentralbank AG and its directors in Zurich, Amsterdam

186

and Paris. Among the people he had seen, both officially and privately, had been Dr Heinrich Zür Strasse. He was reported to be on another such visit at the time of writing and had been seen in Stuttgart.

Mr Schoeman was one of that interesting variety of people: a self-made man. He was reported to be very wealthy. Most of his holdings were in the pharmaceutical industry, but he also had interests in the hotel trade, fast-food outlets and the liquor business. Until recently his business had been confined to southern Africa, but there was speculation that his visits to Europe were a prelude to expansion into that part of the world. Mr Schoeman's principal offices were in Johannesburg, which was also his home. He was a shrewd investor in philanthropy as well as business. His firms sponsored public events of the publicity-gathering kind, and he had recently made a private donation, the amount undisclosed but believed to be in excess of ten million francs, to the international fund of the Agence pour l'Alléviation de Détresse Internationale.

His careeer was set out in synopsis. Born: Uitenhage, Cape Province, Union of South Africa, 1928, the fifth child, second son, of a railway workshop labourer. Education: left school at primary level, subsequently completed high school and BCom degree through correspondence courses. Employment: apprentice fitter and turner, South African Railways; clerk, South African Railways; senior clerk, Department of Inland Revenue.

It went ever upwards, through his first business venture, by way of selective and smart buying into the drug trade and clever work on the Stock Exchange to his present position at the top of the heap. The report ended with a list of the companies over which Mr Schoeman had control.

It was fascinating, both as the raw material for the study of the rising business influence of the Afrikaner and as an individual's story of struggle against the disadvantages of birth and poverty. But what it meant Brand could not fathom. Perhaps if he had known about John Schoeman before the interview with Zür Strasse he might have found some use for the information. But he doubted it.

A photograph was enclosed, obviously enlarged from a group study at some social occasion, for John Schoeman was smiling at

187

someone out of the picture and he was in evening dress with a drink in his hand. The photograph was blurred, but it showed a long, clever face, and the smile was ironic. Brand put the photo aside with the report.

He telephoned the number on Van der Hove's business card.

'Mr Van der Hove, I think we can call off the hunt. It doesn't seem as if you're getting anywhere. Even assuming there is anything behind it in the first place. What is this story about a Mr Schoeman?'

'He is a big contributor to AID. I thought it would interest you.'

'Why should it?'

'He is also connected with other organizations which interest you.'

'I can't make head or tail of it. Let's drop it. In any case, I'm leaving Paris tonight.'

The detective sounded disappointed. 'You return to Denmark, yes?'

'No. I'm flying back to Africa.'

'And you must leave tonight?'

'I've been away for a long time.'

'Please give me your address. Perhaps if it is that I discover anything further I am able to write to you in your distant land.'

'Provided it doesn't cost me more money.'

'That is understood.'

The weather had turned miserable again and Brand spent the day watching television in his hotel room. The French was too fast for him and he was baffled by the comings and goings on the screen. He checked out early to take a taxi to the air terminal. It was there that Monsieur Van der Hove found him.

The little Dutchman was in a state of high excitement. 'Thank the good Lord you have not already left for the airport. *M'sieur*, it is imperative that you come with me at once.'

'You must be joking. My plane leaves at ten. I have to check in by eight o'clock at the latest.'

'Personally I will transport you to the airport. You will be in good time. But this is a matter of great importance.'

'What's it all about?'

188

'You must accompany me. We have an assignation, is that the word?'

'It's quite out of the question.'

'*M'sieur*, would I come here if it was not urgent?'

'Just tell me what it's about.'

'I have traced the source of an inquiry.'

'What on earth does that mean?'

'If you would kindly accompany me you will find the answer to all your questions.'

'I have a plane to catch.'

'You will be in good time for your aircraft. Personally I guarantee this.'

Finally, grudgingly, Brand consented. 'But, for God's sake, I don't want to be late.'

They crossed Paris in a series of taxis, dismissing one and taking another apparently at random. Brand wondered whether there was a genuine chance of their being followed or if it was all merely designed to impress him with secrecy. Van der Hove continued to be evasive to questions. 'All the answers will be given shortly' was all he would say.

Brand was soon confused by the switches in direction. They had travelled south and then east, but later they crossed the river and entered what he thought was Montmartre, although he could not be sure. It was a district of mean streets and sombre buildings. It was already dark; the few pedestrians hurried past as if anxious to reach better, well-lit places. Rain fell on a cutting wind.

'Where the hell are you taking me? It'll take ages to the airport in this weather.'

'Soon. Soon.' Van der Hove was peering through the windscreen past the taxi driver's head, giving high-pitched directions.

They turned into a side street.

'Here! Stop! Stop!' Brand was shooed on to the pavement while the little Dutchman paid off the taxi. He wondered how much was left of Dr Zür Strasse's 5000 francs.

On the corner was a building with a bistro sign outside. The shutters were up, but chinks of light shone through. Van der Hove pushed open the door.

Half a dozen men stood at the bar, a few more sat at rickety-looking tables. The quiet hum of conversation died away, although no one looked at the newcomers. Van der Hove went to the bar and spoke softly to a stony-faced waiter. The man jerked his head towards an inside door. Van der Hove gave him money and he pocketed it with a contemptuous air.

'This way,' Van der Hove said.

Brand looked at his watch. 'It's getting very late.'

People looked at them, curious to hear English spoken. The Dutchman was flustered. 'Please,' he whispered. 'It is for us not to draw attention.'

The door opened on to a darkened room. It was quickly closed behind them. Brand stumbled against his guide, his eyes not yet adjusted. A hand took hold of him by the shoulder and he shook it off, suddenly apprehensive. There was a square of bright light, writhing and contorting, against the far wall. His eyes had adapted to the dark but even so it took him a moment to comprehend that the light was shining on a cinema screen and that a man and two women on screen were engaged in complicated copulation. They had walked into the showing of a blue movie.

'Look here! What the hell?'

Voices hissed at him and Van der Hove said sharply: 'Sit down.'

Now he could see that there were chairs arranged in rows, with people sitting intently watching the action on the screen. The doorkeeper, who had caught him when he stumbled, shoved him roughly into a seat in the back row and Van der Hove sat down beside him.

'What is all this?'

'Quiet. Wait.'

The naked man achieved simulated orgasm and disappeared from the scene. Now the women were making love to one another and there were close-ups of heaving breasts and writhing fingers and an abundance of pubic hair. The sound effects consisted of stagy gasps and squeals.

'If you think I'm going to sit here – '

Van der Hove seemed as engrossed by the show as the other watchers.

'Wait.'

The lesbian scene made way for yet another orgy, with one

190

woman and several men this time. Brand was becoming cold in the draughty room. Van der Hove did not stir.

The door behind them opened. He turned to see. Two men had come from the bar and were standing in the doorway, speaking to the doorkeeper. Brand felt their glances sliding towards him. His lower spine was icy cold.

He had read and enjoyed many of the new wave of clever, realistic spy novels. Now he realized that in one respect they were not realistic enough. There was nothing subtle about being cornered. One's reaction was the instantaneous primitive fear of a hunted beast. He tried to look away but his eyes swivelled back to the hunters like those of a hare in a thicket. He wanted to run.

The doorkeeper came up and whispered something to Van der Hove. The detective rose and Brand followed him. They went out of the dark room through a second door that gave on to a long corridor. The doorkeeper led the way and the other two came up behind. They looked like Corsicans. Both wore scuffed leather jackets. No one said anything. There was a smell of stale food and urine. There were doors leading off the corridor, but they were closed. Their footsteps rang on the uncarpeted floor.

Down a flight of shallow steps. Another door. An open courtyard beyond. Brick walls, the outline of dark buildings. A new smell: dampness and rotting vegetation.

A car stood in the courtyard. Its engine started up and the lights came on, showing a row of dustbins with their lids askew.

The doorkeeper stopped abruptly. He spoke to Van der Hove. The French was too fast for Brand, but he gathered that the Dutchman was protesting about something.

It was a trap and he had to get out. He tried to push past Van der Hove. One of the men in leather jackets barred his way. They scuffled briefly. He wrenched free and heard a ripping sound as his jacket sleeve tore.

The other man had fallen back to block the doorway. He reached into a pocket. A knife blade shone coldly in the car's headlights. Brand stopped short.

He saw the nakedness of the knife blade. There were no heroics, no mocking of death. It was cold and unambiguous and it meant brutality and pain and the odds-on chance of his life ending here and now.

191

He could not quite believe that it was happening to him; would have liked to believe that in a sane world it could not happen. It was ludicrous and exaggerated but unmistakably real.

He did not resist as the men seized him on either side and marched him towards the waiting car. Behind him he could still hear Van der Hove's shrill protests, ending in a gasp of pain and indignation. He could not see what they had done to the detective. He was bundled roughly into the back seat and one of the leather-jacketed men climbed in with him. Doors slammed and the car made a tyre-squealing turn into an alleyway, through an open gate and into streets he did not recognize.

His companion on the back seat was the man who had pulled a knife on him. He sat very close and his body was tense with the excitement of action just past. Brand could hear his fast breathing and smell his sweat.

After a time Brand found courage to say: 'Where are we going?' His voice was a croak.

The man beside him grunted uncomprehendingly and Brand asked in a louder voice: 'Where are you taking me? Who are you anyway?'

They had turned into a wider avenue, joining a sea of lights moving in one direction. The traffic flowed at breakneck speed but, looking through the side window, Brand could see men and women in other vehicles flicking past in the fast lane, all oblivious to his predicament.

The driver turned his head sideways.

'Do not fear,' he said. 'All is OK.'

The fellow was wearing a beret. The theatrical touch, straight out of a Grade B, Paris-by-night cinema thriller, made Brand suddenly and violently angry.

'What bloody right have you got. . . .' He struck wildly at the man next to him, hitting him on the side of the jaw, although without force in that confined space. The man grunted in surprise and Brand tried to hit him again but the other leather-jacketed one, kneeling on the front seat, grabbed his arm and twisted it painfully. They struggled until Brand was expertly subdued.

'Quietly, quietly,' the driver said in a disapproving voice. 'Be quiet and all is OK.'

The uncaring traffic streamed past on both sides. Brand sat

silent while his captors watched him sullenly. He had been muddled about directions while travelling with Van der Hove; now he was hopelessly lost. Had this been the idea all along? He began to wonder about the little Dutchman's role. Unwilling decoy, or a partner in crime?

He thought they were travelling on one of the principal routes through Paris, but had no idea whether it headed north, south, east or west. The names on the occasional illuminated signboards meant nothing to him.

They turned off the boulevard and wound swiftly through busy side streets. Unexpectedly the driver swung the wheel and they slid through a gateway and on to a steep ramp leading down. Neon lights blazed in an underground parking garage. The car continued down to a level marked 'Private' and protected by automatic gates. The driver pulled up at a bank of elevators with more signs, in several languages, warning: 'Private. Permit holders only'. A lift came and the driver held the door open. Only then was Brand allowed out of the car. He looked around hopefully, but there was no one else in the cavernous basement chamber.

There appeared to be only one control button, which the driver operated with a key. They were carried swiftly upwards. The lift stopped and the doors sighed open. Brand stood blinking at the entrance to what, to all appearances, was the brightly lit and sumptuous hallway of a private house.

A young man in a dark business suit was waiting for them.

Brand said angrily: 'What the hell is going on here?' But the young man silenced him with an upraised hand. He spoke dismissively to the driver and his companions, then turned on his heel.

'This way, if you please.'

There was no choice but to follow. They went through the hall into another equally opulent room, either library or study, with tall bookcases against the walls, paintings and pieces of modernistic sculpture in discreetly lit alcoves, expensive rugs on the floor.

A man who had been sitting in a capacious armchair rose at their entrance and came towards them. Brand recognized, with no sense of surprise, the face in the photograph Van der Hove had sent him. The elusive Johannesburg millionaire John Schoeman.

His anger was so great he could hardly speak.

193

'Is this some kind of joke?'

Schoeman's hands were raised in a pacifying gesture. He was smaller than Brand had expected, with a neat, almost fussy way about him.

'Doctor, I do apologize. I realize how upset you must be. But you haven't allowed me to introduce myself.'

'I know who you are.'

Schoeman caught sight of the flapping jacket sleeve. 'You have been hurt. I am so sorry.'

'I was attacked. I was held up at knifepoint, my companion was assaulted, I was dragged into a motor car, and you're sorry!'

'Let's be calm. Let's sit down. Would you like a drink? I think we could do with a drink.' He spoke quietly to the young man, who had stopped in the doorway, and then smiled at Brand. 'I think our . . . uh . . . hirelings perhaps exceeded their instructions and frightened you needlessly, but I assure you there is no cause for alarm.' Schoeman had not quite lost the harsh Afrikaans accent of his youth. It became more pronounced when there was a sarcastic edge to his voice.

'And now that drink.' The young man had pushed forward a trolley on which stood glasses and bottles and ice buckets. He waited politely to serve them.

Brand folded. 'Oh, all right then. Scotch and water.'

The liquor was poured into crystal glasses. Schoeman motioned him to a chair and seated himself opposite. Brand sipped at his drink. It was excellent whisky.

'Thank you, Gerhardt,' Schoeman said.

The urbane young man exited silently, and closed the door behind him.

'I had to speak to you,' Schoeman said.

Brand laughed angrily and helplessly. 'You can't be serious.'

'It would not wait.'

'Did it ever cross your mind that you could simply have come to see me, or asked me to come to you in the normal way?'

'There was no time, doctor. I only learned today that you were planning to leave on tonight's flight. I knew you would not agree to delay your departure merely because I expressed a desire to speak to you.'

'So you had me kidnapped?'

watched the slow progression of sea and desert and arid African bush and tropical forest.

And gradually the puzzle began to fit together.

The aircraft landed at Jan Smuts Airport shortly after dark. Brand had left his car in the underground parking complex.

The first edition of the Sunday newspapers was already on sale. As he unlocked the car a black urchin, staggering under a pile of papers, came entreatingly towards him. He stopped, fumbling for a coin.

Waiting for change, he glanced absent-mindedly at the headlines. The lead story on page one said, in Second-Coming-sized type: 'TERROR ROCKET BLASTS MERCY SHIP'. He had seen the word 'mercy' used often enough in relation to AID to know that to headline writers it was synonymous with hospitals and health. He knew at once what it meant.

To the newsboy's delight he pushed aside the proffered change and read the report in the neon glare from the high roof.

There was a subsidiary headline: 'Doctors Held Hostage'. The report was based on an official army communiqué. It was datelined Leruarua. An unnamed hospital ship operated by a private health agency had been attacked in the operational area by means of a terrorist missile. A number of the hospital staff, among them several doctors, had vanished. They were believed to have been abducted, although nothing certain was known of their fate. An army 'hot pursuit' operation was already in progress.

He read the story again, his thoughts chaotic. He skimmed over the predictable, horrifying phrases while images of death haunted him. Civilians had been shot and a white woman bayonetted to death. The full number of casualties was still not known. The terrorist party was said to be moving north, towards the border.

Shahida. Was she dead?

He had to get there. And fast. Another aircraft? He could not bear to wait until morning. He would have to drive, although it would take all night and most of tomorrow.

Shortly after dawn he stopped for petrol at a forlorn town in the middle of nowhere. It took a while to trace and rouse the

199

disgruntled filling-station owner. He stood next to the car in the morning chill with the garage man, in shirtsleeves and slippers, grumbling at his side. The road ran past the petrol station and then northwards, straight as an arrow. He had an unexpected feeling of sheer elation.

He knew now where the road would lead.

PART FOUR

The river

15

In the first terrible moments after the rocket hit, Shahida could not understand what had happened.

It was raining, as it had rained steadily since the start of the voyage. It was the same rain that had so far kept the helicopters grounded and had enabled the *Faith* to slip undetected into the deeper regions of the marshes.

She was standing on the boat deck with Helmut Fissher, sheltering behind the paddle-wheel box and watching the river bank, grey and misty through the falling rain.

'It's like the monsoon in the Far East,' she said.

'I have never been to the East,' Fissher said.

He was still visibly edgy about Dr Hauge's impulsive decree that he had to accompany them. Shahida thought he perhaps felt that, with his disability, he would be in the way. Or perhaps he had no stomach for adventure. To put him at ease she spoke of Virus H and what they would have to do if the epidemic scare proved to be genuine.

There was a sudden flash of pure white light, turning instantly to a fiery glow, and then the thunderclap of the explosion and screams and dirty brown smoke rising around the bridge.

Shahida's first logical deduction was that the steamer had been struck by lightning. She was still cowering at the rail, looking dazedly at the sky, when the firing started. First there was a volley of single shots, followed by the dry rattle of automatic fire. She saw a group of black men on the shore running raggedly across a clearing between the stunted bushes. They wore khaki-green uniforms, with camouflage markings. They had bandoliers slung criss-cross over their chests and they carried stubby automatic rifles. They fired as they came running.

Fissher shouted something to her, but she did not understand and it took a moment to register that he had spoken in German. She wanted to run to some secure place where she would not have to witness scenes of violence or death. But there was nowhere to go and she could only stand and watch in frozen disbelief.

The *Faith* had been moving ahead slowly, for the channel was narrow here. Now, ponderously, still under way, she slewed over towards the starboard, heading at an angle towards the bank where the attackers had gathered. The gap of green water between vessel and land was narrowing more quickly, it seemed, than the *Faith*'s speed should warrant. As Shahida watched, the surface was churned, as if disturbed by a random rain squall. The leaders among the attackers had reached the edge of the water and were firing at point-blank range.

But the steamer continued its slow turn to starboard, and the turn became the beginning of a circle. She saw that, for some reason, only the portside paddle was turning. Shouts from the land showed that the men there had seen and understood what was happening. Presently they were hidden from her by the superstructure. The *Faith* continued to circle.

Someone jumped from the bridge ladder to the deck beside them, and she screamed. It took her a moment to recognize Captain Da Costa. His face was a shock to her. He had received an ugly scalp wound, a flap of skin torn away above his left eye, from which blood was streaming.

He crawled across the deck towards them. The land came into sight again as the steamer completed a full circle. Another spray of bullets ripped the water.

'Down! Get down!' Da Costa shouted, and they flung themselves to the deck, Fissher shielding his head between raised arms. Da Costa took cover behind the paddle-housing next to them. After a moment the sound of firing died away.

Da Costa wiped distractedly at the blood on his face.

'You OK?'

She nodded and tried to speak and was annoyed when all she could utter was a hysterical sound, half sob, half laugh. She realized that she was probably in shock and that the right treatment was warmth and rest. The thought was comic under the circumstances.

She gained control of her voice.

'What happened?' She was aware of the inanity of the question, for she knew the answer. But she wanted the reassurance of someone else's explanation.

'Got us with a rocket,' he said bitterly.

She stared at him.

'RPG. Or more likely a rocket. The ters get these bloody SAM 7 missiles from the Russians.'

The martial shorthand meant nothing to her. She noticed that he had again discarded his pidgin speech mannerism, like that evening when they had encountered the poachers shooting in the bush.

'But why? Why? They know – ' She broke off, for what she had intended to say was 'They know we mean them no harm' and the statement was as meaningless as the question.

Da Costa was not listening to her. It was as if what he was saying was an explanation to himself, or an expiation.

'Probably the heat of the funnel that drew it. Hit just behind the bridge. Killed my helmsman. Lucky for me I wasn't at the wheel. Killed him stone dead. Bang! Up the arse.' He glanced at her and there was animosity in the look. 'Sorry. But I've lost my helmsman.' He indicated the paddle box with a jerk of the thumb. 'Look. You people stay down behind this thing. OK? You'll be all right here.'

She nodded.

'They shot out the rudder cable. And this paddle gear jammed. If I can get to the rudder . . . shove it over to counter the other paddle . . . might straighten us out. You stay here, you hear?'

Fissher was still lying with his head between his arms. He had not spoken a word since that one incoherent shout immediately after the explosion. Now he looked up and saw Da Costa scuttling away on hands and knees. He attempted to follow, his bad leg dragging behind him.

Shahida tried to stop him, but he pushed her aside.

'Got to . . . got . . . help.' She did not know whether he wanted to help or whether he sought it.

'Mr Fissher, no. You must stay here. Don't. . . .'

He got halfway erect, holding the boat-deck rail and hobbling awkwardly towards the companion ladder, out in the open.

She screamed frantically: 'Mr Fissher! No!'

She saw the bullets hit him, heard the wet-sack blows, saw his body flopping as the bullets tore into it. She saw him die, and did not believe it.

The impact of half a dozen 7.62mm bullets flung him several yards along the deck, wedging his body between the lower treads of the ladder and the deckhouse. She would have to step over the body to reach shelter.

The *Faith* started another circle, once more carrying them out of the target area of the guns on shore. But the steady push of the stream had been working against the flailing paddle wheel, and this time the steamer went only halfway round before running aground on a mud bank with a slow sliding motion and a soft bump. The paddle came to a creaking standstill.

Shahida heard more firing, and yells of triumph from the men on shore. A little later she heard screams and more shooting. She lay on the rough deck planking behind the paddle box. The confined circle of her surroundings had taken on the dreadful familiarity of a place of helpless delay, like an airport lounge or a station platform. She knew it all, the grain of the planks, the white paint flecking from the rusty metal of the rails, the smell of burning, the dust and the heat and the gritty feeling between her teeth. She knew all of it and would never be able to forget it.

She lay there in fear and horror and this was where the soldiers found her.

There were five of them, all armed and equipped like the others she had seen. The first to find her was a bearded man, with blunt, tough features. He climbed down on to the stern deck and saw her and raised his rifle. Then he shouted and the others came down too. They talked among themselves. The bearded man prodded her into a sitting position with his boot. She looked at the circle of black, excited faces and the guns in their hands and waited impassively to be killed.

But when the bearded man put down his rifle and began to undo the front of his trousers she understood that she was not going to be killed, not immediately.

Random firing was still continuing, and elsewhere there was the occasional scream or other sounds of violence, but the afterdeck was an island of relative silence and isolation. When the fourth man raped her she experienced, to her horrified disgust, a brief, involuntary orgasm.

After that shame it did not matter what they did to her.

*

206

Dr Hauge and Captain Da Costa were being driven at the head of the line. Both had their hands roughly bound and they were tied together, against the unlikely possibility that either the old man or his injured companion could somehow run away from their captors. Two of the guerrilla soldiers marched behind them, using rifles to prod the stumbling men. Despite this they made very slow progress.

Shahida was astounded that Dr Hauge was able to keep up at all. She was behind him, also with a guard, and then came William Kgosana, unguarded. She did not know what had happened to any of the others. Probably they were dead.

There had been thirty or more men in the band that had attacked the steamer but now there were only about fifteen in the column marching with the prisoners. The two parties had separated, for what purpose she did not know. A while ago she had heard the sound of shooting, like the faint sputtering of strings of firecrackers. She listened to the distant firing and thought: shoot them; kill them all.

Her bloodthirstiness gave her a satisfying feeling. Kill them. Shoot them.

She would show no mercy towards any of them, not even the one who had saved her from the men who were raping her. He had come on to the stern deck as the bearded man had kneeled to begin raping her over again and had shouted angrily and struck the bearded man with his rifle. He seemed to be their leader, for the others obeyed his shouts and had hauled her to her feet, and then he had asked her questions in an African language. She could not understand and had not even looked at him, for she had closed her mind to what was happening.

Eventually he had given up, shrugging, and they had taken her to where Dr Hauge and Da Costa were being held in the main saloon. Dr Hauge had seen the state she was in and had immediately guessed at the cause. In great anger he had broken away from his guard and flung himself at her captor. It had taken three of the soldiers to drag him away. Da Costa tried to restrain him but he pulled free and at once attacked the gang leader again. This time a soldier hit him with a rifle butt and broke his right arm. The old man fell to his knees, screaming in pain and rage, and when Da Costa wanted to intervene he was beaten too, until the blood streamed from his scalp wound and he collapsed on the saloon floor. They let him lie there while they argued incomprehensibly.

Then William Kgosana had been brought into the saloon. They had been rough with him at first, but after he had spoken to them there had been a subtle change in attitude. Even the man she judged to be the gang leader listened with respect to what William said. They were more kind then to the whites too. Two of them helped Dr Hauge to a settee and they allowed Shahida to go to him.

William had come to help her strap and attend to Hauge's broken arm and Da Costa's injuries. In a low voice William said: 'We must not offer resistance. These people are frightened by what they have done but they are also very excited. We must not provoke them.'

'They are murderers,' she said.

'I am sorry about what has happened, doctor. When men fight. . . .'

'What are they going to do to us?'

'I think they plan to hold us as hostages. They won't harm you.'

'Why have they done this? What have we done to them? Except to try to help.'

He said matter-of-factly: 'I suppose it's because they don't want you here.'

For a moment she believed she had misheard, for the words he had chosen were almost a paraphrase of what Commandant De Waal had said to her: 'Doctor, we don't need you here and we don't want you here.' She remembered the exact words and the hollow silence which had followed them.

'Why don't you tell them to leave us alone?' she asked.

He had shrugged. 'Because I'm a prisoner too.'

Evening came, and with it more rain. During the afternoon, as they marched, the lowering clouds had lifted and it had become intensely hot. But further stormclouds were already forming on the horizon ahead, with dark towers of rain, almost purple in colour, slanting down beneath the great thunderheads. Shahida had wished that it would rain soon, as relief from the heat. But when the storm reached them, amidst all the battle clamour of thunder and lightning and a driving rain directly into their faces, they were soon wet and miserable and chilled.

With darkness the storm abated a little, but it continued to rain heavily. They stumbled on into the wet and muddy night.

It seemed to her that their course was erratic. She guessed this was deliberate, in order to shake off pursuit, but at times she suspected their captors had no more idea of their final destination than she herself.

She was very concerned about Dr Hauge. The shock of the broken arm and Fissher's death, combined with exhaustion and exposure, was making the old man progressively weaker. Finally he was unable to walk and their captors fashioned a crude litter for him, taking turns to carry it. Curiously, they did not seem to resent the labour. They walked along, two to a side, talking among themselves, with the white man's heavy body jolting between them. At times when they were careless he protested, but mostly he lay without moving, and Shahida suspected he was barely conscious of what was happening.

She was worried, too, about what might have happened to Sister Cook. She remembered with agony that she had heard a woman screaming during that terrible time on the afterdeck. She hoped the screams had been her own.

Da Costa, of all of them, seemed to accept their predicament with the least show of concern. He made light of his wound and the beating he had received and tried to encourage her even to the point of making wry jokes. He was kind, too, in not asking questions about the things that had been done to her.

But neither could hide from the other the one basic fact: that they were bitterly afraid.

They hid in the bush during the day, dispersed over a wide area in small groups as a precaution against being spotted from the air. For the same reason no cooking fires were permitted, so they were given no food, only meagre rations of water. The white prisoners were kept separate, with two guards. William Kgosana went away with some of the other soldiers. Shahida had lost all trust in him. She believed he was on the side of the people who had attacked them.

209

All day, while they were hiding, she listened for aircraft engines. But there was no sound except the weeping of the rain.

By evening it was clear that Dr Hauge was seriously ill. He had a temperature and she feared the onset of pneumonia. Her attention was on the ailing old man, so she did not hear the approach of soft footsteps over the soggy soil. She was startled when a voice spoke behind her.

'There has been a change of plan, doctor,' William said.

The guards came raggedly to attention. The gang leader had accompanied William. She looked at him. She had still not learned his name. He wore a heavy, drooping moustache, his face was plump, unusual among the Matetwa, and he had little piggy eyes.

She said nothing, waiting for one of them to speak.

William nodded deferentially towards the other black man. 'The general has decided that we are returning to the river. We will start back tonight.'

She thought contemptuously: he calls himself a general. A general of what?

She guessed that the decision had stemmed from the arrival of a group of newcomers to the band, late in the afternoon. They had been armed, like the others, but their uniforms were in tatters and they had the dazed, mute look of survivors. It was cause for hope, for it meant that the hunters were closing in. But she had been surprised to find that she did not really care.

All she knew, all she could think about, was the unfathomable depth of her weariness. At another time she might have taken hope from the change of plans, for it meant they would have water and perhaps food and their wounds would be bandaged and their hurts healed. Above all she wished they could be away, far away, far from the dreadful sameness of this bush land and allowed to rest in beds between cool sheets.

She spoke tiredly: 'You must tell this man to get us to safety. Don't you understand that Dr Hauge is seriously ill? He will die if he has to stay out here in the rain.'

William looked at the old man lying limply on the litter.

'I can see. I did medical training once.'

'Didn't your training teach you to value life?'

He gave her a wry smile. 'What one is trained for and what one experiences are often two different matters.'

She said in exasperation: 'Please, this isn't a time to be clever. What is needed is to get Dr Hauge to hospital. And Captain Da Costa can't go much further, either.'

He shrugged. 'Unfortunately. . . .'

She turned pleadingly to the other man: 'Can't you do something to save this old man?'

He ignored her and spoke to William.

William told her: 'The general says, when one makes a revolution, single lives are not so important.'

'He would save his own skin if he could.'

Da Costa, listening in silence, stirred uneasily at her anger. He looked at her reprimandingly, as if to remind her of their danger.

'Doctor,' said William, as if anxious to prevent an argument between friends, 'perhaps the difference between you and the general is that you believe in healing but he believes in fire.'

'And you, Mr Kgosana? What do you believe in?'

He smiled at her. 'For the time being, doctor, only in survival.'

A cold-blooded attack, by means of long-range weapons, on an innocent target like a hospital ship, was an obvious occasion for public horror and indignation. As Brand drove northwards he listened to a succession of sketchy radio news bulletins. Gradually the details were filled in. He heard with shock, and unable fully to credit the truth of the story, that one of the victims had been positively identified as a German citizen by name of Helmut Fissher. Who else was dead? The newsreader announced ominously that names of other victims were being withheld until the next of kin had been informed.

Brand reached Leruarua early in the afternoon, exhausted after the long drive. The events of the following days ran together in his flagging mind.

First there was a conference at the Health Bureau with Dr Van Jaarsveld and his minister. Van Jaarsveld said, as if the admission was painful and had to be drawn from him: 'The situation is unclear. We know they've left the ship and that they have hostages. But there has been no further contact.'

Brand said, angrily: 'What the hell is being done? Are my people still alive?'

211

Van Jaarsveld became angry in turn: 'None of this would have happened if your people hadn't done such a damn-fool thing.'

Makaza was more conciliatory. 'I'm sure they'll be all right. They are valuable goods, you see, and provided they survive the initial . . . ah . . . excitement their chances are good.'

He sounded as if he knew something he was not disclosing. Probably he did. They were all trying to cover up something. All lying.

'They'll be shuttled back to some safe town and some money will change hands and that will be that. There's machinery for this kind of thing.'

This dispassionate air, as if the transaction really involved nothing more than some unspecified goods, infuriated Brand more than Van Jaarsveld's reproaches. But he curbed his temper. It was a luxury he could not afford.

He studied the military intelligence report. The attack had been carried out by a terrorist group under the leadership of a self-styled general named Thobega. This name was probably assumed, for it was also the word for the ceremony of slaughtering an ox in honour of a man who has slain in battle, the report said learnedly. General Thobega was known to be a follower of the Shinyana faction, which had its base in Luanda.

The motives for the attack were unknown but it was presumably another random hit-and-run demonstration along classic terrorist lines. A rescue party had reached the ship and found the bodies of Mr Fissher and the helmsman. The rest of the crew were still alive. They had hidden in the engine room during the attack. Other civilians who had escaped unhurt included several black nurses. The survivors had been taken to the military base at Sekhong.

The body of a white woman had been discovered, shot and mutilated, in a cabin.

Brand spent a bad time before confirmation came that the body was that of one of the American nurses, Sister Cook. Of course he felt sorry for the poor woman. But it might have been Shahida who had been killed.

'Shinyana,' he said. 'Shinyana. Where have I heard that name before?'

Makaza gave him a sour look. 'He was one of the extremists. He ran away to SWAPO.'

212

'Ah,' Brand remembered. 'He was the leader of the party which was banned.'

'He wasn't a leader. A communist, a rabble-rouser.'

'I recall that his name came up in conversation once, minister. But on that occasion it apparently meant nothing to you.'

Makaza met his gaze defiantly. Then he looked away. He did not reply. Then he left, apparently to consult the Chief Minister. Time was running short, he said gloomily. Some decision had to be taken. He looked at the white men as if he blamed them personally for all that had happened.

As soon as the minister was out of the room Dr Van Jaarsveld shifted his chair closer to Brand's.

'I'll be frank with you,' he said. 'This business has very unfortunate implications.'

Brand gave him a quizzical look. In his experience prefacing remarks such as 'to tell the truth' or 'candidly' usually indicated that the speaker was preparing a lie.

'I don't quite know how to explain this,' the director said. His voice was sombre, but Brand caught the theatrical note. The man was overplaying the role, like a town gossip bursting with scandal but pretending reluctance.

'What is it?' he asked with thinly disguised dislike.

His tone did not escape Van Jaarsveld, who flushed slightly. He said defensively: 'It's all very complicated. Whenever politics gets mixed up in something it gets complicated.' He hesitated. 'You must understand it's not easy for me. I'm not interested in politics. I just want to get on with my job. I was Secretary of Health here under the old administration and I've tried to do my best for these people now that they're in charge. I've been here for twelve years. I don't want to be thrown out because of politics.'

I understand you well enough, Brand thought. You don't want to lose your job.

'There's a risk of that happening?'

Van Jaarsveld answered obliquely. 'My minister has been misbehaving himself.'

'What do you mean?'

'He has had contact in secret with this fellow Shinyana. I thought I had better warn you.'

'Makaza has?'

213

'Yes.'

'About the question of hostages?'

'No. This dates back quite a while.'

'What do you mean by secret contact? What has he been up to?'

'It's all politics. I don't know much about it.'

'Does the Chief Minister know?'

'I doubt it.'

'Who does know? Who told you?'

'I can't disclose that.'

'A South African source?'

'All I want is to warn you. I'm not prepared to be interrogated.'

'Well, thanks for the warning, then.'

He could not work out the motive behind Van Jaarsveld's disclosure. I'll wager that, even if it's true the Chief Minister doesn't know about his Minister of Health's double game, it won't be long before he finds out, he thought. Is Van Jaarsveld trying to get his version of events on record?

At the next meeting, Makaza was accompanied by an army officer. There was more discussion, more plans were prepared and rejected. Eventually Brand began to suspect that the huge flap was a skilful bit of misdirection. There was great concentration on the practicalities, on the business of who was to do what and where and when. Brand spoke to Paris on the telephone to receive AID's authority to negotiate for the release of the hostages. Pauchet seemed feverishly anxious to end the matter with a minimum of delay or publicity. Which was understandable, Brand thought, remembering what Schoeman had told him.

The army officer was next to be called to the telephone. He returned to do the briefing wearing an expression of grim satisfaction. A heli-borne reaction force had gone in after the terrorists, he said. There had been a contact and several of the fugitives had been killed.

Brand looked at him in dismay.

'And the hostages?'

It appeared stragglers had got away because of the difficulty of following up tracks in the rain, but there had definitely been no hostages.

'And if you find them, how are you going to distinguish between hostages and the others?'

214

The officer hedged. It would depend on military priorities. Everything reasonable would be done. The plan was now to establish a cordon against which to drive the fleeing terrorists. There they could be mopped up at will.

'That's all very well from your point of view, colonel,' Brand told him. 'You speak of mopping people up as if they're puddles of dirty water. But what about the lives of my people?'

Every step would be taken to secure the safety of all the hostages, said the officer.

'Are you prepared to negotiate for their release?'

Naturally negotiations would be undertaken, provided this was feasible, the colonel said.

'I have my organization's authority to conduct negotiations. I think it should be left to me. Can that be arranged?'

The officer protested that the cordon was to be established by an armoured strike force, and it was inconceivable that civilians should accompany a combat force going into action. But when Makaza put his weight behind the idea the colonel agreed to consult his superiors. Dr Brand might conceivably be permitted to join the strike force. But if the request was granted, he said discouragingly, there would be no time to waste. The armoured column was assembled and ready to move to its jump-off point.

'I'm ready right now,' Brand assured him.

The officer was silenced. He looked to the others for support. But they had their own preoccupations; they were engaged in mending their own fences.

The command vehicle rode in the centre of the column, so that it was impossible to escape the great cloud of dust raised by the swiftly moving vehicles.

Even without the dust the journey would have been intolerable. The road was the worst Brand had ever encountered, a deeply rutted alley which wound endlessly through a wasteland of scrub bush. He was weary beyond belief but it was impossible to achieve more than an uneasy doze as the line of vehicles alternately droned and whined their way along the sandy track.

At the onset he had been allowed to travel with head and shoulders up through the machine gunner's hatch. Jolted and flung from side to side against the severely functional bits and pieces of armour plating, he had regarded this as a dubious privilege. There was little to be seen in any case, except the vehicles ahead and behind, dim and monstrous shapes in the enshrouding dust. He had stood behind the helmeted commander and watched the young man's lean, tough body swaying rhythmically, absorbing the pitch and plunge of their progress. His gunner, up in the turret beside him, had the number '21' stencilled at the back of his earphone-sprouting helmet. Brand doubted that the youngster was even that age yet.

When they neared the target area he was instructed by means of signs, because of the engine noise, to climb down into the interior of the vehicle. The hatch was closed behind him and he was shown how to fasten his seat webbing. He sat in line with the young soldiers, occasionally exchanging a smile or a grimace as the armoured troops plunged ahead.

His thoughts flitted back and forth between past and present and future. Back home, at the university (was there significance in thinking suddenly of Canada as 'home'?), he had been involved, with other theoretical liberals, in arguments and discussions about the options open to movements of national liberation. He could understand the frustrations which gave rise to acts of terror. But could he still be sympathetic, face to face with the irrational cruelty which was the real horror of terrorism and with people he knew and cared for as its victims?

It was as much an increase in tension inside the armoured car as the sudden burst of speed which alerted him that something was happening. The young men around him sat alertly, eyes watchful under steel helmets. The radio was gabbling and the vehicle commander was speaking unhurriedly into it, but Brand could not distinguish a single word. He tried to look out through the thick armoured glass in the slit opening in front of him. He saw another vehicle racing alongside, wallowing in its wake of dust. They crashed into a thorn thicket and the other armoured car vanished from sight. The column had changed to an open formation and was off the road, racing through the scrub.

He tried by means of exaggerated gestures and mouthed interrogation to find out what had happened, but the soldiers were preoccupied and had no time for him. In the distance, muted by the

216

surrounding uproar so that it came to him like sounds under water, he heard the roar of heavy guns and the sustained clatter of small arms fire. Their own gun joined in, firing a rapid salvo, and then the machine gun was chattering too, and still Brand could see nothing, could not understand or make himself understood, could make out no target, could hear only the savage and concentrated bombardment under which nothing could possibly survive.

He looked at the young men who were his companions in this wild chase. There was an expression not of gloating or even excitement but of tranquillity about their faces, as if they had caught a glimpse of salvation and knew that it lay simply in destroying the enemy.

The wounded had been cared for. Now there was time for the dead.

The dead had been arranged in two rows in order to facilitate their disposal. But they were sprawled in attitudes of abandon which upset the tidiness of the scene. It was as if, by an individual disposal of arms and legs, they sought to testify mutely that they were still resisting.

Three of the white soldiers were going methodically down the rows, emptying pockets, removing ammunition pouches, leaving the bodies face up. A small pile of firearms had been collected. Other soldiers were patrolling the perimeter, moving restlessly, faces alert and rifles at the ready. Still others were watching the body count.

Brand counted too, involuntarily. Seven. All of them were men, all of them black and in camouflage uniforms. Small result for a big effort. Seven dead terrorists. He had tried consciously to think about them as guerrillas, soldiers of the other side, so as to preserve his own neutrality, even if it was only in his mind. But it was strange how quickly you came to regard them as terrorists when they started shooting at you.

The column commander had come to stand by his side. His battledress was stripped of rank marks, identical to the troopers, but Brand remembered that he was a major.

'You OK?' the major asked.

Brand nodded.

'We hit this bunch all right. I think we got the lot.'

'What happened to the hostages? To my people?'

'They must have left them behind.' He saw Brand's face and added: 'I'm sure they'll be OK.'

'They would hardly have been OK if they *had* been with these people. You didn't give them much of a chance.'

The major pursed his lips. 'They had RPGs with them. Rocket grenades. Did you know that? Some of those things can knock out a tank. You don't give someone a chance when he's throwing that kind of crap at you.'

'Is there any way of finding out what's happened to the hostages?'

'We're trying to establish the situation, sir. My radio op is making contact.'

'Can we be certain these are the people you were looking for?'

'Quite certain, sir. They must have split up. They usually do that. Guess this bunch thought they could travel faster and make it over to the other side.' The major looked at the bodies. 'Guess they thought wrong.'

A dry wind had sprung up and was blowing sand among the bodies. A bit of paper neglected by the soldiers during the search was blown towards Brand. He trapped it with a foot. It was an envelope. While the major watched he picked it up and opened it. Inside was a letter. The folds were worn, as if it had been unfolded and read many times. The letter was in an unschooled hand and in an African language Brand did not recognize. The closing salutation was in English. It read: 'with love and kisses'. Folded in with the letter was a snapshot of a young black woman. She was posed against an anonymous wall. The quality of the photograph was poor: there was too much light on the wall and the girl's face was screwed up against the sun. But she was laughing.

Brand folded the letter and put it and the snapshot back in the envelope. He handed it to the army major.

The recall command came shortly afterwards. The commander listened on his radio and then summoned Brand up into the turret beside him.

'We've been ordered back. They're sending a chopper to pick you up.'

'What's happened?'

The major shrugged. He had pulled his dust goggles down round his neck and his face was caked with sweat and grime, except for the ring around the eyes where the goggles had been. 'Don't ask me. They only tell you as much as you need to know.'

The helicopter pilot had more information. The terrorist party had split. The group wiped out in the attack had been trying to escape across the border. A larger group (and scouting parties had established that the hostages were travelling with this group) had turned back to the south, moving under constant observation. It was thought that the objective might be the river. Interference with the movement of the terrorists had been forbidden, because of the risk to the hostages.

They were still in the air when the final message came. The fleeing band had reached the river and had occupied the stranded and deserted steamer. It had been quickly surrounded; its destruction could have been accomplished in a short time and with little effort. The army was clearly chagrined at having to hold back. But for the hostages, it would have been so easy.

16

The steamer had appeared derelict even lying on her moorings back at Leruarua. Here, against a backdrop of wild bush and reed-tangled river, her abandonment was almost theatrical. She lay tilted sideways, half aground on a mud bank, and streamers of weed trailed from her bows and from the motionless paddles. A pied kingfisher had found a lazily convenient perch on the portside deck rail and was watching for prey in the shallows beneath. There was no sign of life on board.

'Watch it,' Commandant De Waal warned Brand. 'There are some of them up on the bridge. They've got a machine gun up there and they're trigger-happy.'

They were in cover high up on the bank, surveying the ship and the bush around it. Two patrol boats hovered upstream, judiciously out of range of the stranded vessel. Spread through the marshes,

Brand knew, was the better part of a battalion of troops, under orders to keep their distance and hold their fire.

'Have you any idea how many of the' – his hesitation over the word was lessened by now – 'terrorists are on board?'

'We estimate fifteen of them.'

'They're heavily armed?'

'Not really. They threw away their grenade launchers. Too heavy when you're on the run. They've got perhaps two LMGs – light machine guns – and I guess most of them still have their goon guns.' He saw Brand's bemused expression and explained: 'AK-47s. They would have kept those. And they might have explosives.'

'What do you aim to do?'

The officer smiled faintly. There was an air of soldierly disdain about him that Brand remembered from their last meeting. Commandant De Waal had no great regard for muddle-headed civilians.

'We sit tight and wait. They've got to come out of there sooner or later.' He lifted his binoculars and examined the steamer through the screen of vegetation. 'The only thing that bothers me is that she might get afloat again. The river is rising. It's all that rain we've had. And the forecast is for more rain.'

'What happens if they threaten to harm the hostages?'

'We'll cross that bridge when we get to it, doctor. Fortunately, it's a kind of diminishing return situation. They haven't got so many hostages that they can afford to waste any of them.'

'I don't much care for that word – waste.'

De Waal looked at him thoughtfully. 'I don't care much about any of this, doctor. But seeing that we're in it we've got to figure a way of getting out.'

'Can we try the radio again?'

'If you wish.'

A constant listening and calling watch was being maintained over the frequencies on which the VHF transceiver on board operated. A command post had been established among the trees. The radio operator sat in a tent, surrounded by a clutter of equipment. He pulled off his earphones when they came in.

'Still nothing, commandant.'

'May I try?' Brand asked.

220

The soldier made room for him.

'My name is Dr Brand,' he said into the microphone. 'I've been sent to negotiate with you. I am not from the army or government. Is anybody listening?'

Silence greeted him.

He tried three more times, then handed the microphone back with a shrug.

'All we can do is sit and wait,' De Waal told him.

They waited.

The army logistical support was exceptional. The operation had been executed as smoothly as if it were all part of a routine exercise planned months ahead. Equipment and commissariat were flown in on a scale that would have suited preparations to besiege a city.

The first evening meal to which Brand was invited was almost symbolic as a triumph of normality. It consisted of that most thoroughly South African custom, a *braaivleis* party – a barbecue in the bush. A row of khaki-clad chefs, under the watchful eye of a cookhouse corporal, served out lamb chops and sausages and *sosaties* as nonchalantly as if they had been in the mess halls of their home base.

Brand was given a stretcher in a tent alongside the headquarters emplacement. The weather had deteriorated again and there was nothing to do all day except lie on the cot and listen to the rain on the taut canvas above his head.

At times his mind was filled with thoughts of violence. Violence would solve this problem very quickly. It was the military answer, and De Waal and his men were ready, waiting to provide it. Meet violence with violence: that was the answer to all problems, wasn't it? The men on board the ship – call them terrorists, then – saw things in those terms. And the men waiting for them on land had an equally simple solution.

He thought: is it the modern panacea? The sick patient is the entire world. How then to cure its ills: the intruding germ of revolution, the pains of change, the suffering of the body politic, the slow decay of the body corporate? The patient decides on self-cure, and reaches for the gun, the rocket-propelled missile, the stick of gelignite. The difference between wooden club and high-tensile-steel cannon is a matter only of distance, not of degree.

So what had changed?

Nothing, except individual perception. When our own innocence ends, we see the death of innocence all around us.

It was Shahida who proposed that the steamer should be repaired and refloated.

She asked William: 'How far are we from that camp?'

'Motloboga? We almost made it there, doctor. It can't be more than ten kilometres or so.'

'While we're sitting here it could just as well be ten thousand.'

William laughed. 'Why would we want to go there?'

'It's the reason why we came.'

'Don't you think we have enough worries? In any case, how do we get there?'

'Captain Da Costa thinks the flood could lift us off. But with the steering gone we'll simply go round again.'

'So you want him to fix it? I don't know whether General Thobega would agree.'

'Tell him it would place him in a better position. He would be better off on a floating ship than marooned here.'

'I don't see how that would improve matters for us.'

'We might be able to do what we came here to do.'

'Set up a hospital?' William shook his head wonderingly.

What methods of persuasion he used on the leader of their captors she never learned. But the result was that Da Costa was freed and allowed back on his bridge and into the engine room to assess the damage. Some of the guerrilla soldiers, under his caustic direction, were put to work repairing the wreckage they had caused. The boilers, by good fortune, were intact. The steering cable needed only a few clamps, but the jammed paddle-gear was a major problem. Da Costa swore furiously as he examined the smashed wheels and cogs. It took him days to put together a makeshift arrangement, mostly of timber banded with iron, that would turn the useless starboard paddle.

'We won't get more than four or five knots out of her,' he predicted gloomily.

222

'That doesn't matter,' Shahida said. 'We don't have far to go.'

She also was allowed on the bridge with Da Costa on the day he announced himself ready for the attempt to get the *Faith* afloat again. The furnace was stoked by a wood-gang impressed from the ranks of the terrorists, and smoke poured from the tall funnel. The first creaking turn of the paddles produced great gouts of mud splashing over the vessel's stern. There was activity among the watchers ashore and a brief outbreak of firing. Shahida ducked behind the flimsy shelter of the wheelhouse, hearing the clatter of automatic weapons which had become a familiar but still hated part of her life. But the guns grew silent and she felt the deck stir under her feet. The steamer shifted and lodged again and the paddles groaned and rained more mud over the afterdeck.

Then, miraculously, the battered vessel slid into the fast, ochre-coloured flood, the paddles turned freely and the *Faith*, slowly and laboriously, headed up against the stream.

It was a voyage that seemed aimless to those on shore who shadowed the steamer's flagging progress. Northwards lay the labyrinth of the headwaters to the marsh, where she could not navigate, and at the end of the river to the south was the deathtrap of the falls.

But it was the riverside camp Motloboga, the Place of Despair, that was her destination.

The steamer anchored offshore. Working with cool disdain under the guns of the watching soldiers, men from the ship were seen to be constructing a rough-and-ready floating causeway. It was a weird contraption, logs suspended over a long row of dugout canoes, jutting out at all angles. Shahida was vividly reminded of a floating restaurant she had visited in a Hong Kong harbour, an elaborately tiered vessel surrounded by a tattered armada of junks and sampans.

The people from the encampment were suspicious at first. They were afraid of the armed men on board and of the soldiers who waited on land. But they remembered Shahida and eventually they brought their sick to the strange hospital on the river.

Dr Hauge had been the *Faith*'s first patient, and Shahida was very happy about her success with him. He had been brought

223

aboard on his litter, unconscious and close to death. But antibiotics had cured the incipient pneumonia, and rest and supportive therapy had taken care of the effects of exhaustion and exposure. The old man was almost himself again, irascible in captivity, swearing at the guards when they interfered with his liberty. In spite of the cast on his arm he insisted that he was well enough to work.

They were busy with their first patients when a shrill outcry broke out among those still on land waiting to cross the log ramp. In a moment of hollow dread Shahida believed the besiegers had launched an attack, with no regard for the sick and maimed between them and the ship. Her fear was reinforced by the guards, who had retreated to the deckhouse and were readying their weapons.

But then they saw the cause of the uproar: a group of children had spotted a troop of monkeys swinging through the bush and had given vociferous chase. The guards watched them indulgently. One of them, who spoke a smattering of English, leaned towards Shahida.

'Nice food.' He made a gesture conveying food to his mouth with both hands.

'The monkeys?' Hauge said. 'Do they eat the monkeys?'

'Monkeys?' the soldier said, grinning. 'Chil' chase monkeys. Eat. Sure.'

The excitement died down and they went back to work. But Dr Hauge was distracted, and after a little he left her, to sit down with his eyes closed. She was concerned, and about to go to him, when he sat suddenly upright and called to her.

He told her: 'A monkey bit the child.'

She thought he was rambling and said, to humour him: 'No, doctor. It's all right. They were chasing the monkeys but they didn't get near them.'

His face darkened and he said sharply: 'Don't be a fool, girl. I know what I'm talking about. A monkey bit the child who died of Virus H disease. And these people eat monkeys. That is the link.'

She stared at him, not understanding.

He said: 'They could not get the virus to grow in monkey cell cultures.'

'So?'

224

'It was put down to a failure in laboratory technique. But it could mean that the monkeys are immune.'

'You're saying that monkeys serve as a host for Virus H?'

'Probably.'

'But a bite could not be a causative factor because saliva could not transfer the disease. It's a blood-borne virus. Blood would have to be involved.'

'Were there not other wounds? I recall something from the postmortem.'

'Of course!' she said excitedly. 'The child's hands were lacerated. Perhaps it happened while he was catching the monkey.'

'If he planned to eat it he would have skinned it before cooking. There would be fresh blood. His wound could well have become infected.'

'With Dr Hamilton it needed only a little scalpel cut.'

'Why didn't we consider this before now?' he asked.

'We never thought that monkeys might be used as food. William led Dr Brand and me to believe that there was a religious significance. We understood that monkeys were holy to these people.'

'Was he being deliberately misleading?'

'I don't think so. I think the real reason is simply that he didn't know.'

'Didn't know the customs of his own people?'

'They're not his people. He's a stranger here.'

She thought about what she had said. Had there been hidden significance in her choice of words? She had known all along that the black man was a stranger, and not only in the sense of being a foreigner to the country. Sometimes she was afraid of William. But he fascinated her too. She believed he was the key to their survival.

She told William about the troop of monkeys and Dr Hauge's conclusions.

Then she said: 'Mr Kgosana, we have not yet seen anyone with anything remotely like Virus H disease.'

He looked away. 'Really, doctor?'

'I want to know the truth. Was there really an epidemic? Were there any new cases at all?'

'That was the story people told.'

'I think you know better. Why did you bring us here?'

'These people need medicine. What difference does it make what diseases they have?'

'I don't think you're telling the truth.'

'Why would I lie?'

Later he returned, as if anxious to appease her.

'I have made inquiries about the monkeys.'

She was weary and she looked at him blankly.

'What you told me about the monkeys. Whether they might carry the Virus H disease.'

'Oh. Yes.'

'It is very strange. These people know about a disease they call the *tala kgatla* sickness, and the strange thing is that *tala kgatla* is their word for raw monkey. Is that not strange?'

'So they identify the disease with the monkeys?'

'That is right. They fear it very much, for the people who get the sickness mostly die.'

'Is it common, then?'

'It is not common, but they know about it. There are outbreaks sometimes and people die. Mostly this happens when there is great hunger and people are reduced to eating anything they can lay their hands on, including monkeys. Cooking a monkey makes it safe, which is why they call it the raw monkey sickness. If we had known the name we might have discovered this long ago. It's very strange.'

It was, she reflected, even stranger than he thought. They had first suspected Marburg disease, and Marburg, she remembered, had once been known as green monkey fever. It was the name scientists had given it. They, like primitive people, could at times be very literal.

The attack came exactly as she feared, but even so she was not prepared for it. She had noticed, without attaching much significance to the fact, that there were an unusual number of young and fit-looking men among the waiting patients that day. Some of them had drifted away from the queues and the guards were trying to force them back, shoving and prodding with their rifle butts. There was a commotion and she looked to see a guard struggling with one of the young men, who wore a bright-coloured

226

blanket draped over his shoulders. She saw Dr Hauge walking over angrily to remonstrate with them.

And the young man threw off the blanket to reveal the assault rifle he had carried in concealment under it, and she saw another of the men hurl something at the guards, and there was the ear-splitting blast of an exploding grenade.

There were people at the water's edge and others on the makeshift causeway, in the act of crossing to the steamer. They had turned to face the source of the explosion and their body attitudes had gone slack, as if they were passive spectators at a drama which did not concern them. She saw a man fall, writhing in the sand, and now there were ripping sounds in the air which she suddenly realized were bullets going by.

The frozen tableau came to an abrupt end. The people on shore scattered. A young man leaped from the catwalk log he had been straddling and landed in the water with a great splash. A woman with an infant in her arms crouched on the pontoon, screaming. People were running everywhere now, or swimming, for some had sought refuge in the water.

But the brief and brutal action at the centre of all the pandemonium was already over. The half-dozen raiders, realizing the failure of their attempt at infiltration, had withdrawn with the swift efficiency of trained soldiers, leaving one dead, the young man with the blanket.

The terrorist troops, in an eruption of fear and fury, went on firing at every conceivable target, real or imaginary. Several people on shore were hit as they scrabbled desperately to escape the bullets.

In fear that the attack might be renewed, Thobega ordered the gangway to be cut loose. The dugouts and the timbers that had supported it were left to drift away on the stream. Then, in spite of Captain Da Costa's furious protests, the terrorist leader had the mooring ropes cast off. The steamer, without power and twisting helplessly in the turbulent water, was carried far downriver before Da Costa could free the anchor. Ignoring the firing still in progress, and cursing and kicking everyone within reach, he managed to heave the heavy weight over the bows. Even this did not immediately check the *Faith*'s headlong rush. The anchor dragged for a distance before it fouled an underwater obstacle and brought

the steamer up with a jerk. She lay pitching and rolling with th
muddy water slicing past her bows.

During the rampage after the attack, equipment had bee
smashed, doors and whole partitions in the saloon wrenched t
bits, cabin portholes staved in.

And at some time, either during the original skirmish or durin
the disorder that followed, Dr Hauge had been killed.

They found him lying on his back close to the body of the dea
raider. There was a gash at his temple and wounds in his shoulde
and arms. Blood had matted on the mane of grey hair and it wa
impossible to tell how he had died, whether from grenade shrapne
or in the subsequent crossfire.

Shahida remembered the old man saying something abou
grubbing to identify a pinprick of matter while people starved an
were killed. For what did any of it matter? If you removed yoursel
far enough, then humanity and its struggles, its victories an
defeats, could be reduced to the scale of the warring of viruses an
antibodies.

Brand was furious about the abortive raid. Commandant De Waa
had given him no advance warning and it seemed to him
deliberate attempt to provoke the terrorists to retaliation.

'You've only succeeded in stirring up a hornets' nest,' h
accused.

'When you're dealing with terrorists in a position of strength it i
essential to catch them psychologically off-balance,' De Waa
retorted. He sounded as if he were quoting from a textbook. 'It i
when a terrorist believes he is in control of a situation that he is leas
likely to bargain.'

'Do you bargain by shooting people?'

'If it had worked we would all have been out of here by now.

'It couldn't have worked. You'd have had to shoot the lot o
them.'

'I will if I have to.'

'And in the process you'll kill the hostages too. That's a hell of
way to solve the problem.'

'Dr Brand, I make the military decisions around here.'

They glared at one another. The radio operator listened wit

fascination while pretending that his earphones prevented him hearing anything. Then he stiffened and cupped the phones between his hands.

He said diffidently: 'Commandant.'

'What is it?' De Waal asked crossly.

'I think they're calling us, commandant.'

'Then answer them, man.'

The young soldier spoke into the microphone. 'Charlie Foxtrot Zulu answering last station. Do you read?' he listened for a time and repeated the call. He shook his head. 'He's gone off the air, commandant.'

'Call him again.'

Only after a number of attempts was there a response. The soldier looked apologetically at his superior.

'He wants to speak to Dr Brand, commandant. He's calling for him by name.'

De Waal gestured curtly and Brand took the young man's place.

'Wait,' De Waal said. 'I want to hear this.' He said to the operator: 'Uncouple that phone. Switch on your speaker.'

A tinny voice came from the loudspeaker. 'I have a message for Dr Brand.' De Waal was listening intently. Brand saw his face stiffen.

'Go ahead,' he said. 'Brand here. I'm listening.' Awkwardly he imitated the radio operator's technique and added: 'Over.'

'I have a message, Dr Brand,' the voice said.

'That's Kgosana,' the officer said grimly. 'The bastard. He's gone over to them.'

Brand asked: 'Is that Mr Kgosana?'

'Yes, doctor. I am speaking on behalf of General Thobega.'

De Waal snorted contemptuously. Brand silenced him with a gesture.

'Go ahead with your message.'

'The general wants me to tell you that if there is another attack on his men then all three of us who are still hostages will be shot.'

'Listen, I want to negotiate with him to free you.'

'He is prepared to let us go free, but he has certain demands.'

'What are they?'

There was a pause while William apparently consulted someone else.

229

'He wants to cross the border without interference and he wants transportation to get there. After that he will let us go.'

De Waal shot out a hand forcefully in a gesture of rejection. 'Tell him: no way.'

'Wait, please,' Brand said. He released the transmit button. 'This man is threatening to take innocent lives,' he said to the officer. 'We have to think about this.'

'Our policy is: no negotiating with terrorists. That's final. Tell him to surrender and then we'll talk.'

Brand lost his temper. 'The hell with all of you.' He used the microphone again. 'Listen, I'm coming on board.' He turned his back on De Waal's protesting motions. 'I want to see this general of yours face to face.'

'How will you get aboard, doctor?'

'I don't care. I'll bloody well swim if I have to. Get Da Costa to steer back towards shore to pick me up.'

'We don't have steam, doctor. And in any case the general would not allow it.'

'Tell him I'm coming alone.'

'It might be dangerous for you to do this thing. The general is suspicious about the length of our conversation. He fears we are planning something.'

'Don't bullshit me, Mr Kgosana. I know what's going on.'

'He has instructed me to stop speaking,' William said.

'Tell him, damn it,' Brand said furiously.

He had operated the microphone too quickly and blotted out the other transmission, so that a portion of the message was lost.

'. . . then the hostages will be shot.'

'Wait,' Brand said desperately. 'Tell him I'm coming alone to speak to him. Do you hear me?'

But the radio was silent.

'I can't allow this,' De Waal said. 'All you're doing is handing the man another hostage to use against us.'

'Try and stop me,' Brand said.

The radio operator watched them out of the corner of his eye.

'What do you think you'll achieve?'

'You wouldn't understand if I told you.'

Brand thought: I hardly understand it myself. But I do know that I have stood by for long enough. I have stayed here, with Shahida

230

only a river's width away but as remote as if she had been transported to another world. I have wanted to tear down pillars of vengeance and I've done nothing. Now I've watched as she built a hospital out of her own prison and I've seen it destroyed. I must act, even if only to match her spirit.

'I have to go.'

The officer spoke appeasingly. 'Look, I can pass this message, all the demands and so forth, on to my command. Although I doubt that the decision will be any different.'

'Save yourself the trouble. I'm going.'

Commandant De Waal eyed him for a moment. 'OK. I can't stop a man cutting his own throat.' But there was a reluctant note of respect in his voice. 'Corporal.'

The radio operator snapped to attention.

'Commandant.'

'Ask the officer of Bravo Company to come here.' He turned back to Brand. 'At least they can give you covering fire if those bastards start shooting at you.'

The rising waters had swallowed the narrow strip of beach, and Brand was forced to make his way along the steep banks, elbowing through scrub bush and crashing through expanses of reed with apprehensive thoughts of crocodiles and hippo.

The *Faith* had drifted down to the spit of a drowned island of which only the tops of trees still showed above the flood. He found a vantage point on the bank opposite it and waved frantically to attract attention. There was no response from the steamer and no one moved on the decks. From here she seemed once more abandoned. He waved again and shouted. His voice was puny against the tumult of the rushing river.

He stood looking helplessly at the lifeless vessel. Would no one answer him? He would have to return tamely to De Waal and admit defeat. Would De Waal assist him to get across? There might be more shooting. Damn them. Couldn't they see him?

There was a patch of reeds, almost submerged, at the base of the headland on which he stood. Something long and dark, bobbing among the reeds, drew his attention. His first thought was that a crocodile had spotted him, but closer examination showed it to be

231

one of the dugout canoes cut adrift from the steamer's gangway, upended and awash here among the reeds.

He scrambled down the bank and tried to free the heavy craft from the tangle of driftwood where it had caught. He had to venture waist-deep to reach it, and the sharp papyrus blades slashed his face and arms as he struggled, sweating and fearful. The waterlogged canoe was a dead weight. When at last he shoved it clear of the reeds the stream almost snatched it from him and he had to plunge up to his chest after it.

He pushed the dugout ashore, turned it over to empty out the water, and sat down on the prow to think over what he had to do. The thing was no more than a tree trunk, roughly shaped with sharp ends and hollowed out. There was no paddle, but he found a plank, probably also part of the wreckage from the gangway, which would serve.

He looked once more at the *Faith* and then at the tumbling, foam-streaked water which separated him from her. He launched the canoe and climbed carefully into it. It capsized at once and he went under the dark water.

At the third attempt he came to an uneasy compromise with his craft's innate instability and the need to sit erect in order to propel it. He learned that he could keep his balance by sitting with his knees splayed and leaning forward. Slowly, dipping his plank paddle with great care, he rowed out of the relative calm of the shallows to where the river tore past in full fury.

He was not altogether prepared for its force. He saw at once that he would not make it across in one attempt, for the stream would carry him far down beyond the steamer. He would first have to go upriver, then trust to luck and judgement to fetch up where he wanted to go.

Cursing aloud and soaking wet, Brand navigated his clumsy canoe along the swollen river. He wondered if De Waal and his soldiers were watching him and laughing at his ungainly progress. Or, conversely, whether there were guns on the *Faith* already trained on him. But there was no time really to think about it. It needed all his strength and concentration to keep from tipping over and to hold the keel-less and unmanageable craft on approximately an even course.

He could not tell how long it took him to complete the crossing.

His sole concern was that he was coming to the end of a journey and that Shahida Karim was waiting for him.

17

She had always been slender; now she was almost gaunt. He thought, anxiously examining her face, that she had lost more weight than she could afford. The strain of the ordeal showed itself in other ways, the bruised look of her eyelids, the slight droop of her fine-curved mouth.

He took a step towards her; her eyes opened wide, incredulously, and her body responded with an arching movement, as if from unendurable longing. Then, to his surprise, she blushed painfully, her lips began to tremble and, putting her hands to her face, she wept.

Da Costa had stumbled to his feet and was babbling excitedly in Portuguese, but Brand had regard only for the young woman. He longed to touch and comfort her but he was embarrassed, and not only because of the presence of others. He had waited for this moment for a long time, but now it had come there was a barrier which he could not overcome or even properly define.

He tried to cross the stateroom to her, but a violent motion of the steamer took him by surprise and he staggered, grabbing at one of the decorative pillars for support. Lying here in midstream, exposed to the full force of the flood, the *Faith* was being flung around like a bobbing cork.

'Perhaps we should sit down,' William Kgosana suggested. He took a couple of lurching steps past Brand and fell into a settee, grandly brocaded but also, in a seamanlike fashion, firmly bolted to the deck. His companion, who was burly and moustached and carried an automatic rifle cradled to his chest, remained at the doorway.

Brand was compelled to take the seat beside the African, and they all sat there, at opposite sides of the elegant room, like awkward guests waiting for a party to begin, swaying in time with the pitching and rolling of the vessel.

233

And, as if he felt the need to take on the role of solicitous host, William said: 'It was very daring of you to cross in that little boat. We were anxious about your safety.'

'You didn't show it. You might have come to my assistance.'

'Captain Da Costa wished to. But it was a question of raising steam. Also the comrade general' – the gesture indicating the armed man at the door was as discreet as the voice – 'was understandably reluctant. He feared treachery.'

'From one man in a canoe?' Brand laughed disbelievingly. He decided to end the preliminaries. 'I have come to talk to him about bringing this business to an end.'

'He has stated his conditions.'

'You know as well as I do that surrender is his only course.'

'He still hopes to strike a bargain.'

'He can forget about it. Does he speak English?'

'Very little. I can translate what you say.'

'All right. Tell him . . .' Brand stopped, frowning. 'Where is Dr Hauge?'

The strained silence gave him the answer.

'Dead? He's dead?'

'It was an accident,' William said.

Brand turned angrily to the black man in the doorway. 'You killed him! You bastards killed a helpless old man!'

The terrorist leader had watched them with an expression intended to be menacing. Occasionally he had fingered his gun. But it was obvious that he did not understand what was being said. Now he looked sharply from one to the other and asked William something. William replied soothingly.

He said to Brand: 'It was no one's fault. He was killed during the attack on us, in the crossfire.'

'Us? Do you include yourself with these people?'

William shrugged. 'In a manner of speaking.'

Da Costa said: 'Don't trust him. He is one of them.'

There was a startled silence. Brand looked at the black man. William's expression was enigmatic.

'Is this true?'

'Is what true? I don't know what Captain Da Costa means.'

'Ask him what side he's on,' Da Costa said. 'He pretends to be prisoner like us. But he is one of them.'

234

'Does he mean I am black?' William asked. 'If so, he's right.'

'You know what I'm talking about,' Da Costa said. He jerked his head at Thobega. 'That one knows nothing. It is William who tells him what to do.'

'I am merely a pawn in the game,' William said. There was mockery in his voice, but it was hard to tell whether it was directed towards them or himself.

'You brought us here,' Da Costa said. 'Why? You said there's a fever epidemic. Where is it? Where are your dying people? You lied. You set up an ambush for us.'

'That was not planned.'

Brand broke in. 'So you admit something was planned?'

'I am only a pawn, doctor. Do you play chess?'

'What the hell's that got to do with it?'

'I spent part of my life playing a lot of chess. I never got to be very good, because I couldn't see far enough ahead.'

'Whose side are you on?'

'The black pieces or the white pieces?'

'Don't try to be clever. Who are you? What do you want?'

'Do you seek a metaphysical answer? Greater men than I have struggled to find it.'

'All right, be clever, then. Did you arrange all this?'

'If you mean did I arrange that doctors and nurses could be brought to a stricken and backward people: yes, I did.'

'Did you know in advance there was going to be a rocket attack on the ship?'

'That was a sad error.'

'I see,' Brand said sarcastically. 'Just a regrettable mistake.'

'An error in the channels of information. Our friends here' – his gaze slid towards the terrorist leader – 'were not informed that the ship was friendly. So they exceeded their instructions. So much trouble in the world is caused by people acting impetuously.'

'You sodding bastard.' Brand grabbed him by the front of his shirt. 'You murderous . . .' William did not resist. His expression was still calm, a little disdainful. Thobega had raised his gun warningly and his slit eyes were watchful, but he made no move to intervene.

Shahida spoke from where she had been sitting in a corner, almost forgotten. 'Leave him alone.'

Brand turned to her, wanting to exonerate himself, wanting her to understand the depth of his despair and disgust.

'What does it matter now?' she asked.

'He tricked you. He almost had you killed.'

'It was not his fault. I believe him.'

'He lied in order to bring you into danger.'

'In order to help people who are sick. Is that the worst thing anyone has ever done?'

She got to her feet and moved to the middle of the cabin, as if she could not bear to be still, as if anger was a spur, and now she stood there, braced against the boat's motion, a slight, defiant figure, her folded arms hugging her small breasts. Brand felt that her wrath included all of them. She was weary and contemptuous of the world of men, with all its squalid conspiracies in the name of great causes. And he understood also the simple ethic by which she lived, the reason she grew impatient with people or policies that obscured the basic rule: love thy neighbour.

Curious, he thought, that such a plain little word could have become so debased that one could hardly use it without being embarrassed. Love. One could say almost anything, could sprinkle conversation with all the other four-letter words and not cause heads to turn. But to use that word was to risk the questioning look, the awkward silence, the averted smile.

Nevertheless, 'I love you' was what he wanted to say to her, in gratitude for the simplicity of her needs.

She had taken on a troubled look, pressing her hands to her side. The steamer rolled and she almost stumbled. As he watched, not understanding, her face became a mask of pain and she uttered a sound between groan and protest, then doubled over.

He leaped to catch her as she fell. Her weight was nothing: that of a bundle of bone and feathers, bird-light, bird-fragile.

The others sat stupefied. Her breathing was harsh, in pained gasps.

He asked her, 'What's wrong? What's the matter?', but she would only shake her head.

The habits of long training and routine asserted themselves. Observe, ausculate, palpate. Look, listen, feel.

'Help me,' he said sharply. 'That table.'

The black man with the gun moved forward as if to intervene.

'Get the hell out of my way,' Brand snarled at him.

The terrorist leader fell back.

They lifted Shahida on to the table. He recognized it, remembered once having admired it as one of the better pieces of furniture remaining from the days of the old mission station at Leruarua; how on earth had it come here? It was a beautifully carved craftsman's work and had probably once been used in the church. It was massively heavy but a little too short, so that Shahida's heels dangled over the ends. He thought about making her more comfortable but decided there were other priorities.

Soft, rapid pulse. Extremities cold and clammy. There was a fine sheen of sweat on her face.

Pallor, sweating, cyanosis, the pearly look of the eyelids. Obviously going into shock. The cause? A coronary was unlikely; the pain which had caused her collapse was in her abdomen. Perforated viscus? Acute pancreatitis? A dozen other conditions suggested themselves. The stormy onset indicated dramatic loss of blood or fluid. Ruptured aorta? Ruptured spleen? The breathing had become fast and shallow, as if she was hungry for air. It clicked into place. Rapid and continued blood loss, for some undetermined reason. Leave it for the moment. Deal with effect, not cause.

He turned to William. 'Is there blood plasma on board?'

'I don't . . . there might be. These people took many things after the attack. They broke many other things.'

'Go and have a look,' Brand said. 'Scrounge for what you can find.'

He did not wait to see his order carried out. His attention was back with his patient.

Violent haemorrhage resulting in acute abdominal pain, accompanied by rigidity of the stomach muscles. The other symptoms were those of blood loss. But what had caused it?

Images intruded: of the girl in her overlarge hospital coat, waiting for him as if by assignation, of the relief on her face when she had seen him, the look of expectation rewarded. The look of lovers meeting.

Think, he told himself. Think.

Da Costa was hovering solicitously. 'Can I help? Is there anything . . . ?'

'Just keep out of the way,' Brand replied roughly.

A dark doubt had already formed in a corner of his mind; the first ragged cloud which was the seed of a storm. A professor, back in the dim past, had urged his class: 'Think ectopic.' A young woman of child-bearing age; a paroxysmal collapse. 'Think ectopic.'

Dear God, no. The thing was unthinkable.

He closed off his mind to the possibility and ranged over a whole catalogue of diseases. What previous symptoms had she shown? He had been unable to take a history and she was already comatose, unable to answer questions. She had seemed well only a short while ago, except that she was so dreadfully thin.

But the cloud was rising steadily over the mind's horizon which it would presently fill. 'Think ectopic.'

William was back in the stateroom. Behind him at the door crowded several of the other guerrilla soldiers, drawn by the commotion. Brand ignored them. His eyes sought and gratefully found the plastic container William was carrying.

'Thank God.'

'Saline. It's all I could find.'

'It'll have to do.'

He worked rapidly to set up the saline drip, ripping open sterile packages of tubes and intravenous needles, connecting the vaculiter which held an isotonic saline solution to replace the lost body fluid. The veins had almost collapsed; he managed to plunge the needle home only after a prolonged struggle. The unsteadiness of the deck under his feet made the procedure doubly difficult. He set the flimsy plastic regulator and the reassuring flow of liquid commenced.

William had found other bits and pieces of apparatus, a stethoscope, a sphygmomanometer, syringes, a set of needles. Brand resumed his examination. The heart sound showed diminished right ventricular return. The vasomotor tone was increasing as the blood vessels constricted because of the lower volume of blood. All the symptoms of a severe haemorrhage.

He stood swaying against the motion of the boat, looking down at the young woman on the table which had once served as an ornament in a church, the adjunct of another ceremony, the bearer perhaps of some other symbolic sacrifice. Shahida lay without moving, her thin face bloodless.

After a time William asked: 'Have you made a diagnosis?'

238

'Massive haemorrhage,' Brand told him shortly. 'I don't yet know what caused it.'

'Have you considered an ectopic pregnancy?'

It was as if, while he was trying to hide somewhere, a hand had been placed on his shoulder and a stranger's voice had spoken his name.

He turned angrily and asked in a choking voice: 'What the hell do you mean?'

'She was raped,' William said.

'Oh God.' The thought of the act was as horrifying as to contemplate its consequence.

'What the hell would you know about ectopic pregnancy?'

William smiled thinly. 'I studied medicine.'

'Where?'

'In South Africa. Later in Russia.'

'I'll be damned.' For a moment Brand examined the black man with curiosity. But William's disclosure, startling as it was, could not hold his attention.

'Did you notice anything else to confirm that diagnosis? Other symptoms?'

'Nothing conclusive. She has become more withdrawn, but that would be understandable under the circumstances. Also she has not had a period since we have been in captivity.' He smiled embarrassedly. 'Forgive my mentioning it but, naturally, living in enforced close proximity. . . .'

'Of course. You . . . could be right. I had considered it. Naturally I didn't know of. . . .'

'Of course not,' William said with warm sympathy.

Again Brand was startled. He looked at William with fresh insight. Is it so obvious how I feel about her? I still haven't worked it out myself, but it seems other people can tell. Does she know? Or is it only William Kgosana who happens to be so uncommonly observant?

'What do you think?' Brand asked him. 'Tubal rupture or tubal abortion?'

'If I remember rightly, a differential diagnosis is almost impossible. And it does not make a great deal of difference.'

'No. It doesn't.'

When you concentrated on the medical condition you could

239

almost reject the thought of its cause. The laws of nature were implacable and did not consult the wills or wishes of the mortals they ruled. When the female ovum separated from its ovary to lie for a few hours in one of the fallopian tubes, sperm might reach it, and nature was not concerned whence it came or how; from a rapist's force or a lover's rapture, in sadness or terror or joy. Normally, the fertilized egg continued its journey to the uterus where the embryo could safely develop. On occasion, however, and for a variety of reasons, the fertilized ovum was not expelled from the tube. The embryo grew and the tube inevitably, catastrophically, ruptured.

He thought about how much time he had and how much he could gain by various stratagems. He thought about the situation in which they were placed and about the skimpiness of the equipment at hand.

'I'll have to operate,' he said.

The *Faith* heaved like a wild thing, tethered by her anchor rope against the fierce rush of the waters.

William shook his head. 'Not here,' he said. 'Not under these conditions. You'd kill her.'

Brand thought of holding a scalpel in his hands, of steadying it against the manic motion, of cutting close to a vital organ or one of the great blood vessels. He saw his hand jerk, the knife slip, the spurt of blood. . . .

'No.' And then, almost in panic: 'But what else can we do? There's no time. Where could we go?'

More of the black soldiers were crowding the doorway, gaping at them.

'Persuade these people to let us land,' Brand said. 'Tell them how serious Dr Karim's situation is.'

'They'll never allow it.'

'Persuade them.'

The gang leader spoke angrily to his followers and some of them fell back. But they still stood engrossed by the events within the stateroom.

'They will never agree. Their lives are at stake. To them it's a simple choice. The hostages represent freedom and safety.'

'At least try to get them to beach the boat. All we need is that she should lie stable.'

240

William said: 'The one choice is as bad as the other, doctor. Once this ship is beached, nothing will get her off again. We would have to wait for another flood and that could take years.'

'You got us all into this mess. Now get us out again.'

William Kgosana stared at him for a long time. Then he looked down at the woman on the sacristy table. He shrugged.

'If you wish.' He gestured towards the door and the inquisitive onlookers. 'Join me, please. It is better if we both talk.'

The argument went on for a long time. William spoke and the terrorist leader answered him in an angry voice. William spoke again and the other black man shook his head. William showed anger too, but the other man continued to shake his head. Brand listened with impotent incomprehension.

At last William said to him: 'Doctor, I have an idea. But it requires your co-operation.'

'What do you mean?' Brand asked.

'I am not the only one who perceives the consequences of beaching the ship. Our friend here has been quick to point out the disadvantages.'

For a moment Brand was puzzled by the black man's suddenly pedantic speech. Then he understood.

'You said he does not have much English?'

'That is correct. However, one or two of his associates are better equipped. Now this calls for a certain amount of subterfuge on your part.'

'What is this all about?'

'You are very concerned about Dr Karim's condition, aren't you, doctor? The sick woman. You are worried, not so?'

'Naturally.'

'Describe her symptoms, doctor.'

'Well, she ... it's a condition of collapse, following an acute haemorrhage.'

'Bleeding. The woman is bleeding.'

'Yes.'

William explained something to the scowling gang leader. His face was grave.

'Now we will have to dissemble a little. Dr Hauge has died too. Would you say that he also showed symptoms of a bleeding tendency?'

241

'You know very well how – '

'Yes, but before that. Would you say the other doctor has also had this bleeding sickness?'

The men in the doorway were silent. Their leader held his rifle as if to ward off something. And Brand understood the direction in which William was trying to steer him.

'Virus H?'

'Yes.'

'Yes. The other doctor may also have had the sickness,' Brand said firmly.

William explained in a loud voice to the man with the gun. Then he spoke to Brand again.

'The people here call it the monkey sickness,' William said. 'They fear it greatly, for they know it is contagious.'

'Yes. It can make others ill,' Brand said. 'Many people can die from it.'

'And both the old man and this woman came seeking the seed of this sickness, not so?'

'That is right.'

'And you now fear that is the reason why the old man was sick and why the woman has become sick?'

'It may already have spread all over this ship,' Brand said.

William nodded solemnly. 'And this monkey sickness . . .' – his pause extracted every ounce of drama from the name – '. . . could cause everyone on the ship to die. Not so, doctor?'

The men around them were muttering to one another. One of them started a shrill argument with his leader.

'It would be best if we all got off the ship at once,' Brand agreed. He was only too conscious that, compared to the black man, his performance was hollow and contrived.

The gang leader said something furiously to William. His reply was muted. They talked back and forth, back and forth.

'What does he say?' Brand asked impatiently.

William did not look at him. 'Be careful, doctor. This individual is exceedingly suspicious. He thinks I have switched sides and that I'm trying to put something across him.'

'What do you want me to do?'

'Go back to your patient.'

It was not easy to give an impression of well-bred contempt while

242

walking across a floor which would not remain still, but Brand tried his best. To act concerned was less difficult. Shahida was in desperate straits.

It had gone beyond pretence, beyond a game of deceit and make-believe. He looked at the arguing men in the doorway with dislike approaching hatred.

'Get out!' he shouted at them. 'All this crap stops right now,' he said to William. 'Get these bastards away from here. I have to operate.'

'How do I persuade them?'

'I don't care what you do. Tell them they'll die if they don't go.' He snapped at Da Costa: 'You! Try and get this bloody wreck of yours under control.'

Da Costa spread his hands helplessly. 'How? I have no steam.'

'Then put her on the beach. Sink her. But whatever you do, do it fast.'

'Beach my ship?'

'Don't argue. Just do it.'

'They will shoot me if I try.'

'And I'll kill you if you don't.'

Captain Da Costa stared at him. Then the tough face creased in a sudden grin. 'OK. So what the hell? Maybe they don't shoot.'

Brand gave him a tight, approving nod. He turned back to William. 'Let's get on with it. I need you here. We're operating.'

18

She lay on the same sacramental table, but it had been scrubbed and draped so that at least it had the appearance of a table in an operating theatre. She was draped too, from the neck down, except for a square opening Brand had cut in a linen sheet before packing it around with absorbent dressings. She had regained partial consciousness, but seemed unaware of what was happening to her.

They had collected the pitifully few instruments – knife, scissors, artery forceps, clamp – and sterilized them too. There was a toilet and washbasin in a cubicle adjoining the stateroom and Brand

243

scrubbed as well as he could, then put on his gloves. It had not taken long to be ready.

William stood at the head of the table. He was alert but calm. He seemed almost to have grown in stature. Brand thought that the man's elevation had come when he had said: 'We.' He had said 'We're operating' to William Kgosana.

The motion had become less violent, more rhythmical. Were they moving? He did not know, for the stateroom door was closed and he could not see outside. Could he take the risk of starting?

William looked up questioningly and he nodded. William worked quickly and expertly with a bottle and a pad and the sharp reek of ether filled the room. Shahida made convulsive movements of her head in protest and then her body went slack. William reached for her pulse. After a moment he repeated the anaesthetic. Her breathing became deeper.

'OK?' Brand asked.

William nodded.

One scared-looking guard had remained posted at the door, but Brand had slammed it shut in his face when they had started preparing Shahida for the operation. Now, in part of his mind, he regretted the gesture. He wished he knew what was happening.

But there was no time to think of outside events.

There were no clips, so he caught the drapes to the skin with a few quick stitches. The girl's flat, gold-skinned belly was smooth under his gloved fingers. He cut into the skin and blood welled. He deepened the incision. He heard William take a sharp breath.

It's a straightforward operation, he reminded himself. One of the simplest in the book. In. Tie off. Out. That was all there was to it. An old hand at the game could do it in ten minutes flat, allowing himself time to deliver a lecture to a circle of students as he went along. But he would have an anaesthetic machine and double banks of instrument trays and monitors and every surgical aid that science could think of. And blood. Bottles and bottles of blood, all neatly cross-matched and ready to feed into the patient who was already so exsanguinated that she was showing signs of anaemia. He wouldn't have to operate on a kitchen table with a kitchen knife. If not quite that, then as near as damn it. A church table and an old scalpel.

He went deeper.

William continued to administer the anaesthetic, slow drop by drop.

'She OK?' Brand asked without looking up.

'OK.'

The boat's movement was definitely easier now. They were in calmer water, no doubt about it. What in God's name was happening?

But he forced his thoughts back to the table.

It was the lack of blood that worried him most. The first bottle of saline was nearly all in, but Shahida had not shown any appreciable improvement. Now there would be operative shock to add to the trauma. And he could not give her the blood she desperately needed. He did not know her blood group and she was unable to tell him. There were no facilities for matching and therefore no possibility of a transfusion.

She could die, he told himself bleakly. Shahida could die right here under my hands. And there won't be a thing I can do about it.

Cut. Dab with a swab. Clamp. Pack the wound around. Cut again. He was slow and fumbling, long out of practice. A surgeon, a real surgeon, would laugh at this procedure. And laugh too, probably, at the hamhanded way he was going about it.

But the surgeon would not be worried sick about the patient on the table. To him it would be just another broken body to be mended.

She could die.

'OK?'

'OK.'

He had reached the peritoneum. Less blood here, for he was past the smaller surface vessels. The glistening membrane stretched beneath his hand. Through it he could see the blue wash of blood inside the peritoneal cavity. His diagnosis had been right. She had bled a great deal.

He held the knife poised.

Without warning, the wild, bucking motion resumed, and a moment later the cabin tilted sharply over, as if the steamer was turning on her side. He staggered half a dozen steps across the floor, and even the heavy table slid a foot or more, with William clinging desperately to keep both Shahida and himself from falling.

245

'Jesus Christ!' Brand said. He looked at the deep incision, aghast. If he'd had the scalpel in there at that moment. . . .

There was the sound of firing: brief separate bursts from a single weapon.

'For God's sake open that door. What the hell is Da Costa up to?'

The guard outside the door had fled. William left it open and it banged rhythmically as the steamer rolled, in counterpoint to Brand's confused calculations. What could he devise to make up for the lack of blood?

William returned alone.

'What's happened?' Brand asked.

'We're still adrift. Captain Da Costa slipped the anchor cable.'

'Where is he?'

'Barricaded up on the bridge.'

'Can't he put the damn thing ashore?'

'He managed to steer her on to the bank. I think that was the big bump we felt. But the river took her off again. Some of the general's men took the opportunity to jump ship and he's a bit annoyed. He's threatening to shoot everyone in sight. But my feeling is that he's getting ready to run too.'

'It was your idea to panic them, my friend.'

'Yes,' William said. 'It was my idea.' He hesitated. 'I will have to go with them.'

'I need you here.'

'I know. Nevertheless. . . .' The black man spread his hands. 'The hunt is up, doctor.'

Another shuddering blow shook the steamer and sent them both staggering. Brand fell heavily. He made no attempt to save himself, but held his gloved hands away from his body to secure them from contamination.

'Leave me,' he said crossly when William moved to help him up. 'Don't touch me. Is Shahida all right?'

Movement had ceased. The *Faith* had come to rest at last, leaning over at a steep angle but mercifully still.

'I think we're grounded,' William said. He went to the door.

'God forbid that she fills up with water now.'

'We're not on the bank,' William reported from the door. 'I think we struck one of the islands. I can see trees.'

'To hell with that now. Come.'

246

William stayed in the doorway.

'She's hard aground. Nothing will shift her off here.'

'For God's sake, man!'

'I have to leave you.'

'How can you go now?'

'I must. I think the others have already cut and run. Like rats, eh? Getting off the sinking ship. I'm one of them.'

'Will you leave me here with a dying woman?'

'There will be help for you presently. There's no help for me. I have to follow my friends.'

'Go, then.'

'Don't you understand?'

Brand looked at him with contempt. 'No. But go if you have to.'

'I will tell Captain Da Costa you need him.'

'Get out of here,' Brand said.

With the steamer motionless and with Shahida's laboured breathing the only other sound, he could hear the endless roar of the river past the *Faith*'s fragile hull.

He went to the door, willing Da Costa to hurry. Through the outside portholes he could see portions of the river. He thought it was like the dark stream of violence which ran through Africa and, at times of flood, destroyed all in its path. He could see the yellow-green of the papyrus huddled below the banks.

Was there an answer of sorts to be found in the reeds? Would those who sought roots in Africa discover that they were not planted in the landscape or even in the dark soil of their origins? Would they end like the papyrus, sustained for a time by the mass of their intertwining structure but fated eventually to be torn away by the onrush of the water?

A sound of footsteps. He turned. The captain of the *Faith* wore an expression of unease which became real dismay when he saw Brand's masked and gowned figure. Behind him came William Kgosana.

Brand did not say anything. The black man met his gaze with a wry smile. He gave a shrug of resignation.

'Ah, well,' he said.

'You're staying?'

'Perhaps the hunters will wait.' He raised his hands to the classic surgeon's position and held them ironically towards Brand. 'After you, colleague.'

'Thank you.'

'I also have a suggestion,' William said. 'You will have to tell me if it could work.'

'What is it?'

'I'll show you. Come.'

They went to where Shahida lay. Da Costa followed them, his pale face determinedly averted. William pointed at the open incision and at the blue sea which showed beneath the peritoneum.

'We need blood, don't we? There it is. All we need. But how do we get it to her?'

It was so simple and yet so brilliant. There indeed was the blood they needed. But how to retrieve it?

'OK. It's a great idea. But there's a danger of clotting and that would kill her. If we have heparin. . . .'

'There's heparin in the store. I'm almost sure of it.'

'Thank God.'

'I noticed it when I fetched the saline. That's what gave me the idea.'

'Bloody smart thinking,' Brand said. He was suddenly animated. 'OK. I'll tell you what we do. We'll use that vaculiter as a transfusion bottle. You go and fetch the heparin. We've got sterile gauze here, that's OK. Get a funnel of some kind. Any plastic funnel will do. And a cup. Preferably a china cup without cracks. That's all we need.'

'What's the cup for?'

'I'll show you. You can handle the transfusion while I tie off the tube. And the captain here can give the anaesthetic.' He looked doubtfully at Da Costa's singlet and jeans, grease-stained from his work with the anchor cable. 'He'd better scrub first. Show him how. And you scrub too, once you've collected those things.'

'What do you plan to do?'

'Here's how we'll do it. I'll open up the peritoneum with a small incision. Then you simply scoop the blood up with the cup and pour it through the funnel into the vaculiter. There will be heparin in there to stop clotting and then we feed it back into the vein.

248

You'll see.' Brand smiled for the first time. 'It'll be as easy as pouring tea through a strainer.'

The last stitches were placed and the incision was closed. Brand stood back and squinted at it. The neatly sutured cut did not look as if it concealed more than a superficial wound.

Is there any mark on me, he thought, to show the abundance I found within myself as my hands laboured within the body of the woman I love?

Say it, he thought. Let them hear it and scream their condemnation if they wish. She is of another race and colour and God knows there are overwhelming obstacles between us. But she is the woman I love.

He realized suddenly that he was utterly, numbingly weary. And yet the critical part of the procedure had been childishly easy. He had located the uterus, pulled it up and clamped it on the broad ligament of the right-hand side. Then he had brought up the sac and clamped it too, on its uterine side. With that the bleeding had stopped and he had gone on, working calmly to remove the ruptured organ. An operation right out of the textbook.

The three of them lingered in the room, unable to leave, talking now in undertones, occasionally in voices raised in elation, of what they had done.

'I think she's going to be all right,' Da Costa said.

'Of course she's going to be all right,' Brand said.

'You're a hell of a surgeon, doc,' William said.

They were emotionally charged, high as addicts on a trip. They said and did things from which, in other circumstances, they would have shrunk. They boasted mildly; their conversation was filled with marvelling expletives, with 'Did you see this?' and 'Did you realize that?' and 'Weren't we lucky?' meaning: 'Weren't we great?'

But then William said, almost with regret: 'I have stayed too long.'

They were suddenly silent, looking at him.

He spoke to Brand. 'The hunters won't wait after all. All that remains is for you to set free the quarry.'

Brand said to Da Costa: 'Stay here. Look after her.' He went out into the corridor and then on to the deck, with the black man

249

following. He saw for the first time how the *Faith* had stranded, hard up against the bank, heeled over so that tree branches touched her funnel.

'Will you get clear?' he asked.

William shrugged. 'Maybe. Maybe not.'

'Why?'

'Why do I have to go? Doctor, my story wouldn't stand up to much investigation anyway. And after this they'll be looking at it through a microscope.'

They stood on the steeply angled deck, watching the flow of the river.

'I would have liked to have known you better,' Brand said suddenly, almost surprising himself.

The black man smiled. 'You think we would have had something to say to one another?'

'Yes. . . .'

'Doctor, all we could have talked about has been said countless times before. But the trouble is that no one listens.' He went to the leeside rail, from where it was only a short drop to the water. He looked down and made a mock-heroic face. 'I've always hated getting my feet wet.'

'Good luck,' Brand said.

'Thank you.' The black man perched on the rail. 'You know,' he said, 'the odd thing is that, although you are on the one side and I'm on the other, we are both men in the middle.'

Then he was gone, with a splash and a shout. Brand went to the rail to watch him swimming strongly, striking out for the near bank.

'Good luck,' he said softly, half to himself.

He noticed, drifting here and there on the river, clumps of water hyacinth. They were, he remembered reading, a menace on the waterways and dams of southern Africa, flourishing and multiplying even as they were carried by the vagaries of wind and current.

If there was no answer with the river and the reeds, was the solution to drift like the hyacinth, content wherever you ended up?

There were no easy answers. Their rescuers would come for them and from that moment on there would be problems he dared not even contemplate. Would he speak out or remain silent?

If only Shahida weren't ill, he thought forlornly, I could take my

250

problems to her. Even if she could not give me answers at least I could share my doubts. We cannot be alone, not even the most solitary of us.

With a kind of rough affection he thought: and what am I going to do about *you*, young woman? You're another of my cares, and not the least of them.

He could not altogether discard his customary caution. He had, after all, been here before. But at another level there was an irreverent, suffusing joy at the thought of her. Love, was it? Yes, damn you, he told himself. It is.

What the hell. We can work it out. We're going to work it out.

He looked again at the flooding river and then, as if for the first time, at the frail, somewhat ridiculous craft which the floods had thrown up against the shore. The *Faith* had sailed for the last time. Next year's floods, if they should reach this high, would have come too late. Termites would have been at the steamer's planking; the African bush and the sun would have worked her decay and ruin.

Did the final answer not lie with this wrecked ship? For, brief as her voyage had been, as she carried men against the torrent, had she not also carried something of men's dreams?